Food Trade and Foreign Policy

Food Trade and Foreign Policy

India, the Soviet Union,
and the United States

Robert L. Paarlberg

Cornell University Press   Ithaca and London

This book was written under the auspices of the Center for International Affairs, Harvard University.

First published 1985 by Cornell University Press.

International Standard Book Number 0-8014-1772-4 (cloth)
International Standard Book Number 0-8014-9345-5 (paper)
Library of Congress Catalog Card Number 84-29335
Printed in the United States of America

Librarians: Library of Congress cataloging information appears on the last page of the book.

The paper in this book is acid-free and meets the guidelines for permanence and durability of the Committee on Production Guidelines for Book Longevity of the Council on Library Resources.

Contents

Tables

Preface

"Food," it has been said, "is a weapon." This book challenges that sensational assertion through an examination of past and present grain trade policies in India, the Soviet Union, and the United States. In none of these countries, as it turns out, is food trade used consistently as an instrument of foreign policy. Moreover, when such use has been attempted, the presumed advantage to those wielding the "food weapon" has failed to materialize. I trace the scant use and frequent failure of food power in the first instance to domestic food and farm policy constraints. I argue that such domestic constraints are, considering the alternatives, a healthy inhibition.

I began this extended inquiry into the use and nonuse of food power soon after the controversial decision of President Jimmy Carter, in January 1980, to impose a partial U.S. grain embargo as one means to punish the Soviet Union for its 1979 invasion of Afghanistan. The difficult implementation of that embargo and its dubious impact upon the Soviet Union are examined at length in the concluding chapter. For balance, a parallel chapter examines President Lyndon Johnson's 1965–67 "short-tether" policy on food aid to India. But the larger burden is to explain the surprising rarity of such food power episodes. An increasing *disconnection* between food trade and foreign policy in each of the countries under review emerges as a major finding, and as the major analytic challenge, of this book.

I have received invaluable support and advice from many quarters. Much information was gained through private interviews with officials of the government of India, the U.S. government, the Food and Agriculture Organization of the United Nations, the World Food Council, and the International Wheat Council. Generous support from the Ford Foundation and assistance from the Institute for the Study of World Politics made much of this research possible. An attractive supplement to this essential support was an invitation from the Rockefeller Foundation to prepare initial portions of the manuscript while I was a guest at the Conference and Study Center in Bellagio.

I owe even larger debts to the Harvard Center for International Affairs, and especially to Joseph S. Nye, Jr., Stanley Hoffmann, Raymond Vernon, Samuel P. Huntington, Eric Nordlinger, and John Odell for their assistance and advice. Others who have provided helpful reactions include Martin Abel, J. P. Bhattacharjee, James Cole, I. M. Destler, Arturo Goetz, Merilee Grindle, Dale Hathaway, Raymond Hopkins, Robbin Johnson, R. P. Kapoor, Robert Keohane, Rip Landes, Clifford Lewis, Anton Malish, Zhores Medvedev, J. S. Mehta, William Pearce, Fred Sanderson, Samar Sen, Lawrence Sullivan, Peter Timmer, Alberto Valdes, and Mitchel Wallerstein.

Don Paarlberg, my father, shared his valuable experience and his reasoned reactions at every stage.

My thanks also to Wellesley College for granting a year's leave to begin the study and later for supporting the final preparation of the manuscript. The intelligence and enthusiasm of my students at Wellesley, together with the support of colleagues such as Alan Schechter, helped me over many a hurdle.

Marianne Perlak, my wife and my partner in every enterprise, did more than her share, as usual. In this case, she has even designed my book.

To Don and Eva Paarlberg, with their son's love and admiration, this book is dedicated.

ROBERT L. PAARLBERG

Cambridge, Massachusetts

Food Trade and Foreign Policy

Introduction

Has food become an important instrument of foreign policy? Do food-exporting nations, such as the United States, have a powerful foreign policy "weapon" at their disposal? Are they using that weapon with increasing frequency? Are food-importing nations taking extraordinary measures to reduce their vulnerability to this food weapon? It has become commonplace to assume that food resources will be used by exporters to gain international influence. Yet the accuracy of this presumption is called into question by one of the first foreign policy actions taken by the Reagan administration.

Alexander M. Haig, president-elect Ronald Reagan's newly designated secretary of state, brought forward the question of food power in a private meeting at Blair House, two weeks before the 1981 inauguration. At that important early meeting, Haig stressed the wide variety of issues the new president would have to view as matters of *foreign policy* interest, and in doing so he specifically included "food policy" as one of those concerns that could "impinge upon our strategic interests." Haig then suggested that he, as secretary of state, should be given enough authority over the conduct of U.S. food policy abroad to ensure that the president would never be "boxed in by the parochial interests of a single department," presumably referring to the Department of Agriculture. If this were accomplished, said Haig, food could be "a particularly valuable instrument of foreign policy in the years ahead."[1]

The immediate concern behind Haig's plea was the continuing partial suspension of U.S. grain sales to the Soviet Union—the so-called grain embargo—imposed by President Carter one year earlier to "punish" the Soviet Union for its military invasion of Afghanistan.

Haig knew that U.S. grain producers, lobbying hard through their friends in the Congress and the Department of Agriculture, would urge that the new president lift the embargo soon after the inauguration, something he had promised to do during the recent election campaign. In the interest of U.S. foreign policy, Haig wanted the president to keep the embargo in place, lest there be any misunderstanding abroad of the U.S. resolve to resist Soviet aggression.

President Reagan's eventual disposition toward the grain embargo, and toward Haig's desire to oversee U.S. food policy abroad, stands as a serious challenge to the notion that nations will habitually seek to exercise "food power." While showing greater firmness toward the Soviet Union in every other policy arena, Reagan rejected Haig's advice on food sales. As Haig would later recall, "my efforts to persuade . . . Reagan, that the embargo was a very important foreign policy issue, did not succeed."[2] The new president proceeded within several months to terminate the grain embargo, and then to deny to Haig any exceptional authority over U.S. food policy. Food export policy would be made within Reagan's Cabinet Council on Food and Agriculture, where the State Department lacked a central role. With the approval of this body, the Department of Agriculture promised to make available to the Soviet Union, in the upcoming year, a record volume of U.S. grain exports. In 1981–82 actual Soviet purchases of U.S. grain reached nearly 15 million tons, close to the preembargo record volume of 18 million tons.

Even after the surprise declaration of martial law in Poland in December 1981, Reagan did nothing to discourage further U.S. grain sales to the Soviet Union. Despite his decision to suspend export licenses for electronic equipment, computers, and oil and gas equipment, the president continued to join the Department of Agriculture in promoting grain sales, announcing unambiguously that the "granary door is open."[3] This eagerness to expand grain sales to the Soviet Union in 1982 eventually became a serious source of resentment among U.S. allies who were being pressured at the time to cut back on their own trade relations with the East.

Several questions come to mind. Why, in this instance, were U.S. grain sales to the Soviet Union permitted to resume at high volume, despite sharp cutbacks in other areas of U.S.–Soviet trade and a worsening East–West crisis? If—as Secretary Haig had suggested to Reagan—food could be a "particularly valuable instrument of foreign policy," why was it not being put to use? And why, if the food weapon was something to be feared, was the Soviet Union willing to resume depending upon sizeable grain purchases from the United States? Observing only this isolated instance, we might be tempted to conclude that international food trade operates without much reference to foreign policy.

Such a conclusion would force a major reappraisal among contemporary students of international affairs. Secretary of State Haig was not alone in believing that food was on its way to becoming a useful and widely used instrument of foreign policy. This dominant presumption—the presumption of "food power"—had been gaining widespread popularity at least since the 1973–74 boom in world commodity prices. At that time, with food and fuel prices both sharply on the rise, the Arab petroleum-exporting countries seized an opportunity, through export restrictions and production cutbacks, to exercise a convincing measure of "oil power" against the United States. It seemed that an equivalent sort of international power should also be available to exporters of food.

This possibility of food power was especially attractive to the United States, which felt disadvantaged as a large importer of oil and hoped to gain some compensation from being the world's largest exporter of food. One early endorsement of the food power presumption came from none other than Secretary of Agriculture Earl L. Butz, who announced in 1974 that "food is a weapon."[4] The Central Intelligence Agency, in an unusual open report, published its concurring view: assuming a continuation of adverse world weather conditions, "[T]he United States' near-monopoly position as a food exporter . . . could give the U.S. a measure of power it never had before—possibly an economic and political dominance greater than that of the post-World War II years."[5] Analysts outside the government endorsed this notion of food power as well. Geoffrey Barraclough wrote in 1975 that a "global realignment" was under way, "in which the weapons (backed, naturally, by the ultimate sanction of force) are food and fuel."[6]

Responsible U.S. foreign policy officials seemed at first reluctant to test this supposed food power advantage. In 1974 President Ford, for example, assured U.S. food customers abroad that "it has not been our policy to use food as a political weapon, despite the oil embargo. . . ."[7] Comparable assurances were then given by Jimmy Carter during his 1976 presidential election campaign. Carter promised that "the singling out of food as a bargaining weapon is something that I would not do."[8] But the Soviet military intervention in Afghanistan in December

1979 prompted Carter to reverse himself. The Soviet Union, having suffered a bad harvest in 1979, was so in need of imported grain that Carter found the opportunity to use food power impossible to resist. In January 1980, when he imposed his partial embargo on grain exports to the Soviet Union, the long-anticipated era of U.S. food power had apparently arrived.

President Reagan's subsequent retreat from the use of the food weapon against the Soviet Union may be attributed, in part, to the disappointing results of the 1980 grain embargo, which Reagan had labeled as "bad for our farmers, bad for our economy, and not that bad for the aggressor we were supposedly going to punish."[9] It could be argued, however, that the notion of food power would have soon lost its luster even without the disappointing 1980–81 embargo experience. The food weapon is not only prone to failure on those rare occasions when it is put to use; it has also shown itself on most occasions to remain unused.

This book steps back from the grain embargo episode to take a systematic and deliberate look at the realities of food power. It first reviews the past and present grain trade policies of three large and significant nations—India, the Soviet Union, and the United States—to ascertain when and how often these nations have manipulated their grain trade in the pursuit of foreign policy objectives (including foreign economic as well as diplomatic objectives). It is discovered that the grain trade policies of these three countries have *not* often been linked to the pursuit of foreign policy objectives. In fact, the manipulation of grain trade policies for foreign policy purposes takes place *less often* now than in the past.

Two exceptional instances are then examined in which the coercive potential of the U.S. "food weapon" was actually put to a test. The first is the decision of President Lyndon Johnson to put a "short tether" on U.S. food aid to India in 1965–67, in search of a wide range of concessions from the Indian government. The second is President Carter's punitive embargo on grain exports to the Soviet Union in 1980–81. Johnson's short-tether policy is judged to have been, at best, only a qualified success. The embargo is judged to have been a considerable failure.

1 The Food Power Presumption

When we reconstruct the recent debate over food power, we find that a pair of critical assumptions dominates. The first presumption is that nations will frequently seek to use food power. The second is that, when they do, food-exporting nations will enjoy a relative foreign policy advantage over food-importing nations. This chapter first reviews the origins of these two popular preconceptions, then reconsiders the terms of the recent food power debate, all as a prelude to testing the validity of these presumptions against evidence from three important cases.

The first presumption can be restated as an assertion that national governments will regularly manipulate their food imports or exports in search of *external* advantages. That is, their food trade posture will be designed to pursue outward-looking rather than inward-looking policy objectives. These outward-looking "food power" objectives may be only *economic* in nature—for example, to earn (or conserve) foreign hard currency to correct a weakened external trade or payments balance. They may include a full range of diplomatic and security objectives as well—for example, rewarding allies with food aid, or punishing adversaries with food embargoes. It is important to note that these sorts of outward-looking policies can be adopted by food-importing as well as by food-exporting nations. Importers can seek a *defensive* kind of food power by reducing the volume of their food imports or by diversifying the source of those imports away from a potential food power adversary.

The second food power presumption, as defined here, predicts that in most food power confrontations, the food-exporting nation gains the greater advantage. Even when food power policies are adopted by importers as well as by exporters, those with food to export are expected to enjoy more commercial or coercive leverage.

In some situations, of course, who gains from food power depends precisely upon who choses to adopt a food power policy. For example, if an importing country actively pursues food power through a strategy of preemptive import reduction or diversification, and if exporters are constrained (perhaps for domestic political reasons) from ever suspending their exports, then a relative advantage will lie with the importer. Accordingly, one must establish the frequency and the energy with which both importing and exporting nations have subordinated their food trade policies to the pursuit of foreign policy objectives in the first place.

Origins of the Food Power Presumption

The idea that nations frequently manipulate their food trade in search of an external advantage and that exporters more often gain such an advantage has a respectable intellectual foundation. It fits neatly with a dominant mode of thinking about modern international relations, in which national governments are seen as competitive or power-seeking members of an "international system," and are naturally inclined within this system to shape their external behavior, including trade behavior, with opportunities for competitive gains uppermost in mind. Many of today's international relations scholars still accept what Leopold von Ranke, the nineteenth-century historian, described as "the primacy of foreign policy."[1] They believe that the pursuit of a nation's power interest abroad enjoys priority over the indulgence of preferences at home.

Since the Second World War, it has been considered "realistic" within this school of thought to expect that governments will use the full variety of resources at their disposal, including military force if necessary, to ensure that their own power-seeking strategies prevail. It is only a small step from this general expectation about international relations to an endorsement of the first half of the presumption of food power. Food resources, these realists would argue, are no different from any other kind of national economic or military resource. Nations that seek power over their neighbors should be expected to shape their food trade policies in any manner that contributes to this end.

The modern presumption of food power also enjoys a certain historical credibility when we recall the national food trade policies adopted by most European powers during the great age of mercantilism. The English Corn Laws, which were consistently in effect for nearly four centuries until 1846, were much more than a domestic political response to the commercial needs of the English landed aristocracy. They were also a mechanism designed to create for England a positive external balance of trade in agriculture, thereby adding to the nation's gold reserves, and hence (by the accepted logic of the day) to England's international power and influence. Nor was England alone in pursuing such "food power" policies. A similar mercantile objective inspired Frederick William I of Prussia to specify the death penalty for anyone found buying or consuming foreign grain.[2] Such a pursuit of external over internal objectives was even more conspicuous in the grain trade policies of Tsarist Russia, which continued its food exports to earn foreign currency even in times of acute domestic shortage.[3] This policy was to be revived under Stalin, who exported grain to the West to earn hard currency even while Russian peasants were suffering from widespread starvation.

Those who believe that nations will be inclined to seek food power might also point to more recent trends in the structure and character of world food markets. Since 1970, nations trading grain have become more interdependent. The share of world grain consumption satisfied through trade nearly doubled during the decade of the 1970s, to reach a significant level above 15 percent.[4] This deepened dependence on international trade can alter the inward-looking character of a nation's food policy. When food exports begin to constitute a much larger share of total national farm sales and export earnings, or when food imports begin to satisfy a much larger share of a nation's food consumption, while also using up more hard currency reserves, food trade policy can take on a larger foreign economic policy significance. And if the foreign food supplier or the foreign food customer happens to be a strategic adversary, as in the case of U.S. food sales to the Soviet Union, diplomatic and security questions may arise as well.

Believers in food power might offer two additional justifying observations. First, in the thermonuclear age, the use of a "food weapon" might become more attractive to decision makers by virtue of being less dangerous. Perhaps the risk of using military force is now so great, particularly in major power conflicts, as to make the more frequent use of alternatives, such as food power, nearly imperative.[5] Second, food power seems more likely to be used today because the United States, the exporting nation best positioned to seek food power, has lately found itself in need of additional power-wielding instruments. With its continuing legacy of global commitments, recently expanded to include security in the Persian Gulf, the United States has experienced a diminished power advantage in the arena of traditional economic and military competition. It would naturally be expected, therefore, to seek a compensatory power advantage within the world's food markets. Once the world's preeminent food exporter begins to seek an external advantage from its food trade policies, it is likely that other nations will follow.

The second presumption, that a power advantage will go to nations with extra food to sell, also has respectable origins, dating once again to the mercantile era. It was more recently reinforced by the conspicuous contribution of North American food exports to an allied victory in both World Wars, as well as by the strategic and diplomatic impact of postwar food assistance, offered by the United States to the recovering nations of Western Europe under the terms of the Marshall Plan. This potential advantage of food exporters was then seemingly reconfirmed by analogy, during the decade of the 1970s, following the success of the Organization of Petroleum Exporting Countries (OPEC). If the exporters of oil could exercise power, why not the exporters of food? Arab oil power, in fact, might be countered directly by U.S. food power.

The popularity of such views was not universal, of course, least of all among agricultural economists, and others who consider themselves food policy specialists. In contrast to some international relations theorists, food policy specialists have long held a more suspicious view of food power. They question not only the foreign policy advantages to be gained by exporters, in markets where supply is traditionally abundant. They also question the ability of governments to seek those advantages in the first place, given the greater power over food policy being exercised by inward-looking domestic interests.

This view usually is put forward as an unhappy fact of life, rather than as a preferred state of affairs. Most agricultural economists consider inward-looking domestic political pressures to be a decidedly inferior source of guidance. Those pressures are just as likely to impede the growth of international economic welfare as they are to block the exercise of foreign policy influence. Economists seeking welfare gains through trade liberalization complain loudly about the introversion of so many national food policies. The views of D. Gale Johnson are representative: "[T]he trade measures that each country adopts are an adjunct of its domestic farm policies. In most cases, a specific trade restrictive or interfering device has been adopted, not for its particular direct benefits, but because it is a device that will make it possible for a domestic measure to function."[6]

To say that internal forces or inward-looking policy objectives more often determine the content of a nation's food trade policy is not to predict that the food trade policies of all nations will be similar. In many industrial countries, to be sure, income support for food producers will be a common domestic policy objective. Particularly among the nations of the European Community, but also in the United States and Japan, food producers have long enjoyed enough political influence to insist upon high farm product prices, often set above market clearing levels. To maintain such internal price guarantees, the governments of these industrial countries may have to adopt highly protective farm trade policies at the border. Import levies or quotas will be set in place, to prevent low-priced foreign foods from entering the protected domestic market, and eventually, if the high internal price guarantees begin to generate excessive food production, subsidized exports may have to be arranged to dispose of the surplus.

In many nonindustrial countries, however, a different internal political bias may shape national food and food trade policy. In the nonindustrial world it is more often urban consumers, seeking *low* food prices, who exercise a disproportionate influence over national food policy.[7] If domestic food prices are held artificially low to satisfy this internal political demand, food production may begin to lag, and an ever-larger volume of food imports may have to be arranged.

In either case, be it a policy of high prices to satisfy producer demands, resulting in exports, or a policy of low prices to satisfy consumer demands, resulting in imports, the nation's food trade posture will have been set in response to internal policy objectives rather than outward-looking "food power" objectives. Such nations may even find themselves on occasion forced to make an external policy sacrifice in order to permit the continued pursuit of their food policy objectives at home. Their foreign policies may be forced to serve their food policies, rather than the other way around.

Why are so many national food trade policies so heavily determined by domestic forces? Food trade policies tend to be a residue of domestic politics in part because food trade itself remains, for most nations, a "residual" activity. Most nations still trade only a small share of their internal food supply. Despite a great deal of talk about "global food interdependence," international trade still satisfies only a small share of total world food consumption. As late as 1970, more than 80 percent of the world's citizens lived in nations that were still more than 95 percent self-sufficient in their food supplies.[8] Specifically for grain, the world's most heavily traded food source, the share of world consumption satisfied through trade until the early 1970s remained at less than 10 percent. With nations continuing to produce so much of their own food supply, it is not surprising to find national food and food trade policies more responsive to internal than to external forces or objectives.

To be sure, such distinctions between the internal and external objectives of national policy can easily be overdrawn. As Peter Katzenstein has observed, "A selective focus on either the primacy of foreign policy and the 'internalization' of international effects, or on the primacy of domestic politics and the 'externalization' of domestic conditions is mistaken."[9] The objective of public policy, in most instances, is to serve internal and external purposes at the same time.

In some instances, perhaps a single food trade policy could be found to meet all of the nation's needs, both at home and abroad. In times of domestic food abundance, for example, a policy of commercial export promotion could serve an external economic purpose of earning foreign exchange, and also ease the cost to taxpayers of supporting domestic farm income. The simultaneous internal and external gains from such a policy would make the internal or external motives behind the policy difficult to disentangle. Alternatively, in times of short food supply at home, a national policy of cutting back on exports might serve an external objective of denying food sales to an adversary state, while protecting domestic consumers from food price inflation. Here too, with internal and external forces pulling trade policy in the same direction, the relative strength of those two forces might prove difficult to estimate. Food *import* policies can at times also perform a double function. For some poor countries, assuming a relative abundance of food supplies at home, a policy of cutting back on food imports could conserve foreign exchange (in the interest of foreign policy) and reduce the nation's vulnerability to a possible food trade embargo (in the interest of national security), while firming up domestic farm prices (in the interest of maintaining production incentives or political support from domestic farmers). Political leaders no doubt would be delighted if a single food trade policy could always serve so many divergent objectives equally well.

Unfortunately it is seldom possible to find a single food trade policy that simultaneously serves the nation's purposes at home and abroad. The distinction drawn here between inward-looking and outward-looking food trade policies is necessary precisely because objectives at home and abroad are so often in conflict. The desire to sell more food abroad to earn foreign exchange may be in direct conflict with the need to contain an increase in food prices at home. The desire to import more food to satisfy consumers at home may be in direct conflict with the need to reduce expenditures of foreign exchange, or to reduce diplomatic vulnerability to international food trade blackmail. One examination of U.S. food trade policy properly emphasizes the "inevitability" of such difficult trade-offs between competing internal and external concerns. This study lists among the "competing concerns" that drive U.S. food trade policy, two that are inward-looking (farm policy and domestic economic policy), and two that are outward-looking (general foreign policy, and global welfare and development policy).[10]

The food power presumption provides a general rule for predicting how nations will resolve such inevitable conflicts. It predicts that they will resolve these conflicts by giving "primacy to foreign policy." It further predicts that, when doing so, food-exporting nations will be likely to gain a relative advantage over food importing nations.

The Food Power Debate

Participants in the debate over food power need not endorse both components of the food power presumption. Even some food power enthusiasts express partial doubt, thereby confusing and complicating the food power debate. To reduce that confusion, consider the four logical positions that could be taken toward the food power presumption, as it has been defined here:

1. Full acceptance. Food power policies are *regularly adopted* by food-trading nations, and those policies provide an *advantage to exporters*.

2. Acceptance of exporter's advantage only. Food power policies may provide an *advantage to exporters,* but they are *seldom adopted*.

3. Acceptance of regular use only. Food power policies are *regularly adopted,* but they are adopted by importers as well as exporters, and so they provide *no relative advantage to exporters.*

4. Total rejection. Food power policies are neither regularly adopted, nor do they, when adopted, provide a relative power advantage to exporters.

Of these four possible views, the first three at one time or another have been explicitly endorsed by prominent participants in the food power debate. A typical sampling of such endorsements is provided in the following discussion. Less familiar than these first three is the fourth view, which stands apart from the others because it rejects both components of the food power presumption. This view has been less popular than any of the other three, but it may yet emerge as the most accurate.

The first view, that food power policies are frequently adopted and when adopted provide a relative advantage to food exporters, has been embraced by a surprising number of analysts, despite their wide disagreement about the *sort* of external advantage food power confers. Most stress external commercial gains, such as the success of the United States during the decade of the 1970s in promoting ever-larger grain exports to help pay for ever-larger imports of expensive foreign oil. Some objected to this sort of food power, in the belief that export promotion could lead to a dangerous misuse of U.S. farm resources.[11] But a larger number in this first category endorsed the external commercial objective, and objected only to the more questionable belief, that food power could also be used within the *diplomatic* realm. During the 1980–81 U.S. grain embargo, for example, many believers in commercial food power criticized the diplomatic restrictions then being placed on exports, arguing that the United States had lost sight of its real advantage:

> The real power we have from our modern, highly productive agriculture is not *withholding* our productive power from other countries, but in using it positively. After all, our strength comes from being able to compete in international markets. A strong export position—a surplus in our trade accounts, for example, enables us to sustain a presence around the world; it enables us to purchase imports of raw materials and other goods and services that we need for our production sectors, and it enables consumers to buy goods and services that can be produced more cheaply elsewhere. It is a pity that we can't get this important fact of life across to the State Department and to the National Security Council.[12]

The most widely quoted believer in U.S. diplomatic food power was in fact former Secretary of Agriculture Earl L. Butz. Having described food as "one of the principal tools in our negotiating kit," Butz went on to give the impression in 1976 that U.S. diplomats were already putting that tool to good use. Butz claimed that the veiled threat of a U.S. grain trade suspension had been used to restrain Soviet influence in the Middle East; he also claimed that the Soviet need for U.S. grain in 1972 had contributed to their acceptance of strategic détente with the United States.[13] Even before the 1980 grain embargo, therefore, some officials were claiming diplomatic as well as commercial gains from U.S. food power.[14]

A second camp of more suspicious critics would argue that the food power presumption, as defined here, is only half correct. These critics would embrace the notion that exporters enjoy a *potential* food power advantage over importers, but they would go on to complain that most food-exporting nations, including the United States, have not made full use of this advantage.

Some in this second camp are openly envious of the early commercial success of OPEC, and fault food-exporting countries for failing to take a comparable collective advantage of their own presumed international market power. "[T]he food producers' monopoly exceeds the oil producers' monopoly," argued Assistant Secretary of State Thomas O. Enders in 1974. "[W]e could make OPEC look sick," said another State Department official at that time, "if we were just to use what our agriculture gives us."[15] Both the United States and Canada were criticized for their joint failure to coordinate export policies in this regard, so as to use their "almost monopolistic control of the world's grain supplies" to better advantage.[16]

Others in this second camp have singled out the United States for failing to take maximum advantage of its own diplomatic food power in the conduct of its relations with the Soviet Union. Samuel P. Huntington, writing in 1978 as a recent coordinator of security planning at the National Security Council, complained that the United States was denying itself an available source of leverage over the Soviet Union through its continuing failure to adopt a grain export strategy which was explicitly conditioned on Soviet diplomatic behavior. Huntington traced this failure not to any lack of imagination on the part of U.S. foreign policy officials, but instead to "a variety of institutional, legal, and political constraints, that have tended to restrict the freedom of movement of American decision makers."[17] Huntington is one of numerous observers in this second camp to attribute missed diplomatic food power opportunities abroad to economic and political constraints at home. A Library of Congress study had observed in 1977 that the U.S. domestic economic system, built as it was on lightly regulated private sector control over grain export flows, "would have to change radically" if the United States were ever to realize its food power potential.[18] This same study also laid stress on the likely opposition of powerful domestic grain producers and traders to any diplomatically inspired interruption of commercial food exports. The importance of such domestic constraints has also been underscored by former Secretary of State Henry Kissinger, in his account of U.S. grain sales to the Soviet Union in 1972: "[W]e had subsidized the deals at a time when the Soviet Union quite literally had no other choice than to buy grain at market prices or face mass starvation. . . . It was painful to realize that we had been outmaneuvered."[19] Kissinger's allegation that the United States was *not* taking best advantage of its food power in 1972 contradicts the more self-congratulatory account earlier offered by Earl Butz. U.S. food power was outmaneuvered in 1972, in Kissinger's account, because of an inappropriate "business as usual" attitude in Butz's own Department of Agriculture, and also because lightly regulated private U.S. grain export firms were far too eager on that occasion to outsell one another.

A third group of analysts sees no such missed opportunity for the United States to exercise food power. This group accepts the proposition that nations may seek food power but it questions the proposition that exporters will enjoy a food power advantage, given the structure and condition of world food markets. Within these markets, they note, supplies are usually abundant and real export prices are usually in decline, giving the relative advantage to *importers*. Food-importing nations can also, on short notice, diversify their trade away from any one supplier, thereby eliminating an exporter's presumed source of leverage.

Such doubts about the presumed advantage available to exporters were raised from the start, even amid conditions of temporary short supply in world markets. In November 1973, for example, a Library of Congress report cautioned against the use of U.S. "food power" to counter the "oil power" of the Arab OPEC nations. This insightful report stressed the "extremely decentralized" nature of the cereals purchases of the Arab oil producers and mentioned the ease with which U.S. grain could be "transshipped," around or through an export embargo. Publication of this report late in 1973 helped to discourage U.S. officials from initiating a retaliatory food embargo against OPEC.[20]

Knowledgeable critics continued to warn of the limited market leverage available to food exporters throughout the remainder of the 1970s. Emma Rothschild pointed out in 1976 that a number of food-importing countries had by then already adopted a secure "defensive" posture, by diversifying their food trade away from the United States.[21] Cheryl Christensen followed a similar line of argument in 1977, expressing doubts about an exporters' food power advantage in more general terms: "An exporter, facing a world of sensitive importers who can avoid being vulnerable by taking simple and inexpensive domestic measures, will probably not have much food power over the long run."[22] Others in this camp were wise enough to predict that even a large grain importer such as the Soviet Union might find adequate means to frustrate any exporter's attempt to exercise food power. Willett and Webster, for example, foresaw in 1977 that embargo strategies against the Soviet Union might "backfire," given the wide availability of "alternative suppliers."[23] Describing U.S. agriculture as "increasingly dependent upon exports," they were among the first to express a fear that the United States would injure itself if large overseas customers, questioning the reliability of the United States as a source of supply, were to develop alternative trade sources.

It was no accident that such doubts about the diplomatic advantage of food power to exporters were becoming more visible by 1977. The brief 1973–75 "world food crisis" was at an end, world harvests were again abundant, and the export price of grain fell into a sharp decline. As this decline continued, some analysts even began to doubt the *economic* advantage that exporters might gain from food power. Dan Morgan, for example, argued in 1981 that the United States was no longer gaining sufficient commercial compensation from its expanded volume of grain exports. Quite the contrary, he maintained, the nation was "subsidizing the rest of the world with its grain."[24] Lauren Soth stated in the same year that U.S. grain had become such a bargain in world markets that in a strictly commercial sense the United States was "being exploited by grain-importing countries."[25] Soth believed that many importers were using their unrestricted access to the U.S. market to gain a one-way advantage: rather than carrying expensive buffer stocks of their own, they judged that in years of tight supply they could turn to the United States, where grain stocks (held at taxpayers' expense) would still be plentiful and export prices still relatively low. Soth maintained that any further expansion of U.S. grain exports under these circumstances might overburden and exhaust the productivity of U.S. agriculture, further eroding the exercise of food power in the long run.

When the total volume of U.S. commercial grain exports then suddenly began to contract, in response to a deep worldwide recession in 1982, plus much higher U.S. currency exchange rates, yet another basis arose for questioning the presumed leverage available to food exporters. It again became fashionable to stress what most agricultural economists had always believed, that supply conditions in world food markets would more often favor importers over exporters.[26] Those who had always been suspicious of food power assumptions could argue credibly once more that "U.S. farmers need foreign markets more than foreign buyers need U.S. farmers."[27]

These insights of critics with partial doubts about food power could be combined to yield a full rejection of the presumption. Perhaps exporting nations in today's world food system will neither gain *nor will they seek* a food power advantage. If the food power potentially available to exporters is small, then a disinclination on their part to seek food power should not be surprising. This disinclination might have been set in the first instance, however, by the inward-looking character of most national food policies.

Most critics of food power have stopped short of exploring this final possibility. Those who doubt the inclination of nations to seek food power seldom sort out the reasons, and too often believe that exporters *would* gain, if only the food weapon could be more widely used. Those who challenge the gains available to exporters also stop short. They make their case well enough by examining those few instances in which exporters sought food power and failed, but they neglect to mention that such attempts are exceptional to begin with. By highlighting the errors made when exporters have sought food power, they obscure a more profound truth—that the "error" of seeking food power is seldom made in the first place.

Here we explore this final possibility—that food power is not only seldom enjoyed by exporters, but also seldom sought. Rather than focusing only upon those exceptional instances in which food power has been used by exporters, we review a larger sample of national food and food trade policies to assess the frequency with which importers as well as exporters seek to exercise food power in the first place.

Chapters 2 and 3 examine the policies of two importing countries,

India and the Soviet Union, for evidence that "defensive" food power strategies (such as trade reduction or trade diversification) have been employed. In chapter 4 the policies of the United States are examined for evidence that "offensive" food power strategies have been pursued. From these examinations it is learned that none of these three nations any longer manipulates its food trade policy in consistent search of an external economic or diplomatic advantage. Neither in an "offensive" nor in a "defensive" mode, does any of these nations consistently seek to exercise food power. Chapters 5 and 6 review two exceptional occasions when the "food weapon" was used: the protracted U.S. threat to suspend food aid to India in 1965–67, and the actual U.S. suspension of commercial food sales to the Soviet Union in 1980–81. On both occasions, despite an apparent abundance of food trade leverage, the United States is seen to have made external gains which are exceptionally modest.

This rejection of both preconceptions about food power suggests an optimistic conclusion, that the use or misuse of the so-called food weapon is a much-exaggerated concern. Of the many threats to the peaceful conduct of international relations today, and of the many threats to the security and stability of the world's food-trading system, "food power" is one of the least substantial.

2 India: Domestic Sources of Grain Trade Policy

India's unmet domestic food needs are colossal by any standard. Approximately one-third of India's 700 million citizens are too poor to afford a minimum diet needed to sustain a healthy level of human activity. Per capita food consumption within India remains well below world standards and has not increased over the past two decades. Half of all the world's chronically undernourished people live in India.[1]

How, then, can we explain India's apparent reluctance to import more food from abroad? India's net foodgrain imports over the past several decades have actually declined.[2] During the 1960s those imports averaged a significant 5.6 million tons per year, but by 1977 India had emerged as a small net *exporter* of foodgrains, and began to ship varying quantities of wheat and rice to the Soviet Union, Vietnam, Bangladesh, Mauritius, and several states in the Persian Gulf.[3] India briefly resumed importing wheat on a small scale in 1981, but it continued for a time its exports of rice. In fact, the Indian Planning Commission expressed a hope that India's rice exports would be able to triple during the period of the Sixth Five-Year Plan, so as to reach a level of 3 million tons by 1984–85.[4] This goal would not be met, but by 1984 India was once again contemplating modest exports of wheat.

India's emergence as an occasional net exporter of small quantities of wheat and rice might suggest that some internal food needs are being neglected in the conduct of Indian grain trade policy, and that external objectives are instead the dominant concern. Perhaps the Indian government has cut its foodgrain imports and has sought instead to export foodgrains so as to conserve foreign exchange, or to reduce India's vulnerability to diplomatic food trade "blackmail." Perhaps India's grain trade policies are functioning as little more than an adjunct to that nation's larger foreign economic and security policies. Those who accept the presumption of food power would expect nothing less.

In fact, India's recent grain trade policies have not been driven by foreign policy objectives. Those grain trade policies at times have been *compatible* with India's external interests and objectives, but they consistently have been determined by a more important set of domestic policy concerns. Appearances to the contrary, changes in India's grain trade policy abroad closely mirror changes in that nation's foodgrain balance at home, particularly as that balance expresses itself through an ever-changing level of government-owned food stocks, and through price trends in India's domestic food market. During those interludes when public food stocks are adequate in India and retail food prices are low, imports decline. It is an unfortunate fact that a significant share of the Indian population remain undernourished even as imports decline, but this tragic fact reflects the low purchasing power and political invisibility of India's many poor citizens, rather than anyone's conscious decision to sacrifice internal food needs in pursuit of external policy objectives.

The Domestic Food Balance

For lack of income, or for lack of sufficient political organization, many Indian citizens are still unable to give effective expression to their need for food. It could be argued that India has gone a long way toward meeting the "supply" side of its massive internal food problems; foodgrain production is now responding well enough to internal consumption demands which register in the market place. Unfortunately, India has been less successful in solving the "demand" side of its food problems. So long as "effective demand" for food within India fails to grow, further gains in Indian food production will only translate into a commercial food surplus and a reduced need for imports, despite the persistence of widespread malnutrition.

A large share of India's 700 million citizens are without adequate income to exercise effective purchasing power in the domestic food market. India's per capita income of $180 is only marginally greater than that of the poorest states of sub-Sahara Africa.[5] According to India's own official estimate, 48 percent of the population remains below a poverty line defined by the income that would be sufficient to purchase a minimum daily food requirement.[6] Poverty persists because so much of that nation's most abundant resource—its still growing population—is neither equipped nor organized to create wealth. Nearly 80 percent of India's people continue to live in the countryside, where the creation of wealth continues to be hampered by natural disadvantages (primarily weather and climate) and by a combination of man-made disincentives to productive labor, including India's own culture and tradition, the impact of its colonial experience, and the inadequate or inequitable distribution within India of education, land, capital, and status.

Such barriers to the creation of wealth in rural India have been relieved only in part by urban industrial development. After a quarter of a century of planned growth, the modern industrial sector still provides jobs to fewer than 15 percent of new workers every year, and to only about 10 percent of the total workforce.[7] With a literacy rate below 40 percent, India's workforce responds slowly, even to industrial development that is centrally planned and generously subsidized.

Rapid income growth of the kind that can trigger larger food demands, including food import demands, has not yet been experienced in India. Over the span of India's first five national planning periods (between 1951 and 1977), per capita income grew at an annual rate of less than 1.5 percent. Three out of four nonindustrial countries did better, and many of those from a higher base. India's present leaders should not be singled out for having failed to generate higher rates of income growth, however. India's economic growth rates since independence in 1947 have been several times greater than those recorded during the earlier half of the century, when the economy stagnated under British rule.[8]

Purchasing power is also unevenly distributed. The poorest 30 percent of households account for less than 15 percent of total consumer spending. The poorest citizens spend a larger share of their income on food, but they spend less in proportion to their numbers than the well-to-do. The poorer half of the population spends more than two-thirds of its budget on food, but these expenditures account for only about one-third of the nation's total food purchases.[9]

A more equitable income distribution within India would no doubt remedy the inadequate diet of many Indian households. By one estimate, if income in India were "equalized" hunger throughout the country could be eliminated, with an accompanying increase in total national food requirements of only about 6 percent.[10] This low increase in total requirements, even if income were equalized, is actually another reminder of India's overall poverty. *Even if evenly distributed,* India's present wealth would be *insufficient* to stimulate a rapid growth in aggregate consumption such as might lead to a dramatic surge in food imports.

Some of India's low-income food consumers have been able to make their demands effective outside the marketplace. Ever since independence, after the food emergencies experienced under British rule during the Second World War, the Indian government has taken steps to provide subsidized food distribution to politically visible low-income urban dwellers, particularly in Calcutta and Bombay. These urban poor do not always have the purchasing power to demand food supplies in the marketplace, but their concentrated numbers and proximity give them a compensating measure of political power.

There are sound social and economic justifications for directing food subsidies toward India's urban poor. The majority of undernourished citizens live in the heavily populated countryside, but rural dwellers engaged in agriculture often have other food sources close at hand to compensate for foodgrain shortages. A larger *share* of urban dwellers routinely suffer from inadequate calorie intake. Also, it is widely believed by Indian officials that concentrations of food marketing power in the countryside can pose a threat to the food security of urban dwellers. Large producers and wholesalers are said to routinely hoard their grain in times of short supply, so as to drive free market prices still higher and beyond the reach of the urban poor.

Even so, it is the greater political power of urban dwellers, including some who live well above the poverty line, that drives India's large and expensive food subsidy program.[11] The plight of low-income urban groups may be offered as the chief concern, but middle- and upper-income urban groups also enjoy access to subsidized "fair price shops." In times of high free market prices, it is not only the poor who are willing to seek out such shops, endure long lines, and accept foodgrains of a lower quality.

In contrast to urban dwellers, the rural poor lack the political means to make their food demands effective.[12] One of India's few programs designed specifically to subsidize food consumption among the rural poor—the Food For Work Program (FFWP)—was created in 1977, not in response to political demands from the poor but for the purpose of moving a temporary grain surplus out of expensive and inadequate government storage facilities.[13] Even in such times of abundance, if only because of their greater dispersion across the countryside, the rural poor do not enjoy the city dwellers' access to subsidized food distribution.

For political as well as economic reasons, therefore, a large part of India's human demand for foodgrain remains ineffective. Under these circumstances, the Indian government can meet its primary obligation to maintain adequate supplies of inexpensive food in urban areas in most years without having to arrange larger imports. Foodgrain imports can be discontinued altogether in those years when abundant domestic production and government procurement push public foodgrain stocks up to an optimal level. If public stocks should begin to exceed that level, a modest volume of foodgrain exports might even be arranged.

Indian foodgrain production has at times grown fast enough to provide such conditions of market abundance. Unfortunately, the internal food market to which Indian officials react is somewhat disconnected from the nation's much larger subsistence foodgrain economy. Only a small share of Indian foodgrain production ever enters commercial market channels, and only a fraction of those marketed supplies are ever procured by the Indian government for purposes such as price management or public distribution. When Indian officials make food policy, they may therefore be reacting to only one part of the nation's larger foodgrain balance. Foodgrain stock levels in government storage, measured against the rate of "offtake" from the nation's Public Distribution System (PDS), may become a narrow but decisive factor in the decision to trade. How trade policy decisions respond to this segment of India's internal needs can be appreciated only by clarifying the link between public foodgrain distribution and India's larger commercial foodgrain market.

More than half of India's total annual foodgrain production never enters a commercial market. Instead, it is retained on the farm, for domestic consumption, for seed, for feed, or for payments in kind to agricultural laborers. The share of grain production finally sent to market, farm by farm, may depend upon the size of the production unit. Large farmers, seeking to maximize income, may chose to market less of their production when prices are low, preferring to hold their grain in storage, hoping for a future price increase. Small farmers, who have more pressing short-run cash income needs, may actually market more grain when prices fall.[14] In an average year, only about 35–40 percent of total Indian wheat production, and 25 percent of all rice production, is commercially marketed.[15]

Much of India's marketed foodgrain is produced in the northern states of Punjab, Haryana, Western Uttar Pradesh, and Andhra Pradesh, where the use of fertilizer, irrigation, and new seed varieties is most advanced. Foodgrain production in these "surplus" states enters a well-developed market chain, moving from small market towns to central regional markets, and from there most often to terminal markets in large urban centers. This grain will have been handled along the way by a series of commission agents, wholesalers, processors, and retail merchants. Much controversy surrounds the degree of control that can be exercised over these markets by large grain producers and wholesalers. The view held by many Indian officials is that producers and wholesalers tend to withhold grain from regional and terminal markets in times of tight supply, thereby aggravating shortages, driving up prices, and earning windfall profits. Government regulation and intervention in foodgrain markets typically is justified as a necessary counterweight to this perceived hoarding tendency within the private trade.[16] The acute sensitivity of Indian grain markets to weather fluctuations certainly provides a natural venue within which experienced traders and speculators can prosper. But the capacity of Indian producers and private traders to control market deliveries is probably exaggerated by government officials.[17]

Whatever its precise structure, India's commercial grain market is a supplier to a public as well as to a private foodgrain purchasing system. Acting through the Food Corporation of India (FCI), the Indian government annually purchases about one-quarter of all foodgrains entering commercial market channels. These foodgrains are then subsequently sold by FCI, at subsidized prices, through an extensive network of several hundred thousand designated fair price shops (a disproportionate share of which are located in urban areas). The Indian government operates this public distribution system on what it calls a "no profit no loss basis." Within the open commercial market, where prices move with relative freedom, the procurement agents of FCI seek to make adequate annual purchases of grain at a predetermined "procurement price." This grain is then held in publicly owned or rented storage while being distributed throughout the year at a predetermined "issue price," which is set to fall below open market retail prices.

Through the many adjustments that can be made in managing the PDS, the government enjoys a central means to pursue its various domestic marketing objectives. Price stability in the open market, which is usually the primary domestic objective, can be preserved by alternately drawing down and then replenishing the foodgrain supplies in the government's central pool. Supplies coming into the central pool can be managed through yearly adjustments in both procurement prices and in quantitative procurement "targets." In parallel fashion, yearly or monthly "offtake" from the PDS can be adjusted or maintained at a desired level through a variety of formal and informal means, including both the adjustment of "issue" prices, and the opening or closing of additional fair price shops in low- or high-income neighborhoods. By offering stronger promotion to the offtake of either wheat or rice through fair price shops, the government can also adjust the balance among separate commodities in the central pool. PDS operations also permit the government to pursue diverse farm income policy objectives, as the setting of annual procurement prices has become a principal means of rewarding commercial farm interests for their continued political support.

Management of this PDS can at times become expensive. The budgetary costs of subsidized food distribution can grow quite large (increasing to $800 million by 1980–81).[18] Containing these costs is no simple task, as consumers oppose a sudden rapid increase in issue prices, while producers firmly resist any proposal to reduce the procurement price. If the gap between these two should widen, the implied public cost of food subsidies will grow. The PDS can also disrupt India's fragile financial and monetary system. By renting grain storage facilities, or by contracting for massive grain transport operations in an emergency, FCI may find itself responsible for an inflationary expansion of the nation's money supply.

In an effort to minimize budgetary costs in particular, the Indian government tries to use various administrative means to reduce procurement and distribution costs. For example, it places restrictions upon the private movement of grain from surplus to deficit states, hoping to bottle up grain in surplus areas so as to depress free market prices, thus making the government's preset procurement price seem more attractive to farmers. In one extreme circumstance in 1973 the Indian government briefly banned all private wheat trade, in a vain hope that producers would have no choice but to sell to FCI. At other times, grain producers and rice millers have been forced to sell minimum quantities to the government under a mandatory "levy." Officials concede that the procurement of adequate quantities of grain for subsidized public distribution would not be affordable without some element of compulsion.[19]

Using this wide variety of policy instruments, officials at the "Centre" of the Indian government in New Delhi may appear to enjoy a commanding position in relation to the nation's foodgrain economy. But they are in reality highly dependent upon the cooperation of powerful local authorities in India's separate states, which may be under the control of an opposition party. For example, the single most important annual food policy decision—setting the procurement price for wheat and rice—is heavily influenced by state authorities. Procurement price decisions are customarily initiated at the Centre by the Agricultural Prices Commission, which forwards a recommendation based upon a review of production costs to the Food Department in the Ministry of Agriculture, for eventual consideration by the Cabinet. But state authorities are consulted at every step in this process, and the final price decision almost always is adjusted *upward,* following a conference (held individually or collectively) with Chief Ministers from individual states. Even if the Centre manages to secure state approval for procurement prices and for separate state procurement targets, it must still entrust the procurement operation itself to state authorities. The secretary of each state procurement agency administers the procurement effort, issues orders to collection agents, arranges financing, handling, and storage, interprets rules, adjusts controls, and enjoys considerable leeway overall to proceed as he sees fit. The result is quite often no more than a haphazard approximation of the procurement strategy designed at the Centre.[20]

India's fair price shops are also administered by state authorities, through a process that involves licensing retailers, registering households, issuing ration cards, and determining the amount that can be purchased by each family each month. Authorities in New Delhi can exercise some control over state purchases of grain from the central pool, but subsidized distribution is otherwise greatly influenced by the administrative competence and the political loyalty of the state authorities involved. It is within this problematic administrative and domestic political context that government officials at the Centre must manage India's external food trade.

The logic by which the Indian food system generates external trade requirements can be easily understood in the abstract. With only a few exceptions, foreign trade in foodgrains is a government monopoly in India.[21] The Food Department at the Centre seeks to arrange grain imports whenever annual procurement from domestic production begins to fall behind annual offtake from the PDS. After crop failures due to inadequate monsoon rains, the gap between procurement and off-take can widen quite rapidly. If open market prices increase following bad weather and a bad harvest, more consumers will be attracted to the fair price shops, and offtake from the PDS will increase. Those consumers who were previously unwilling to accept the lower-quality grains available in fair price shops, and those who previously found the use of those shops inconvenient or time consuming, now turn to the PDS to gain the growing price advantage. For producers, meanwhile, high open market prices provide less incentive to sell grain to the government. If open market prices move too far above the FCI procurement price, the postharvest procurement effort may falter, and the annual replenishment of public grain stocks falls short. A failed procurement then compounds the government's short supply position, because public knowledge of dwindling stocks at the Centre drives open market prices still higher, further stimulating offtake and further inhibiting procurement. The government at the Centre must protect itself from such an accelerating drain on public grain stocks if it is to avoid opposition charges of mismanagement, and if it is to protect the security of urban food consumers. Whenever FCI grain procurements within India fall far enough behind PDS offtake to threaten a loss of control over urban food prices, Centre officials consider making up the difference with imports.

India's occasional foodgrain exports may also be explained through reference to the workings of the public foodgrain procurement and distribution system. After a period of good weather and abundant production, as open market prices fall, producers are more likely to sell to the government at the preset procurement price, and FCI procurements rise. Simultaneously, as urban consumers find it affordable once again to buy higher-quality foodgrains through convenient private retail outlets, subsidized sales through fair price shops lag. With procurement on the rise and offtake in decline, the government begins to accumulate oversized public stocks. Accumulation of such public stocks beyond a certain level is unnecessary either to guarantee domestic price stability or to supply the PDS. Burdensome public storage costs increase and additional private storage facilities may have to be leased, as stocks continue to accumulate, making more difficult the management of the money supply as well as the budget. As storage turnover time increases, the quality of foodgrain in storage also begins to deteriorate. The short-run option to increase the offtake of grain from public stocks through rural FFWPs may be limited by practical or political considerations. At this point the government at the Centre may decide to bring its PDS into better balance by arranging for a modest volume of foodgrain exports.

To underscore the decisive role these inward-looking considerations continue to play in setting Indian grain trade policy, consider India's recent trading experience in two distinct international foodgrain markets—wheat and rice. Since its independence India at various times has been both an importer and an exporter of these two foodgrains, both of which are vital to its own domestic diet. On no occasion, however, has the pursuit of an external economic or diplomatic objective set the pattern of this trade. Appearances to the contrary and official rhetoric notwithstanding, India has not paid close heed to its foreign policy interests when arranging its food imports or exports.

Rice Trade Policy

After China, India is the second largest producer and consumer of rice in the world. Rice is the staple food of the eastern and southern regions of the country, but it is consumed to a varying extent by almost the entire Indian population. Indian rice production has recently averaged about 50 million tons per year. For a brief period after 1978, a small share of this annual production total, roughly half a million tons, was allocated by the Indian government for export.

India's recent rice exports appeared at first glance to be incompatible with that nation's unmet domestic food needs. In response to internal needs, after all, India was for many years a noteworthy *importer* of rice. On the eve of the Second World War, India's annual grain imports, most of which were rice, stood at 2 million tons. It was the interruption of these rice imports after the Japanese occupation of Burma in 1942 that helped trigger the calamitous 1943 Bengal Famine, in which more than one million people died. India continued to import rice after the war on a somewhat reduced scale, averaging 0.5 million tons of rice imports per year through the decade of the 1960s. But then in the 1970s, quite suddenly, India transformed itself from a small rice importer into a small but nonetheless significant rice *exporter*, with net exports exceeding 1 million tons in 1981 (Table 1).

These rice exports briefly provided the Indian government with a variety of external economic and diplomatic benefits. Yet it was not in search of such external benefits that the government first authorized exports of rice. Indian rice export policy was instead a function of the

Table 1. Indian net rice trade, 1961–1984 (thousands of metric tons)

Calendar year	Net trade	Calendar year	Net trade[a]
1961	−384	1973	+ 8
1962	−391	1974	+ 35
1963	−478	1975	− 161
1964	−630	1976	− 203
1965	−723	1977	− 15
1966	−783	1978	+ 139
1967	−451	1979	+ 337
1968	−443	1980	+ 423
1969	−472	1981	+1,073
1970	−179	1982	+ 623
1971	−227	1983	− 145
1972	−117	1984	− 650

a. Plus signs indicate net exports by India.
Sources: U.S. Department of Agriculture, *Foreign Agriculture Circular*, Grains, FG-20-79, December 1979, p. 59; FG-13-84, October 1984, p. 18.

prevailing domestic foodgrain balance, at least insofar as that balance revealed itself to the government in the level and stability of free market prices, and in the availability of adequate government stocks for public distribution.

As late as 1971–75, government-held rice stocks at year's end averaged only 1.8 million tons, not enough to guarantee continuous public distribution and internal price stability. During most of these years, as a result, India kept up its habit of importing rice.[22] Beginning in 1976, however, government-owned rice stocks suddenly began a marked increase to levels well above 4 million tons. In response to this more comfortable stock position, imports were discontinued. Government rice stocks nonetheless continued to grow, reaching nearly 6 million tons at the beginning of the November 1978 marketing year. It was at this point, when it found itself holding public stocks equal to roughly 150 percent of annual rice distribution through the PDS, that the government first authorized a small volume of rice exports.[23]

It is important to realize that the Indian government had no export objectives in mind when it first began to accumulate these large surplus stocks of rice in 1976. The surplus was largely a result of a sudden and unforseen increase in rice production in two northern states, Punjab and Haryana. Because of a local dietary preference for wheat products in these two states, consumption failed to keep pace with local production; the resulting surplus was sold to the government. Between 1971 and 1976, for example, with rice production in Punjab and Haryana increasing from 1.1 million tons to 2.1 million tons, sales to the government more than doubled, from 0.8 to 1.7 million tons. Over the next five years government procurement of rice from these two states nearly doubled once more, to more than 3.1 million tons, or more than half of the nationwide rice procurement total.[24]

This sudden emergence of much larger rice procurements from Punjab and Haryana in the 1970s probably should not have been a surprise to food policy planners at the Centre. The government had recently begun offering much-improved price incentives to Indian rice growers, increasing the procurement price for paddy by 39 percent between 1972 and 1974. Further increases were then provided by the farmer-oriented Janata government after 1977. These improved price incentives were designed to coincide with the introduction after 1971 of much better strains of "high-yielding" Indian rice varieties; rice cropland using those varieties nearly doubled between 1971 and 1976.[25] Planners had hoped all along that the expanded use of these high-yield varieties in combination with expanded irrigation might lead to increased output in India's rice-consuming southern and eastern states, during the *rabi* season (January to April). They failed to anticipate that large rice production gains would also be registered in India's northern wheat-consuming states during the autumn *kharif* season. Planners had been hoping that these northern states would employ their well-irrigated croplands during the *kharif* season to produce maize and millet, an important food supply for local low-income consumers. But the new government price guarantee, plus irrigation, suddenly made rice a more attractive autumn crop in the north, where resourceful Punjabi farmers quickly mastered the necessary cultivation techniques and began growing an ever-larger rice surplus, largely for sale to the government.

This rice surplus produced in India's northern states was difficult for the government to distribute within the rice-consuming areas of India itself. Transport and storage requirements differ for rice compared with other foodgrains such as wheat, and are on the whole more difficult and more costly. Partly for these reasons the PDS traditionally had handled a much larger volume of wheat than rice. Nor was there an obvious commercial market for this surplus rice elsewhere within India, in part because many rice consumers have strong preferences for local varieties. Moreover, an earlier government campaign to substitute wheat for rice in the Indian diet had succeeded all too well, further reducing opportunities to distribute surplus rice through fair price shops. For reasons of speed and convenience in preparation, particularly in urban areas, workers had been acquiring an irreversible preference for wheat products. Despite a concerted government effort to resubstitute rice for wheat in foodgrain issues from fair price shops, and despite a more successful public distribution of rice through the newly initiated FFWP beginning in 1978, total annual rice issues continued to lag behind government procurements. Only at this point, as government stocks continued to grow, were exports at last authorized.

Internal political considerations may have also constrained the consumption of public rice stocks within India, opening the way for rice exports by 1978. Two of India's most important rice-deficit states—Kerala and West Bengal—were during these years under the control of Marxist opposition parties and hence out of political favor with leaders of the Centre. Neither the Janata coalition, which governed between 1977 and 1979, nor the Congress leadership under Indira Gandhi, felt much political pressure to invest in accelerated rice distribution for these states. Such an effort would only strain the nation's limited storage and transport capacity, while producing political benefits at the state level for the leaders of the opposition. India's decision to initiate a small volume of rice exports in 1978 is therefore intelligible entirely through reference to inward-looking policy calculations.

A rice export policy that began as an effort to reduce surplus government stocks at home was then briefly managed to provide some secondary trading and diplomatic advantages abroad. Evidence for this secondary goal first surfaced when India's rice surplus was sharply reduced following a severe drought in 1979. Government-owned rice stocks, which had nearly doubled after 1977 to reach a high of 8.4 million tons in November 1979, fell to 5.5 million tons by November 1980, and then to a mere 3.5 million tons by November 1981.[26] Despite this drop in its surplus stocks, the Indian government momentarily continued to authorize an *expanding* volume of rice exports.

Particularly noteworthy in its *external* commercial and diplomatic significance was the April 1981 decision of the government to sign a bilateral agreement making available to the Soviet Union 500,000 tons of Indian rice in 1982, along with various other Indian agricultural commodities, in exchange for Soviet crude oil and petroleum products. Although this was India's third one-year rice-for-oil barter with the Soviet Union, the first having been signed in April 1979 when India's rice surplus was still very large,[27] the 1981 agreement committed the Indian government, at a time of tightening supply, to *expanded* rice exports to the Soviet Union (up from 410,000 tons in calendar year 1981 to 500,000 tons in calendar year 1982). The 1981 agreement also committed the Indian government to make available to the Soviet Union 100,000 tons of barley and 200,000 tons of maize in calendar year 1982, once again in barter for petroleum products and crude oil. These coarse grains, widely used as a food source by many low-income Indian consumers, had not recently been in surplus, and total exports in the year before this agreement did not exceed 35,000 tons. Considerations other than domestic availability appeared to be influencing Indian grain export policies.

The need to barter whatever was on hand to ensure continued access to affordable petroleum imports was no doubt a factor in India's decision to continue promoting rice exports in 1981. India's Sixth Five-Year Plan (1980–85), which had been published earlier in 1981, emphasized that the Indian economy had become "extremely vulnerable to increases in oil prices and to deterioration in our terms of trade generally."[28] The Plan stated its specific objective "to increase production of export-oriented agricultural and agro-based commodities . . . rather than exporting [only] what is available in excess in the country." A variety of ambitious agricultural "export targets" were then set out in the Plan, with rice leading the list, designated for an ambitious 3 million tons of exports by 1984–85. India's rice exports may have begun in response to the sudden and unexpected emergence of an internal surplus in 1978, but later they briefly came to be seen, at least by some planners, as a valuable means to secure a high-priority external economic objective.

One might suspect that India's rice exports were also being continued in pursuit of external diplomatic objectives, within the context of India's important diplomatic and strategic ties to the Soviet Union. These ties, first made explicit in the August 1971 Treaty of Friendship, had been loosened somewhat between 1977 and 1979, when India's Janata government had announced a policy of "genuine non-alignment," while seeking to improve its relations with the United States, China, and Pakistan. But upon the return to power early in 1980 of Indira Gandhi's Congress party, diplomatic relations with the Soviet Union regained more of their earlier significance. In May 1980, for example, India concluded an important $1.6 billion arms purchase agreement with the Soviet Union, under which two-thirds of India's army and air force equipment, and three-quarters of its sophisticated armored strike force equipment, would continue to be of Soviet origin. Later that spring India also became the first major nation outside the Soviet bloc to recognize the Heng Samrin regime in Kampuchea, brought to power as a result of an earlier Soviet-supported Vietnamese invasion of that country.[29] Was India's subsequent willingness, in 1981, to export an ever-larger quantity of its rice on Soviet account part of a larger diplomatic bargain between the two countries? Perhaps India was under pressure to export rice to secure from the Soviet Union its imported arms as well as its oil.

In fact, such external economic and diplomatic objectives were never decisive, even at this juncture, in shaping Indian rice trade policy. India's rice export policies were still ultimately driven by considerations of domestic foodgrain availability. This became clear in 1982, when the Indian government finally moved firmly to cut back on rice exports, despite the persistence of foreign exchange and oil import requirements. Though it originally hoped in 1982 to export as much as 1 million tons of rice, the Indian government eventually reduced sales to only half that amount when domestic rice production and procurement were further lowered by yet another drought. And in March 1982, when time came to renew its annual rice trade agreement with the Soviet Union, India agreed to only a six-month extension, and to exports of only 175,000 tons of rice during the abbreviated period of that extension. The next year a ban was placed on the further export of ordinary varieties of Indian rice (limited quantities of high-priced, high-quality *basmati* rice could still be sold abroad), and India's rice-for-oil barter arrangements with the Soviet Union were suspended.[30] By mid-1983 India was returning to its earlier status as a net importer of rice, as it resumed entering the world market for substantial rice purchases.

India had taken care even before its 1982 drought never to permit its rice exports to run too far ahead of domestic supply requirements. As early as 1980, after the 1979 drought, rice exports had been officially constrained below original export targets, to ensure adequate supplies for domestic public distribution. In 1981 the announcement of total export authorizations was also prudently delayed, pending detailed reports on monsoon damage to the autumn rice harvest. Even with public rice stocks much reduced in 1981, the FCI had never sacrificed its ability to make as much rice available, on a monthly basis, as would be required for public distribution.

It could also be noted that the terms of India's rice-for-oil barter with the Soviet Union were always studiously protective of India's own internal food concerns. The Soviet Union originally asked the Indian government for grain export commitments of wheat as well as rice, for commitments in excess of the quantities contained in the 1981 agreement, and for commitments on an extended five-year basis, rather than one year at a time. Despite their anxiety over foreign exchange earnings and access to affordable petroleum supplies, Indian officials had resisted these demands, insisting upon more restricted and more tentative rice-for-oil agreements.

As for the rice export targets contained in the Sixth Plan, Planning Commission members argue that there was never a rigid timetable for increasing rice exports.[31] The commission felt less urgency in promoting its exports of rice than in promoting nonfoodgrain agricultural exports. In the cases of some manufactured food products, an export opportunity not taken immediately might be lost for good, but rice was seen as a product for which there would always be a foreign market. India's rice exports, therefore, were never heavily driven by external economic considerations. Domestic rice stocks available for public distribution, rather than external trade obligations or external trade opportunities, remained the dominant concern.

This was not necessarily the wisest policy for India to follow. Some economic experts in India have long advocated that rice exports should be promoted somewhat apart from the changing level of foodgrain production at home. Compared with wheat, ton for ton, rice usually brings a higher price in world markets. By exporting 1 ton of rice, in a good year, India might be able to earn sufficient foreign exchange to import as much as 2 tons of wheat, thereby meeting both its foreign exchange and domestic foodgrain requirements with greater efficiency. Indian experts note that both China and Pakistan, on occasion, have used this rice-for-wheat trading strategy to good advantage. Unfortunately, because of the way in which the Indian government is organized, it is difficult to reach an operating consensus on sophisticated trade strategies of this kind. Too many separate constituent interests might object. Rice-deficit states, which have misgivings about rice exports, could join in a coalition with wheat-producing states, which object to wheat imports, resulting in a formidable political barrier at home to any such rice-for-wheat strategy. Indian political leaders also fear that such a strategy would be misrepresented by clever opposition leaders. Because a larger tonnage of cheap wheat could be imported with the money earned from a smaller tonnage of exported rice, India might often emerge from this strategy *in terms of tonnage alone* as a "net importer" of food. A domestic political audience, long conditioned to view "net imports" as a disadvantageous trade posture, might be aroused to object.

Even less have India's rice exports been driven by external diplomatic concerns. Appearances to the contrary, India did not feel any need to export rice, after 1979, to ensure the continuation of its security assistance or its diplomatic support from the Soviet Union. Quite the opposite: it was the Soviet Union that was busy courting India. After its invasion of Afghanistan in December 1979 the Soviet Union experienced an uncomfortable interlude of diplomatic estrangement from most of the nonaligned states in South and Southwest Asia. It was therefore in no position to place any additional strain on its ties to India. It was instead willing to exchange oil for rice on terms that proved highly favorable to India. A Soviet desire to accommodate India, more than India's need to export rice to accommodate the Soviet Union, lay behind the terms of these barter agreements.

India's rice-for-oil agreements with the Soviet Union were consistently advantageous from India's standpoint. First, consider that India managed through these agreements to secure access to an expanded quantity of Soviet oil after a period of tight world supplies, without having to yield on any one of a variety of Soviet requests for larger quantities of rice, for quantities of wheat as well as rice, or for barter commitments on more than a one-year-at-a-time basis. Second, it is worth noting that these barter agreements with the Soviet Union made it easier for India to export its rice surplus than might otherwise have been the case. India often encounters severe difficulties when it seeks to export large quantities of rice through private trading channels to non-Soviet-bloc customers. It was not uncommon for Indian rice to be weeks late in arriving at dockside for export, and private grain-trading companies often found it costly to schedule their business with India under such circumstances. But the Soviet Union, which operates a less cost-conscious transport system and is always seeking ways to spend the rupee surplus it accumulates in its two-way barter trade with India, is more willing to absorb such costly delays. Without the Soviet market, India might have found it more difficult to expand its exports so quickly when its domestic rice surplus developed after 1978.

Soviet purchases of Indian rice, after 1979, were actually a part of a larger pattern of Soviet concessions to India to ensure that country's much-valued friendship. Even with Indira Gandhi in power in New Delhi, the Soviet Union could not afford to take India's friendship for granted. India, which did not wish to be locked forever into an exclusive dependence upon the Soviet Union, for a number of years had been diversifying its sources of military supply; by 1980 India was actually less dependent upon the Soviet Union for weapons than it had been a decade earlier.[32] By 1980 India had successfully negotiated supply agreements for sophisticated fighter aircraft with Britain and France, and in October 1980 it was even on the verge of completing a $350 million purchase of arms from the United States, the first of its kind in sixteen years.[33] A parallel diversification of India's external economic ties was also giving pause to the Soviets. When the Indian government announced less restrictive policies toward private industry late in 1980, closer contact with Western business firms seemed at last a real prospect. In order to preserve much-valued ties to India, and especially to preserve India's tolerant attitude toward Soviet policies in Afghanistan, Leonid Brezhnev himself paid a visit to New Delhi in December 1980, and showered India with additional economic aid, announcing a further increase in oil deliveries, despite India's refusal of additional foodgrain deliveries in return.[34] India was not manipulating its food exports in search of a diplomatic "food power" advantage over the Soviet Union—on this occasion it was the Soviet Union, through its willingness to import rice on India's terms, that was making sacrifices to gain a diplomatic advantage.

To a limited degree, the conscious pursuit of diplomatic gain did govern the *destination* of some of India's rice exports, but only for a short time *before* the onset of large sales to the Soviet Union in 1979. In 1978, India found it convenient to initiate its exports of non-*basmati* rice through a series of small-scale commodity loans and grants to a number of friendly or neighboring countries—including Vietnam, Bangladesh, Mauritius, Kenya, Yemen, Kuwait, Kampuchea, and several states in Eastern Europe. At this early juncture, India's Ministry of External Affairs (relaying requests from recipient country governments) did take a lead role in the export authorization process. By 1979, however, when India's rice exports began to reach a commercially significant total volume, large-scale barter agreements with the Soviet Union became the preferred means of export promotion. In a curious sense, therefore, India's diplomatic calculations actually began to play a *diminished* role in its rice export policy once the Soviet Union emerged as the principal destination for its exports.

India's distinct preference for the pursuit of inward-looking policy objectives is evident, even within the context of its brief decision to export rice. This discovery does not fit well with the presumption of "food power."

Wheat Trade Policy

Just as domestic conditions and objectives usually offer the better means to understand Indian rice trade policy, so do they provide the better means to understand Indian wheat trade policy. Here again, first appearances are deceptive. In public, Indian officials have long stressed, as a foremost policy objective, the pursuit of "self-sufficiency" in their wheat supplies. Self-sufficiency, usually taken to mean the elimination of imports, would carry some obvious foreign policy attractions. Doing without wheat imports would not only save foreign exchange, it would reduce India's vulnerability to coercive food trade blackmail. Because India on several occasions since independence has actually managed to discontinue its wheat imports, despite continued malnutrition at home, we may be tempted to assume that the pursuit of such external economic or diplomatic objectives has in fact taken precedence. We might conclude that when India reduces its wheat imports it is pursuing a "defensive" sort of food power.

Official Indian pronouncements go a long way toward strengthening this impression. Oversized wheat imports in years past are routinely criticized for having exposed India to "dependence, the tutelage of others and the manipulation of markets and prices by producing exporting countries for self-serving ends."[35] Former Prime Minister Indira Gandhi at times explained India's reduced volume of wheat imports by pointing to just such external considerations. She cited a variety of external commercial and diplomatic dangers associated with importing wheat, ranging from the manipulation of prices by big exporters to the use of food exports as a "political weapon" against importers, and went so far as to urge other developing countries to follow India's lead, and to "do their utmost to attain self-sufficiency within the shortest possible time."[36]

Rhetoric aside, external economic and diplomatic objectives have never been so decisive in the shaping of India's wheat trade policies. On those several occasions since independence when India did approach self-sufficiency in wheat, external gains may have been realized, but they were largely secondary to the pursuit of inward-looking food policy objectives. Indeed, whenever inward-looking objectives subsequently required that wheat imports be resumed and that self-sufficiency be abandoned, outward-looking economic and diplomatic considerations never stood in the way.

Wheat at one time played only a modest role in the Indian diet. Today, however, wheat products such as bread have become an important convenience food for millions of urban dwellers in India, even beyond traditional wheat-consuming regions in the north. Per capita wheat consumption nationwide increased from 32 kilograms during the early 1960s to 50 kilograms per year by the late 1970s.[37] But this new appetite for wheat did not produce a steady growth in imports, because India's own domestic wheat production was able to grow roughly in pace with internal consumption. Indeed, the Indian government occasionally has been able to discontinue its wheat imports entirely, and even to arrange a small volume of wheat exports. On repeated occasions since 1947, due to domestic production gains, India achieved a brief commercial self-sufficiency in wheat supplies.

India's first flirtation with self-sufficiency in wheat supplies came and went in the mid-1950s, following two consecutive years of excellent weather. Indian officials were eager to reduce their wheat imports, to be sure. The uncertain dependability of imported food was impressed upon India during the wartime Bengal Famine of 1943, which was in part the result of an unforeseen interruption of foodgrain imports from Burma. From the first days of India's independence, in fact, the Foodgrains Policy Committee had recommended that dependence on imported foodgrains, primarily wheat, be eliminated in an orderly and planned fashion. A "Grow More Food" campaign was launched soon after 1947, one object of which was to attain complete self-sufficiency in foodgrains by 1952.[38]

This early campaign produced meager results, however, and wheat imports had to be continued until 1953–54, when two years of excellent weather at last produced a surge in domestic foodgrain production. During these two years total Indian foodgrain production increased by a surprising 30 percent, and as ample public stocks began to accumulate, wheat imports were cut back accordingly, from a high of 4.8 million tons in 1951 to 0.8 million tons by 1954, and a mere 0.5 million tons in 1955 (Table 2). Subsidies were introduced, to promote wheat consumption in traditional rice-consuming areas, but even then government-owned wheat stocks continued to accumulate. At one point early in 1955, in the mistaken belief that foodgrain self-sufficien-

Table 2.   Indian net wheat trade, 1951–1984 (thousands of metric tons)

Year	Net trade	Year	Net trade[a]
1951	− 4,800	1968	−5,670
1952	− 3,930	1969	−3,820
1953	− 2,040	1970	−3,550
1954	− 830	1971	−2,010
1955	− 510	1972	+ 490
1956	− 1,370	1973	−3,600
1957	− 3,620	1974	−4,680
1958	− 3,210	1975	−7,400
1959	− 3,850	1976	−6,510
1960	− 5,120	1977	−3,804
1961	− 3,490	1978	+ 223
1962	− 3,630	1979	+ 627
1963	− 4,540	1980	+ 348
1964	− 6,250	1981	0
1965	− 7,440	1982	−2,265
1966	−10,310	1983	−3,700
1967	− 8,660	1984	−2,500

a. Plus signs indicate net exports by India.
Sources: For 1951–76, see R. N. Chopra, *Evolution of Food Policy in India* (New Delhi: Macmillan India Ltd., 1981), p. 292; for 1977–84 (July–June ending years) see U.S. Department of Agriculture, *Foreign Agriculture Circular*, Grains, FG-4-81, 28 January 1981; FG-19-83, July 1983; FG-13-84, October 1984.

cy had been attained, the Indian government actually authorized a small volume of wheat exports.[39] In a more fateful development, during this early and highly deceptive period of short-term foodgrain abundance, Indian planners made a decision to redouble public investments in urban industrial development, and to reduce agriculture's investment share in the Second Five-Year Plan (1956–57 to 1960–61).[40]

A return of average weather late in 1955 soon forced a reappraisal. Wheat production fell, and with consumption still on the rise retail wheat prices began a steep climb. In hopes of containing these free market prices the government promptly discontinued all wheat export authorizations and stepped up subsidized internal distribution through a network of 5,000 newly opened fair price shops.[41] In order to sustain this public distribution effort, by mid-1956 substantial wheat imports once more had to be arranged. These costly imports were first resumed on a commercial basis during the second quarter of 1956; then in late August the Indian government signed the first of its several long-term agreements with the United States to import large quantities of U.S. wheat under the generous concessional provisions of the 1954 Public Law (P.L.) 480 food aid program (discussed in detail in Chapter 4).

As a matter of national pride, Indian officials had long been rhetorically opposed to accepting food aid. Even before independence, in 1946 India's food minister publicly expressed profound distaste for the process of arranging and receiving food aid from abroad: "It is a tragic sight to see India's representatives going from one end of the earth to another—literally from Persia to Peru—with the begging bowl in their hands for food."[42] Yet this rhetorical aversion did not prevent Indian officials from accepting a rapid expansion of wheat imports after 1956, on the attractive concessional terms made possible under P.L. 480. Indian industrial development planners saw P.L. 480 wheat, distributed through the recently expanded fair price shop system, as a convenient means to keep food prices in check during the upcoming period of anticipated deficit financing. Indian officials also calculated in 1956 that P.L. 480 wheat imports, which were to be sold for rupees that would then remain on India's account, could assist directly in the financing of India's ambitious Second Plan. India's 1957 Foodgrains Inquiry Committee made this calculation explicit, by endorsing larger food aid shipments because "imports under the P.L. 480 concessional terms would not only relieve us of our immediate foreign exchange commitments, but also help us to build a rupee fund which can be utilized for development purposes."[43]

With the return of less favorable weather, and with the industrial development objectives of the Second Plan uppermost in mind, Indian planners quickly fell back into a habit of importing wheat. By 1960 a second P.L. 480 agreement with the United States was negotiated, to permit an even larger volume of wheat imports. One stated purpose of this new agreement was the building of a 5 million ton wheat reserve in India, nominally in pursuit of Indian "self-sufficiency." But short term public distribution needs, plus the lure of rupee funds for India's Third Plan, remained the prime motivation. When one Indian official was asked in 1961 about the location of his nation's food reserves, he replied, "Oh, our reserves are in Kansas."[44]

India showed a striking disregard at this time for the larger diplomatic implications of its growing food aid dependence upon the United States. Even before the initiation of P.L. 480 sales in 1956, India had shown itself quite willing to take food aid from the United States whatever the risk of unwelcome diplomatic side effects. India's first large concessional wheat purchase from the United States came in 1951, despite growing bilateral diplomatic tensions over Korea, despite a humiliating delay in U.S. congressional approval, and despite repeated congressional efforts (only narrowly defeated) to attach unacceptable foreign policy conditions.[45] Bilateral relations were not that much better five years later when India signed the first of its many P.L. 480 agreements. Differences with the United States were then widening over a variety of sensitive issues, including U.S. arms aid to Pakistan, and the Dulles Plan then under discussion at the London Suez conference. India's new economic ties to the Soviet Union were a further source of tension; Vice-President Richard Nixon had described these ties as "inconsistent with freedom."[46] Such diplomatic disputes were kept in the background, however, as India went ahead with its P.L. 480 imports. Domestic critics were told that these imports were unrelated to India's foreign policy. Despite diplomatic tensions, concessional wheat imports from the United States, which began in 1956 at a modest level of 3.1 million tons a year, grew rapidly in the next decade to reach unprecedented levels above 10 million tons per year by 1965 and 1966.

External diplomatic calculations did eventually play a role in India's decision to reduce this increasing dependence on concessional wheat imports. In the aftermath of India's border war with China late in 1962, the United States had made a clumsy attempt to use India's increased need for economic assistance as a basis for seeking Indian concessions to Pakistan on the sensitive issue of Kashmir.[47] Then after India's brief war with Pakistan in September 1965, in an even stronger effort to force a negotiated end to the Kashmir conflict, the United States suddenly suspended all further military and capital assistance to both India and Pakistan. Although U.S. food aid to India was not terminated in 1965, a lesson was drawn in New Delhi that any form of continuing aid dependence on the United States might prove costly to India's diplomatic independence. At this point, the earlier rhetoric of foodgrain self-sufficiency for India was strongly revived.

Such diplomatic concerns notwithstanding, the significant initiatives taken by India in the early 1960s to boost domestic wheat production and thereby to reduce P.L. 480 imports were responsive as much to internal as to external policy objectives. Even before P.L. 480 imports had come to be seen as a threat to India's diplomatic independence, they had been recognized as a threat to the health of India's domestic foodgrain economy. It was, in fact, this prior domestic concern that inspired the earliest official initiatives, taken in 1964, to reduce India's wheat imports.

Well before India's war with Pakistan in 1965, planners had noticed that large imports of inexpensive P.L. 480 wheat, when pushed into the Indian market at low prices through fair price shops, reduced production incentives for India's own hard-pressed wheat farmers. Not long after India received its first P.L. 480 wheat imports, free market wheat prices within India began to lag conspicuously behind the price increases then being registered throughout the rest of the economy, putting a profit squeeze on commercial wheat producers. From 1959 to 1963 Indian wheat prices actually *declined* in nominal terms, even while India's general price index was tending upward.[48] In part as a result of this price disincentive passed on to domestic producers, the amount of acreage under wheat within India had stagnated. As one Indian analyst later explained, "With P.L. 480 wheat continuing to glut the market, wheat farmers lost interest in growing sufficient wheat to feed the Indian people. The American farmers had taken over the task for them."[49]

The internal damage being done by too much inexpensive wheat from abroad became impossible for India to ignore by 1964. Domestic production had by then fallen so far behind internal demand that prices finally stopped their downward trend and began an upswing, despite the continued *expansion* of cheap imports. Not even the signing of a larger P.L. 480 agreement in 1964 was enough to ensure internal price stability. Despite a good crop due to excellent weather and continuation of record imports, Indian wheat prices began to climb at an annual rate above 20 percent. Expanded imports of U.S. wheat, which began some years earlier as a convenient adjunct to domestic policy objectives, were recognized by 1964 to be an inadequate substitute for expanded wheat production at home.[50]

Indian officials also anticipated that in the near future there might be a limit to the quantity of wheat available to them from the United States on a concessional basis. Before reaching this limit they decided to seize the opportunity, provided by the development of high-yielding wheat varieties, to place renewed emphasis on domestic wheat production. C. Subramaniam, who became India's Food Minister at this critical juncture in 1964, recalls setting as his aim that India should achieve "self-sufficiency in foodgrains as early as possible."[51]

The first step taken under Subramaniam's leadership was to increase price guarantees offered to Indian wheat producers. In October 1964, a new Foodgrains Policy Committee recommended a 15 percent increase in wheat procurement prices. This provision of improved price incentives was then institutionalized through the formation of the Agricultural Prices Commission in January 1965. A final initiative, taken before the 1965–66 harvest season, was Subramaniam's bold decision to to import and promote the immediate use of high-yielding varieties of wheat, even though those varieties had not yet been fully tested in the Indian environment.

For two difficult years, these important initiatives bore little fruit. A disastrous drought in 1965 and again in 1966 *reduced* domestic wheat production, so much that India was forced to rely even more heavily than before on U.S. food aid. With a return of good weather in 1967–68, however, India's "green revolution" in wheat at last got under way, soon *doubling* total production. By 1971 India's P.L. 480 wheat imports could be terminated altogether. India's rhetorical objective of "self-sufficiency" in wheat was being vigorously and successfully pursued at last, but only after a key *internal* policy objective, food price stability, had apparently become attainable by no other means.

By 1970–71, as Indian wheat production reached nearly twice the level that had been recorded in 1964–65, foodgrain stocks grew to a record level of 8.1 million tons.[52] With foodgrain procurement from domestic production exceeding public distribution for the first time since independence, the Indian government decided to terminate its future P.L. 480 wheat imports altogether, and bravely announced itself once again self-sufficient in wheat supplies.

India's domestic wheat production success was not the only reason for the decision to terminate wheat imports. India's diplomatic aversion to U.S. food aid was by 1971 considerably strengthened, after President Lyndon B. Johnson's sustained attempt in 1965–67 to manipulate U.S. food aid promises to obtain a variety of difficult domestic policy reforms and unwelcome foreign policy concessions from the Indian government. This U.S. attempt to exercise "food power" over India, in its hour of greatest need (examined at length in chapter 5), provided added incentive to reduce future dependence on concessional wheat imports. Moreover, by 1971 India found itself falling into a still more difficult diplomatic conflict with the United States. A brutal war of succession in neighboring East Pakistan had brought on a renewed U.S. attempt to manipulate aid to India in search of diplomatic concessions. India's diplomatic relations with the United States in fact reached an all-time low at precisely the moment that India announced its P.L. 480 import termination, in late December 1971.

Since 1969, U.S. policies in Asia had been moving the United States closer to China, just as India had been moving closer to the Soviet Union. Immediately after Nixon's first trip to China in August 1971, India signed the twenty-year Treaty of Peace, Friendship and Cooperation with the Soviet Union. A civil war was by then under way in East Pakistan, providing an occasion for outside intervention and setting the stage for a severe U.S.–Indian diplomatic conflict. When Prime Minister Indira Gandhi served notice that she held West Pakistan entirely responsible for the crisis, the United States came quickly to the defense of its ally, and threatened India with yet another termination of economic aid and military sales.[53] Undeterred by this threat, India continued to provide support to Bengali resistance fighters in the East, eventually provoking Pakistan into a desperate attack against Indian military forces in the West on 3 December. Three days later, as India's superior army was taking the offensive against Pakistan, the United States made good its earlier threat to terminate most categories of aid. P.L. 480 wheat shipments to India were allowed to continue, just as they had been in 1965, but within a few weeks' time India itself took the initiative to terminate U.S. food aid, announcing that it would not accept any more P.L. 480 grain after 31 December 1971.[54]

Though it is tempting to view this decision to end P.L. 480 wheat imports as an instance in which India's diplomatic requirements were weighed more heavily than its domestic food requirements, evidence to the contrary abounds. As noted previously, 1971 was a year of unprecedented gains for Indian wheat production. By late autumn, as the diplomatic crisis reached its climax, India's limited grain storage facilities were so overburdened with supplies procured at home that additional wheat imports of any kind from any source were no longer necessary. In November, even before the war began, India gave preliminary signals of its plan to phase out wheat imports in recognition of this diminished internal need. And when the Indian government finally terminated all food aid imports in late December, the decision was announced without reference to foreign policy motivations. Agriculture Minister A. P. Shinde explained at the time that India had decided not to purchase the remainder of its authorized P.L. 480 imports "because of adequate production within the country." Shinde noted that the availability of an unprecedented 8 million ton stock of wheat and rice was enough to provide for "any emergency next year," without imports.[55] Indian agricultural planners perhaps were irritated by the suggestion that India's trade action was anything other than the logical conclusion to their own highly successful long-term campaign to boost domestic production. As early as 1966, yet another Food-grains Policy Committee had specifically set 1971 as its target date for achieving total self-reliance in wheat supplies.[56] It was a fortunate coincidence for India that this goal was attained precisely when diplomatic circumstances made a termination of imports most desirable.

Unfortunately for India, self-sufficiency in wheat supplies proved as fleeting in 1971 as it had in 1955. India's 1972 autumn harvest was gravely damaged by late and inadequate rainfall. Hoping to prevent higher food prices, the Indian government unloaded its newly acquired domestic buffer stock into the market—too quickly, by most accounts. By the end of the year foodgrain stocks were back down to only 3 million tons, and knowledge of the government's weak stock position began to inspire a rapid rise in prices. By October 1972, with food prices 16.5 percent above the preceding year's level, the government was forced to abandon its one-year policy of "self-sufficiency" in wheat supplies.[57]

When India finally made its decision to resume wheat imports, its initial purchasing strategy was then far too cautious, despite a foreign exchange position described as "satisfactory . . . to finance such imports as may be considered necessary."[58] For whatever reason, orders were initially placed for only 1.5 million tons of wheat, not enough to prevent domestic food prices from continuing to soar, at annual rates above 20 percent. Additional imports therefore had to be hastily arranged, so that total wheat imports reached 3.6 million tons in 1973 and climbed to 4.7 million tons in 1974.[59]

India's constant readiness to import wheat whenever domestic needs might require was underscored during this sudden revival of imports in 1973–74, which paralleled a sudden increase in commercial wheat import prices. Because of poor worldwide grain harvests in 1972, because of most traditional importers' reluctance to slow purchases, and because of an unprecedented increase in the volume of Soviet wheat imports, world wheat prices had actually doubled during the twelve-month period *prior* to India's belated decision to resume imports. Remarkably, wheat import prices were to double once more the next year. India thus found itself reentering the world market at the worst possible moment, at the onset of what later came to be known as a "world food crisis." The fact that India was willing to spend whatever foreign exchange would be necessary to buy wheat for domestic distribution in this sharply rising world market, testifies to the greater priority India assigned to internal over external policy objectives.

Rising world prices in 1973 did eventually limit India's total volume of wheat imports. By late May of that year, India had been able to sign contracts for only 1.65 million tons of wheat, short of the 2 million tons of imports authorized at that point by the Indian Cabinet. Additional good-quality wheat was at that point only available at astronomical prices, so India briefly suspended its purchasing effort until July, anticipating that the U.S. harvest would have then begun to moderate prices. But a continuing decline in government stocks soon forced a decision to resume imports whatever the cost; the Cabinet revised India's foreign exchange budget sharply upward to accommodate the anticipated size and high cost of these additional purchases. India proceeded to purchase an additional 2 million tons of grain that summer, despite world prices as much as six times higher than India's own preset domestic procurement price.[60]

Finally, by September 1973 purchases were suspended a second time, although 2.5 million tons of newly authorized imports had yet to be obtained. Not only were wheat prices even more prohibitive by September, supplies were by then so tight that imports could no longer be scheduled on a timely basis through commercial channels at any price. India was only one of several wheat-importing nations forced out of the market under these circumstances.

Nevertheless, when India suspended its commercial wheat imports in early September 1973, its domestic needs were not necessarily being sacrificed. By the end of September India had managed to secure from the Soviet Union a 2 million ton "wheat loan," which proved in some respects to be more advantageous to India than a commercial wheat contract. Soviet ships, already at sea carrying Australian wheat originally destined for the Soviet Union, were immediately diverted toward Indian ports and began arriving in India only ten days after the loan agreement was announced.[61] For reasons of prompt delivery it made sense for India to turn from commercial markets to a Soviet commodity loan to secure its needed volume of wheat imports in 1973.

India's wheat trade policies were soon destined for yet another sudden change. While India was still placing orders for sizeable wheat imports, good weather returned and Indian wheat production entered another period of sustained growth. In 1975–76 India's foodgrain harvest was an all-time record, 20 percent above the average of the three previous years. Government procurements in that year set a new record as well; public foodgrain stocks rapidly grew. New import orders were at last discontinued in June 1976, but delivery continued on previously arranged purchases from abroad, so that India's grain imports in 1976 totaled 6.5 million tons, only slightly less than the high of 7.4 million tons taken during the preceding year. And still the good weather continued, so that by April 1977 government stocks of wheat swelled to more than 11 million tons, more than twice the annual requirement for public distribution. For a third time since independence, India found itself in a position to discontinue imports and to claim self-sufficiency in wheat supplies.

India's new wheat surplus was not an unmixed blessing. The government was unable to hold the surplus for lack of public storage facilities; it had to improvise various means to reduce the size of public stocks. Incentives were devised to increase public sales of wheat through fair price shops, where customers purchasing rice were required to take wheat as well. Wheat from public stocks was allocated to the newly created FFWP. Government wheat stocks nonetheless continued to exceed not only projected requirements for public distribution and price stabilization, but physical storage capacity as well. Millions of tons of foodgrains had to be left uncovered on abandoned airfields or adjacent to rail shipment points, subject to damage from moisture and rodents. So burdensome was its wheat surplus by 1977 that the government decided to relieve the pressure on storage by arranging a modest volume of wheat exports.

It must be emphasized that India did *not* initiate wheat exports in 1977 to pursue foreign economic policy objectives. It did not at that point suffer from any lack of foreign exchange. One observer noted in 1977 that India was finding it "no easier to digest [surplus] foreign exchange than food."[62] World wheat prices by 1977 were much too low to provide obvious foreign exchange benefits from export sales. Previously forced to buy wheat in a rising world market, India was now being forced, again by domestic circumstances, to sell in a falling market. In part as a consequence, most of India's wheat exports after 1977 had to be arranged in the form of commodity loans or loan repayments to neighboring or "friendly" countries. Even this proved difficult, given the low quality of India's surplus wheat. In 1977, for example, India sought an opportunity to repay in kind the 2 million ton wheat loan it had received in 1973 from the Soviet Union. But the

Soviet Union had no desperate need for wheat at the time and agreed to the repayment only "with reluctance."[63] Most of this Indian wheat eventually found its way to Vietnam, on Soviet account, where quality considerations were less constraining. India also managed to give or loan small quantities of wheat to several neighboring and Middle Eastern countries as "famine relief."

By 1978, therefore, India could not only consider itself self-sufficient in wheat supplies; it had actually emerged as a small net exporter. India enjoyed some external gains from this shift in its trade posture, but it is essential to recognize that the shift itself had been responsive most of all to a change in domestic circumstances. India was still preoccupied with its foodgrain balance at home; it was not pursuing "food power" abroad.

This most significant interlude of Indian self-sufficiency in wheat supplies did not come to an end until 1981. Government wheat stocks in India began a modest decline soon after 1977, as had been hoped, in part due to the decision to export. But by 1979, when bad weather returned, this decline began to take on a more precipitous appearance. To keep a lid on internal prices after 1979, the government had to draw down stocks sharply, to support increased wheat distribution both through fair price shops and through the FFWP (renamed the National Rural Employment Program). Public wheat distribution was lifted from a level of 6.9 million tons in calendar year 1978 to 7.5 million tons in 1979, and then to 8.9 million tons in 1980.[64] This dramatic increase in public distribution sufficed to contain adverse price effects, but by April 1981 government wheat stocks fell to an unacceptably low level of 3 million tons. At this point the Indian government abandoned its pretense of self-sufficiency and arranged once more for a modest volume of wheat imports. A purchase of 1.6 million tons of wheat from the United States was announced in July 1981, and 0.7 million tons of Australian wheat were purchased before the end of the year.

In India, no prearranged formula exists to connect government stock levels and import policy. Despite frequent official assertions that an agreed-upon "buffer stock" policy is in place, India's grain import decisions tend to be determined by political as well as by purely technical considerations. Had dwindling stock levels been the government's only concern, wheat imports might have been resumed well before July 1981. Agricultural experts in the Planning Commission and Food Department foresaw the need to resume wheat imports as early as a year before the decision was finally taken in 1981 by the prime minister and the Cabinet. Before resigning itself to renewed imports, the government did try several less conspicuous policy adjustments. Late in 1980, for example, allocations of wheat to the National Rural Employment Program were reduced and then eliminated entirely. Allocations of wheat to flour mills were cut back sharply and subsidized wheat distribution through fair price shops was reduced as well, at one point from 750,000 tons to 600,000 tons a month.[65] This attempt to forestall imports by slowing the depletion of public wheat stocks proved unsuccessful, as consumer demand for wheat was simply shifted out of the public sector and into the free market, where retail prices began a distinct upsurge. These higher free market prices early in 1981 complicated the task of rebuilding public stocks to safer levels through their adverse effect on government procurement from the new spring wheat harvest. Now fewer farmers were eager to sell wheat to the government at the lower and previously fixed procurement price. Despite its excellent 1981 wheat harvest, therefore, the Indian government failed to obtain more than 6.5 million tons of wheat (well short of the 9.5 million tons procurement target). When knowledge of this procurement failure became widespread, of course, speculative pressures on free market prices intensified. At this point, in July 1981, renewed wheat imports at last were arranged.[66]

India's momentary reluctance to resume wheat imports in 1981 might imply that some overriding external concern—such as shortage of foreign exchange or reluctance to narrow India's diplomatic options by entering once more into a dependent wheat trade relationship—was constraining the Indian government. In fact, most of the constraints that delayed India's 1981 wheat import decision were internal rather than external. When India's 1981 import decision was finally announced in July, it drew stiff criticism from domestic political groups both right and left. None of these groups, however, was especially concerned with the *external* implications of the decision. On the right, an organized block of well-to-do commercial wheat farmers, primarily from the northern surplus states, protested the import decision on the grounds that it revealed the government's insufficient concern for maintaining adequate production incentives.[67] Left-wing opposition forces, primarily from the largest food-deficit states, such as West Bengal, were also critical of the wheat import decision. Their charge was that the Congress party leadership in New Delhi had "mismanaged" that year's wheat procurement effort, by failing to dislodge private stocks of wheat from wealthy producers and speculators.[68] Facing such a broad range of domestic critics, the government was understandably reluctant to resume wheat imports in 1981, but for domestic rather than foreign policy reasons.

The inward-looking calculations that drove India to resume imports of wheat in 1981 come into sharper focus when the adverse external implications of the decision are taken into account. India made its decision to resume costly wheat imports at a time when its foreign exchange position was exceptionally tight, largely as a consequence of steeper oil import costs after the OPEC price increases in 1979, along with a sudden interruption in remittances from Indians working abroad, due to the outbreak of war between Iraq and Iran in early fall 1980. India's declining foreign exchange reserves were equal in value to only about three months' worth of imports at the time the 1981 wheat import decision was made.[69] The Indian government's willingness under these circumstances to spend nearly 10 percent of its remaining reserves to resume imports of wheat indicates a readiness to sacrifice external economic objectives to meet internal foodgrain requirements.

External diplomatic objectives also were sacrificed to some extent when India resumed importing wheat. A purely diplomatic calculation would have required that India *not* turn to the United States to arrange its first overseas wheat purchase in five years, as U.S.–Indian diplomatic relations were once again at a low ebb. But the Indian government decided to buy U.S. grain, even while it expressed bitter objections to a U.S. decision to supply Pakistan with F-16 fighter aircraft, a continuing U.S. refusal to supply India with nuclear fuel for its Tarapur reactor, and a singling out of Indian manufactured goods for severe U.S. economic trade restrictions in the form of countervailing duties (ostensibly because of India's reluctance to terminate export subsidies). One additional cause for resentment in 1981 was the opposition of the Reagan administration to India's pending International Monetary Fund (IMF) loan request. Bilateral relations reached a nadir in late summer, when India refused to welcome the newly appointed political counselor to the U.S. embassy in New Delhi. The United States retaliated by sending home a ranking Indian diplomat from the embassy in Washington. With so many diplomatic incentives to snub the United States, India nonetheless made its first 1981 wheat purchase from private export firms in the United States.

India turned to the United States for wheat in 1981 on strictly economic and technical grounds. India's specific requirement was for two high-quality wheat varieties, white and hard red winter, varieties not readily available in Europe or from suppliers in the nonindustrial world. Moreover, U.S. prices were lower than those offered by Australia, even taking into account the significant differential in shipping costs.[70]

Before making its initial U.S. wheat purchase, India approached both Australia and Canada; neither was confident enough of its supply position to make the kind of offer India could accept, and only later in the year was Australia able to provide the final portion of India's 1981 import needs. By first approaching the Canadians and the Australians, India revealed a preference for diversifying its wheat imports away from the United States, but government-to-government deals with the Wheat Boards of these two countries were also attractive to Indian officials at the time on strictly nondiplomatic grounds. Among political circles within the Indian government, such deals tend to diminish the risk of appearing "corrupted" through negotiations with "profit-making" private business corporations.

In considering the diplomatic sensitivity of recent Indian wheat imports, however, a point of larger significance deserves to be made. Previously, when India's wheat imports still took the form of P.L. 480 "assistance" from the United States, diplomatic calculations could not be entirely avoided in the arrangement of those imports. Legitimate fears developed, fears of food aid "blackmail." India's foodgrain imports from the United States now take the form of commercial purchases, negotiated directly with the private trade, and therefore are free from any appearance of diplomatic conditionality. Because India no longer imports food on a concessional basis, it has less reason to view its food imports as an admission of weakness or dependence. As a result, India is less reluctant to arrange those imports, even from the United States, and feels less compelled to counterbalance every import decision with a show of diplomatic bravado. To some extent India has consciously chosen this posture as a "paying customer" in world food markets. Even with severe balance of payments problems, India has decided to pay cash for its food imports. India has not only declined to renew any P.L. 480 (Title I) concessional food imports from the United States; it has even declined to make use of the Department of Agriculture's Export Credit Guarantee (GSM-102) program. Given India's history of cautious borrowing and its debt service ratio of less than 12 percent, India enjoys such strong commercial credit ratings as to make U.S. government credit guarantees less essential in any case.[71]

On balance, India's status as a paying customer in the world grain market further insulates its grain trade behavior from the realm of Indian foreign policy. By paying cash for its occasional wheat imports, the Indian government frees itself from its own (often exaggerated) fears that exporting countries will seek to enmesh India in a web of charity, only to exact payment at some later date, or in some other form. Importing food is no longer viewed by Indian officials as tantamount to incurring a diplomatic debt. In a curious way, India has become less concerned about the diplomatic cost of importing grain as the financial cost of doing so has increased.

Trade policy developments since India resumed importing wheat in 1981 confirm these trends. Although originally characterized as a "one-time" event, India's 1981 imports were followed in 1982 by still-larger purchases, this time exclusively from the United States. Very bad weather in 1982—a late and erratic monsoon—had cut into India's fall harvest of grains (primarily rice) making the larger volume of imports necessary. Between August and December 1982, therefore, the Indian government purchased roughly 4 million tons of U.S. wheat. These wheat imports were a most attractive means to replace the domestic rice shortfall in 1982, due to the very low import price of wheat prevailing in world markets at the time (half the cost, ton for ton, of imported rice).[72]

By 1983–84 the responsiveness of Indian wheat trade policy to its ever-changing domestic foodgrain balance was being reconfirmed following yet another cycle of abundant harvests. A record 1983 wheat harvest of 42.5 million tons was followed by an even larger 44.6 million ton harvest in 1984. Wheat procurements in 1984 exceeded FCI targets, and resulted in burdensome government wheat stocks above 17 million tons, the largest quantity ever held in public storage.[73] Efforts were launched to promote domestic wheat consumption, through subsidized FCI sales to Indian flour millers. But as public stocks in surplus states continued to grow (inadequately protected, under temporary polyethylene cover, or piled on airstrips), all wheat purchases from abroad were again discontinued, and plans were made to renew exports. With India's foreign exchange position stronger than before (India had voluntarily surrendered a $1.2 billion portion of its earlier IMF loan), there was no external commercial incentive, and no new diplomatic incentive, to cut back on wheat imports.[74] Trade decisions were being made, as always, in response to inward-looking supply and demand calculations.

Summary

The presumption that nations adjust their food trade policies in pursuit of external economic or diplomatic objectives is no guide at all to understanding Indian rice and wheat trade behavior. The official rhetoric of the Indian government pays frequent homage to the national goal of "self-sufficiency" in foodgrains as a means to reduce expenditures of foreign exchange and to minimize vulnerability to diplomatic food trade blackmail. But in its behavior the government has never sacrificed any of its internal foodgrain policy objectives, such as price stability or adequate public distribution, in pursuit of such external goals. It is the accumulation of government-owned stocks at home rather than trade balance concerns or diplomatic designs abroad that leads to fewer imports and occasional exports, and the Indian government has consistently shown itself willing to ease exports and to resume imports when necessary to cover unmet domestic foodgrain needs, whatever the level of world prices, whatever the cost in foreign exchange, and whatever the diplomatic embarrassment or inconvenience. Indeed, as both a paying customer, and an occasional exporter in international grain markets, India can forget most of its earlier anxieties about the "food power" designs of other major powers.

3 The Soviet Union: Retreat from Food Power

We have seen in the case of India that inward-looking and outward-looking food policy objectives need not be in conflict. India's grain trade policies are driven by internal needs, but are seldom grossly incompatible with various external economic and diplomatic interests. The same cannot be said for grain trade policies in the Soviet Union, where external economic and diplomatic objectives have recently been sacrificed. In pursuit of dietary affluence at home, the Soviet Union has been driven to import troublesome quantities of expensive foreign grain, a significant share of which has come from its strategic adversary, the United States.

Against the record of their own history, Soviet leaders would not be expected to jeopardize external economic or security interests to pursue a purely inward-looking objective, such as dietary development. In times past, Soviet leaders consistently pursued the opposite strategy: they denied adequate food supplies to their own citizens while *exporting* grain to earn foreign exchange and to preserve their diplomatic influence over strategic allies. The present abandonment of such a policy challenges directly the popular presumption that nations always seek "food power." The Soviet Union, which for many years sought "food power" with ruthless determination, now does very nearly the opposite.

It is not for any lack of foreign policy ambition that the Soviet Union has transformed itself from the world's single largest grain exporter into the world's single largest grain importer. The external economic objectives of the Soviet Union remain as ambitious as ever, and remain focused on the need to earn foreign hard currency to finance imports of Western industrial products and technology, deemed vital to continued productivity growth within the Soviet economy. How, then, could the Soviet Union permit the grain trade, once its principal *earner* of foreign exchange, to become its principal *loser* of foreign exchange? It is only slightly less puzzling that the Soviet Union, which still views itself as locked in a momentous ideological struggle with the United States and prefers by tradition to avoid any trade dependence upon its potential adversaries, should now be exposing itself, through its heavy volume of grain imports, to Western food trade blackmail. With a political system that allows for substantial control over the behavior and expectations of its own citizens, why should not the Soviet Union of today be as determined as in years past to pursue food power—to sacrifice some of its internal dietary aspirations so as to minimize both the commercial expense and the diplomatic risk associated with grain imports? We may seek an answer through an examination of evolutionary forces that have been transforming Soviet grain trade policy ever since the Stalinist era.

Grain Trade Policy under Stalin

If ever a nation in the modern world intended to pursue "food power," it was the Soviet Union under Joseph Stalin. Grain exports were maintained by Stalin despite desperate internal food needs, first to earn foreign exchange to finance rapid industrial and military modernization, and later to consolidate political control in Eastern Europe. Russia's rise to superpower status was in part accomplished through this relentless exploitation of domestic agricultural resources. It is perhaps no accident that the modern presumption of food power found its original expression in the words of a Soviet diplomat, Maxim Litvinov, not long after the October Revolution. "Food," said Litvinov in 1921, "is a weapon."[1]

Stalin's mercantile grain export policies were in large measure simply a continuation of the equally ruthless agricultural trade policies of the Russian tsars of the nineteenth century. Roughly one-third of Russia's foreign exchange earnings during the nineteenth century came from grain exports, and agricultural exports overall at times accounted for as much as 75 percent of the total. This pattern persisted until the outbreak of the First World War. In 1913 Russia exported 13 percent of all the grain that it produced, enough to constitute one-third of the world export total, making Russia the single largest grain-exporting nation in the world.

Setting an example that Stalin was later to follow, Tsarist Russia maintained this heavy volume of food exports despite desperate food scarcities at home. As one official conceded in 1904, "grain and millions of eggs are shipped abroad while epidemics due to undernourishment are spreading like a village fire among the population."[2] Tsarist planners, seeking foreign exchange to promote industrialization and railroad construction, were willing and able to subordinate internal food policies to this external economic requirement. During one period of dire rural famine near the end of the nineteenth century, Russia's finance minister was alleged to have said, "We will be underfed, but we will export."[3]

Stalin's rediscovery of this ruthless grain export strategy came after an interlude, under Lenin, of food policies that paid greater heed to the Soviet Union's own internal food requirements. Agriculture had been thoroughly devastated by war, revolution, and civil war. By 1922, the most efficient commercial agricultural estates had either been divided or disrupted and the total land area sown to grains had been sharply reduced, to only 64 percent of the prewar level. In part because of this internal devastation, and in part because the new Soviet regime found its trade opportunities constrained by a difficult foreign marketing situation, Soviet food exports briefly came to a halt. Faced with a domestic food emergency, Lenin at one point even approved the importing and distribution of "famine relief" food aid from the United States.[4] Small peasant cultivators were then given an opportunity under the lenient guidelines of Lenin's New Economic Policy to painstakingly rebuild the nation's rural economy. The famine was eventually overcome, and by 1928 grain production had recovered to nearly the prewar level.[5]

Recovery, however, proved short-lived, as Stalin was soon to begin using agriculture as the resource base for his more single-minded pursuit of rapid industrialization. Once he had overcome his internal opposition in 1929, Stalin initiated a policy of forced rural collectivization to speed the extraction of resources from the countryside. Coercive methods were employed, not only to procure grain, but also to confiscate peasant properties. Many of the most skillful and prosperous peasant farmers were uprooted or eliminated in the process. Seeking political control as well as economic resources, Stalin viewed the independent kulak class as a threat to the final "socialist transformation" of the countryside. As private holdings were forcefully and systematically liquidated, the percentage of collective farm peasant households swiftly increased, from 1.7 percent in 1928, to 23.6 percent by 1930, and finally to 93 percent by 1937.[6]

One of the early effects of forced collectivization was a fall in grain production, followed by a terrible rural famine in the winter of 1932–33, which cost the lives of several million newly collectivized Russian peasants. Stalin was not deterred, however, from a continued extraction of resources from the countryside. Because rapid industrialization required significant quantities of imported machinery and advanced technology from the West, exports of grain to earn foreign hard currency were maintained. The Soviet Union's annual grain exports, which had averaged only 1.2 million tons between 1925 and 1929, increased to 5.4 million tons in 1930, and were maintained at 4.4 million tons in 1931 and at 1.4 million tons in 1932, despite the onset of desperate domestic shortages (Table 3). Stalinist indifference toward domestic famine relief during this period was summarized in the remark of a provincial party officer: "To have imported grain would have been injurious to our prestige. To have let the peasants keep their grain would have encouraged them to go on producing little."[7] In fact, export earnings were more important than prestige. Soviet grain sales abroad accounted for a vital 20 percent of total export earnings during the early years of forced collectivization.[8]

Stalin's desire to maintain grain exports, whatever the domestic food policy consequences, and to push for immediate collectivization in the countryside, whatever the short-run production cost or the long-run

Table 3.   Soviet grain exports, 1904–1937

Year[b]	Exports[a] (million metric tons)
1904–8 (average)	8.4
1909–13 (average)	10.9
1925–29 (average)	1.2
1929	1.0
1930	5.4
1931	4.4
1932	1.4
1933–37 (average)	1.2

a. Five principal grains (wheat, rye, barley, oats, corn).
b. Crop years beginning 1 July.
Source: Lazar Volin, *A Century of Russian Agriculture*
(Cambridge: Harvard University Press, 1970), pp. 232, 344.

damage to efficient peasant farming, was later to draw harsh criticism from those in the Party who stepped forward after his death to expose Stalin's most serious policy "errors" and "excesses." At the time, however, as an uncomplicated exercise of Soviet "food power," this ruthless strategy was not without its foreign policy compensations for the Soviet leadership. Rapid industrial development and total political control, both of which were by-products of forced collectivization, provided Stalin with additional means to counter and eventually to overcome the looming external threat posed by German remilitarization in the 1930s, realized in Hitler's surprise invasion of the Soviet Union in June 1941.

One blind spot in Stalin's overall food power strategy before World War II was the scant attention paid to meeting minimum internal consumption needs, should a military emergency actually arise. On the eve of the German attack the Red Army found itself with only four to six months' supply of grain.[9] This left Stalin with no choice but to request Lend Lease food shipments from the United States, as a matter of military survival. Without U.S. food assistance during the Second World War (primarily high-calorie foods such as fats, oils, dairy products, and sugar) the Soviet Union would not have been able to feed both its army and its defense industry workforce. Even with Lend Lease aid, food supplies for the civilian population were desperately short, calling forth unprecedented sacrifice. The Soviet Union's demonstrated capacity on this occasion to accept acute food deprivation in order to defeat a foreign enemy became an enduring part of the official legend surrounding the Great Patriotic War. In Leningrad alone, during the tragic period of the German blockade, from December 1941 into early 1942, civil order was maintained even though 632,000 people died of starvation.[10]

The German military invasion also did widespread damage to the productive capacity of Soviet agriculture. Between 1941 and 1945 roughly half of the total prewar crop area was overrun by the German army. By one Soviet account, the invaders destroyed and plundered 1,876 state farms, 2,890 machine tractor stations, and 98,000 collective farms; wrecked or stole 137,000 tractors and 49,000 harvesting combines; destroyed 285,000 collective farm buildings; and destroyed or carried away 7 million farm horses, 17 million head of cattle, 20 million pigs, and 27 million sheep and goats.[11] Even in those areas not invaded, manpower and supplies were so widely disrupted that Soviet grain production and government procurement were reduced by more than 50 percent. Reconstruction from this wartime damage moved so slowly that as late as 1953, the time of Stalin's death, the Soviet Union was not yet producing as much food annually as it had produced in 1913.[12]

Despite the devastated condition of Soviet agriculture and the unprecedented sacrifice asked of the Russian people, Stalin insisted upon an immediate resumption of grain exports as soon as the war came to an end in 1945. External objectives, as before, took priority over domestic needs. Stalin's newest external priority was to secure Soviet control within the recently occupied (and equally devastated) states of Eastern Europe; to this end grain was forcibly procured from the hard-pressed Soviet peasantry and shipped west. Soviet grain went to Poland, for example, as one means to help consolidate Stalin's control over the new Lublin government. As Khrushchev later explained, these grain shipments were used to "heal the wounds" that remained from earlier Soviet mistreatment of Poland, particularly at the time of the 1939 Molotov–Ribbentrop partition agreement.[13] These grain shipments to Poland were to become a persistent feature of postwar Soviet trade policy and a continual drain on the nation's own meager food supply.

Khrushchev was to have serious misgivings about this sort of grain trade policy, which served external objectives first and domestic consumption needs last. His rise to power after Stalin's death in 1953 would produce a significant change in Soviet agricultural policy at home to ease the adverse impact of such export strategies.

Grain Trade Policy under Khrushchev

During his struggle to gain full political control after Stalin's death, Nikita Khrushchev sought an affordable means to restore the health of the much-drained agricultural sector. Khrushchev, who came to power with a keen interest in agricultural policy, was appalled to learn that food production under Stalin had been even lower than officially reported. Under pressure from Stalin, the statistical bureau had systematically exaggerated annual agricultural production—on average by 20 percent.[14] A sharp turn away from these self-deceiving and self-defeating Stalinist agricultural policies at home was to become one of Khrushchev's earliest policy achievements.

By the early 1950s, with postwar reconstruction nearly complete, Khrushchev felt an obligation to reduce the domestic sacrifice burdening the nation's long-suffering consumers. In a speech immediately following Stalin's death Khrushchev announced that "communist society cannot be built without an abundance of grain, meat, milk, butter, vegetables, and other agricultural products."[15] This desired abundance would require, in turn, a reversal of those Stalinist policies that denied resources and incentives to food producers. Throughout the Stalinist period, as the products of Soviet agriculture were being used to maximum political and industrial advantage at home and abroad, the agricultural sector itself was being starved of new resources. Investments in land improvement, irrigation, and fertilizer production had been given low priority compared with investments in heavy industry. Compulsory sales of food to the government at low prices, intended to provide one-way benefits for the industrial labor force, took both incentives and resources away from the equally large and important agricultural labor force. The Soviet farm sector was also made to pay what Stalin himself had called a "supertax" in the form of higher relative prices for manufactured inputs, as an additional "tribute" to the priority task of rapid industrialization.[16]

The agricultural sector could scarcely afford such prejudicial treatment, plagued as it is by so many natural disadvantages. In total land area, the Soviet Union is three times larger than the United States, but only about one-quarter is suitable for agricultural use. Soviet soils in some regions are among the richest in the world, but many of these regions are subject to cold climate, or inadequate and irregular rainfall. More than half the arable land in the United States receives annually at least 700 millimeters of precipitation; only 1 percent of the arable land in the Soviet Union receives as much moisture. In those regions where rainfall is adequate, the soil tends to be poor, or the weather too cold. Plentiful moisture in the extreme northern latitudes, for example, is rendered useless by severe winter frost and an abbreviated growing season. The warmer regions south and east of the Ukraine are unfortunately the driest. Light and irregular rainfall during the summer growing season here is often accompanied by high temperature, scorching wind, and devastating dust storms. Because the inadequate moisture levels are also highly changeable, year-to-year variation in Soviet farm output is typically three times greater than in the United States.[17]

To better provide peasants and collective farm managers with the means to overcome these natural disadvantages, in August 1953 Khrushchev initiated a remarkable series of agricultural policy reforms, increasing capital investment, offering higher prices for farm products, and granting tax and debt relief to owners of small private farm plots. He made his break from the Stalinist tradition explicit in a September 1953 report to the Central Committee, where he identified violations of the "Leninist principle" of permitting farmers to have a material interest in the results of their work as the greatest barrier to agricultural progress.[18]

As Khrushchev consolidated his power he persisted in efforts to restore the health of Soviet agriculture. State investment was increased dramatically, almost tripling by 1958. Procurement prices for farm products, which under Stalin had failed even to cover production costs, were raised sharply in 1953, 1956, 1958, and 1962. Finally, under Khrushchev's tireless leadership, the Soviet Union also launched its grand attempt to increase grain production by bringing under mechanized cultivation a vast expanse of so-called virgin land, in Siberia and Kazakhstan. Between 1953 and 1962 total sown area east of the Volga and Urals nearly doubled.[19]

Khrushchev's efforts successfully brought Soviet agriculture to a new plateau. Production gains were at first slow to develop and they were not all sustained during the last several years of Khrushchev's leadership, but gross agricultural output during 1956–60 reached a level more than 40 percent above the standard of the preceding five years. It was precisely during these middle years of rapid growth that Khrushchev decided to commit Soviet agriculture, once more, to producing grain for export as well as for home consumption.

Some Soviet experts questioned Khrushchev's assumption that Soviet agriculture was strong enough to provide simultaneously for significant dietary improvements at home and for an expanding volume of exports abroad. Characteristically, he dismissed their calculations as too cautious, boasting (after a particularly good grain harvest in 1956) that Soviet meat production would surpass U.S. meat production within five years.[20] Alongside such benefits for consumers at home, Khrushchev also predicted that the Soviet Union would regain its preeminence as an exporter of grain. Speaking to the Twenty-Second Party Congress in 1961, he announced that the Soviet Union in the near future would occupy a position in international grain markets that would "make the Messrs. Imperialists aware of how our agriculture is growing."[21] True to his word, Khrushchev did briefly restore the Soviet Union to its earlier position as a significant net exporter of grain. In 1962, total Soviet grain exports rose to a level of 8.3 million tons (Table 4). Fewer of these exports were for hard currency, as direct sales

Table 4. Soviet grain trade, 1956–1964 (million metric tons)

Year[a]	Production	Imports	Exports	Net[b]	Feed use	Stock change[c]
1956	125.0	0.9	5.4	+4.5	33	+12
1957	102.6	1.5	6.2	+4.7	34	−11
1958	134.7	1.7	7.7	+6.0	39	+12
1959	119.5	1.0	6.8	+5.8	40	− 2
1960	125.5	0.8	7.0	+6.2	41	+ 1
1961	130.8	0.8	8.4	+7.6	45	− 3
1962	140.2	0.6	8.3	+7.7	43	+ 2
1963	107.5	10.4	4.7	−5.7	32	+ 3
1964	152.1	2.6	4.3	+1.7	44	+20

a. Year beginning 1 July.
b. Plus sign indicates net exports.
c. Plus sign indicates addition to stocks.
Source: Michael D. Zahn, "Soviet Livestock Feed in Perspective," in U.S. Congress, Joint Economic Committee, *Soviet Economy in a Time of Change*, vol. 2., Table 1, p. 174.

to the West were significantly constrained by Cold War tensions. But an external objective was nonetheless being served. Soviet grain exports (primarily wheat and wheat flour) were a useful device to preserve influence and to balance trade flows within the Soviet circle of allies in Eastern Europe and beyond. During the early 1960s, more than 70 percent of Soviet grain exports moved toward such socialist countries.[22]

Khrushchev's dream of continuing to produce grain for export while pursuing more ambitious dietary objectives at home was badly shaken near the end of his time in power when a widespread drought in 1963, coupled with excessive cultivation of fragile soils in new lands, suddenly cut Soviet grain production by 20 percent. Feedgrain production—and hence livestock production—was particularly hard hit. Acting largely on his own instincts, Khrushchev had hoped to solve the feedgrain problem by planting corn, which was prized for its high energy-conversion value, and because it needed no processing to be fully digestible. Between 1953 and 1962 Soviet acreage planted in corn had been expanded tenfold. Unfortunately, due to its deficient rainfall and a short growing season, the Soviet Union was poorly adapted to corn production, a point the 1963 failure clearly dramatized. In his earlier enthusiasm for grain exports, Khrushchev had also neglected to build a domestic reserve supply large enough to help cover serious shortfalls. The resulting feedgrain shortage forced a 25 percent cutback in rations of grain to livestock, during which precious inventories of cattle, hogs, and poultry had to be subjected to a damaging "distress slaughter." Hog inventories were reduced by more than 40 percent; they required a full nine years to regain their 1963 level.[23]

Khrushchev's ambitious grain export policy was also severely damaged by the 1963 production setback. Soviet grain exports fell from 8.3 million tons to 4.7 million tons, and might have been eliminated altogether had it not been for strong pressure from Eastern European allies.[24] Feeling an obligation to continue a minimum volume of exports for reasons of foreign policy, but not wishing to further reduce Soviet livestock herds, or cut too deeply into domestic bread supplies, Khrushchev was forced to take extraordinary measures. In 1963 he turned to the world market for an unprecedented 10 million tons of grain *imports*.

Internal food needs, for the first time, were pressing the leadership to sacrifice important external objectives. In order to cover the hard currency cost of these grain imports (estimated at $800 million), it became necessary for the Politburo to authorize record sales from closely guarded Soviet gold reserves.[25] With gold then selling at $35 an ounce, the implied drain on Soviet reserves would be significant. A diplomatic price was likewise paid. Most of the grain imports in 1963 had to be purchased in the West, principally from Canada and Australia, as only meager supplies were available in the socialist world.[26] Khrushchev was even forced to turn to the United States, an acute embarrassment.[27] Although the final volume of Soviet wheat purchases from the United States proved small (largely due to U.S. maritime restrictions, which drove up costs), any dealing with the United States was nonetheless distasteful, as propagandists in the West played the Soviet grain purchase for all that it was worth. President John Kennedy boasted, at one point, that the purchase would "advertise to the world as nothing else could" the failures of Soviet agriculture compared with U.S. food abundance. Kennedy may have viewed the sale of U.S. grain to the Soviet Union as compatible with his new diplomatic strategy of détente, recently initiated in the aftermath of the 1962 Cuban missile crisis, but for Khrushchev, who had been humiliated in that crisis, the purchase of U.S. grain was an additional source of injury. This sense of injury was deepened when the United States insisted on a Soviet pledge that none of the U.S. grain be resold to Cuba and Chancellor Konrad

Adenauer of Germany began arguing that any U.S. sale of grain to the Soviet Union should be conditioned on the Soviets' tearing down the Berlin Wall.[28]

With the help of imports and some rationing, Soviet domestic bread supplies were maintained at adequate levels after the 1963 harvest setback. But by 1964 domestic meat production had declined 20 percent, wiping out all of the gains that had been made since 1958, and giving the lie to Khrushchev's boast that per capita meat production was soon to overtake that of the United States. These dramatic agricultural policy setbacks played no small role in Khrushchev's removal from power in October 1964; it was left to Khrushchev's successors to search for a new agricultural strategy less prone to sudden reversals and humiliating setbacks.

Grain Trade Policy under Brezhnev

The new food strategy embraced in 1965 by Khrushchev's successors was both cautious and bold. It was cautious in the sense that it rejected any radical change in Soviet farm sector planning or management procedures. It was bold, however, in its generous commitment of scarce financial resources to the farm sector.

From the start, Leonid Brezhnev made no effort to conceal his intent. At a landmark plenary session of the Central Committee, held five months after Khrushchev's departure, Brezhnev directly criticized Khrushchev for not having allocated adequate investment resources to agriculture. He then insisted that total capital investment in agriculture be increased by more than half during the upcoming Eighth Plan period (1966–70).[29] Compared with Khrushchev's last Plan, deliveries of fertilizer, machinery, and equipment to farms were to double. Nor was this to be a "one-time only" increase in agricultural spending. Agriculture's share of new fixed investment continued to grow throughout the eighteen years of the Brezhnev era, from 19.6 percent of the total in the Seventh Plan (1961–65) to 23.2 percent in the Eighth Plan (1966–70), and up to 26.2 percent in the Ninth Plan (1971–75). Total direct farm investment in the Soviet Union over 1970–77 was by one calculation six times larger than the value of new fixed farm investment in the United States. Slower overall economic growth rates eventually would lead to a squeeze on new investment throughout the Soviet economy later in the 1970s, but even then Brezhnev refused to reduce the investment share going to agriculture. Agriculture's enlarged share of total state investment was maintained at 26.5 percent in the Tenth Plan (1976–80), and was initially projected at a full 27 percent for the Eleventh Plan (1981–85).[30]

Soviet agriculture had long been seriously undercapitalized.[31] Even so, Brezhnev's strategy of throwing money at agricultural problems was bound to produce a less-than-satisfying result. Khrushchev's greatest gains in farm output, registered during the 1950s, had been accomplished by extensive rather than intensive means, by bringing new cropland under production. Now, with no "virgin lands" left to be exploited, production gains could only come from higher crop yields, and the Soviet style of farming was poorly designed to provide such yields.

If economies of scale were all that mattered in agriculture, Soviet farmers would be the most efficient in the world. The 28,000 collective farms (*kolkhozes*) average about 15,500 acres; the 20,000 state farms (*sovkhozes*—the favored form of farm organization since the 1950s) are even larger, averaging 49,200 acres.[32] As a comparison, private farm units in the United States average only slightly more than 400 acres. Unfortunately, even in grain production, economies of scale beyond a certain point can count for very little. Meanwhile, gigantic factorylike state and collective farms present management with an impossible problem of labor supervision. Wage-earning agricultural laborers in any system lack the incentive of ownership and therefore require an extra measure of supervision. Unlike industrial assembly line workers, they must receive constant instructions on when to shift from one task to the next throughout the planting and growing season. Work standards in agriculture are also more difficult to maintain, as the quality of any single day's efforts may not be known until months later, when the harvest begins. In the Soviet Union these unique supervision and work quality problems tend to grow in direct proportion to the size of the wage-labor farming unit. Opportunities to increase the productivity of labor, presented by good weather at planting or harvest time, often go to waste.[33]

Production inefficiencies in Soviet agriculture also arise beyond the farm. Hard-pressed state farm directors and collective farm chairmen constantly must cope with remote central planning agencies, which preempt innovation and flexible management at the farm level by issuing rigid sales quotas and production directives. Central planning, Soviet-style, is poorly suited to efficient food production over such a large land area, where timely adjustments constantly must be made to local climate, soil, and rainfall conditions. Also due to central planning, vital interconnections that must be made with other economic units beyond the farm (shippers and customers, or suppliers of fertilizer, machinery, and spare parts) are seldom reliable or responsive because they are noncompetitive and not even contractual in nature. Agricultural production chains instead are linked together through a cumbersome system of bureaucratic directives, usually weakened by numerous distortions in administered prices. Farm managers have no choice but to accept fertilizer at an administered price from a predesignated supplier, and the suppliers, with no fear of competition, have little incentive to provide the fertilizer on time or in good condition. Productive agriculture, which depends on an intricate sequence of timely actions throughout the growing season, is poorly served by such a system.

What the Soviet agricultural system may lack in production efficiency, it makes up in its compatibility with the conservative institutional needs and preferences of planning officials and party bureaucrats. Those who argue for radical change are likely to be penalized rather than rewarded. It is noteworthy that several more productive modes of farming have been tested within the Soviet Union, including not only small private plots managed by individual farm households, but also, within the state sector, the *zveno* or "link" system. But even when these alternative institutions produce positive results, they are easily discredited for being out of step with the state farming orthodoxy and receive only scant and fleeting encouragement.

Soviet farmers have long been permitted to maintain private household plots (usually less than an acre) to grow high-quality foods—including livestock—either for their own consumption or for sale through numerous collective farm markets. These private plots constitute less than 4 percent of the total Soviet agricultural land area; nonetheless, they account for as much as one-quarter of total agricultural output and are a vital source of fresh vegetables, milk, and eggs. It is no doubt a disadvantage that these household plots depend upon an overintense labor input, which could not be sustained on a much larger scale and would be unsuited in any case to grain production. Still, Soviet officials might be expected to give more notice and encouragement to the kinds of production incentives found on these smaller private plots and to introduce such incentives, where possible, into larger state farm operations. Too often Soviet planners do just the opposite. The private plots are an ideological embarrassment and seldom, except in short-term emergencies, enjoy more than grudging support from middle-level party leaders. The plots are recognized as useful for augmenting rural income and preventing unwanted migration of labor from farm to city. Throughout the Brezhnev era various leadership campaigns were launched to promote the private sector—in 1964–65, 1969, 1972, and 1976–77—but all met middle-level resistance and quickly ran out of steam.[34] A final Brezhnev campaign launched in 1981 was designed specifically to involve the private sector in meat production, but only as an adjunct to the public sector.[35]

More glaring, perhaps, has been the Soviet failure to improve incentive structures on large-scale state and collective farms. Collective and state farm workers have been given steadily higher wages and a variety of collective bonus systems. But costly schemes of this kind do little to encourage what is most needed—an incentive for "unsupervised initiative" on the part of individual farm workers. The one experimental innovation in Soviet farm organization that has succeeded in stimulating individual initiative has never been widely adopted. The so-called link system, first developed after the Second World War, assigns to a small group of farm workers (a dozen or so) full responsibility for every phase of the production cycle on a small specified portion of the larger farm unit. Where experiments with the link system were permitted, the results often were spectacular, with grain yields in some instances tripling and output per worker increasing as much as twenty times. Ideological purists dislike this system for its resemblance to small-scale private ownership; others feel directly threatened by its widespread adoption because numerous administrators and unskilled workers might become superfluous if efficient "production links" were introduced on a large scale. For whatever reason, advocates of the link system have met repeated frustration.[36]

Brezhnev's decision to commit lavish resources to this institutionally flawed agricultural production system was only a partial solution to Soviet food problems. Indeed, despite ever-larger investments the average annual rate of growth of total Soviet farm output continued in decline during the Brezhnev era, from a respectable 4.8 percent in the 1950s to 3.0 percent in the 1960s, and a mere 1.8 percent in the 1970s.[37] By the end of the 1970s, to Brezhnev's credit, total farm output had reached two and a half times the level of 1950. Yearly grain production had recorded major advances, growing from 82.5 million tons in 1953, the year of Stalin's death, and from 152 million tons in 1964, Khrushchev's last year of leadership, to a record harvest of 237 million tons by 1978, the best year recorded under Brezhnev. Yet this trend in production gains could not be sustained at an acceptable cost, because marginal returns on every new investment remained very low. And when total investment growth itself was brought to a virtual standstill near the end of Brezhnev's tenure (falling from 7 percent a year in the mid 1970s to 1.5 percent in 1981), and then when Soviet agriculture was struck by a six-year streak of bad weather (1979–84), further significant production gains were not realized. After the record-breaking 237 million ton harvest of 1978, Soviet grain production fell to 179 million tons in 1979, languished at 189 million tons in 1980, dropped to a mere 160 million tons in 1981, and then recovered to only 180 million tons in 1982.[38] This stagnation of Soviet agricultural growth, which was to plague the last several years of the Brezhnev era, helped to reduce Gross National Product (GNP) growth rates in the rest of the economy from an average of nearly 4 percent between 1970 and 1978, to less than 2 percent between 1979 and 1982.[39] These reduced overall growth rates, in turn, exerted an even tighter squeeze on new resources available for investment in agriculture.

Despite these serious farm production problems, Brezhnev's most important domestic agricultural policy decisions actually focused on food consumption. It was a rising food *consumption* trend that finally transformed the Soviet Union into the world's single largest net grain importer. Domestic grain consumption, first stimulated by Khrushchev, received a further push during the first half of the Brezhnev era, following a decision to place top priority upon increasing domestic meat supplies. To help satisfy this consumption goal, Soviet livestock herds would have to expand, along with imports of livestock feed. Well before the prolonged bout of bad weather that so heavily damaged Soviet grain production after 1979, the rising numbers of livestock required a substantial expansion of grain imports. Under Stalin, the effective suppression of domestic consumer demands had made it possible for the nation to produce and export a grain "surplus." When Brezhnev decided to encourage those demands, it should have been expected that the "surplus" would disappear, and that the Soviet Union would begin to require a significant volume of grain imports.

Internal demands for dietary improvements first appeared in the 1950s, during the post-Stalinist period of political decompression, rapid urbanization, and—most important—officially sponsored growth in real wages. Soviet consumers became steadily more visible, more vocal, and better equipped with disposable income to demand a wider variety of high-quality food. Khrushchev's early boasts about soon overtaking the United States in per capita milk and meat production did much to encourage these demands. But to supply consumers with high-quality animal products (such as milk, meat, butter, and eggs) would require a dramatic expansion of Soviet livestock herds, made possible in turn only through an equally dramatic expansion in livestock feed supplies. When the Soviet leadership began to encourage rapid dietary improvements, they could have anticipated—based upon experience of other advanced industrial nations—that their national requirement for foodgrains (such as wheat to produce bread) might fall on a per capita basis, while their requirement for feedgrains (such as corn to feed animals) would rapidly increase. In fact, this is exactly what was about to take place. While the direct food use of grain remained relatively steady in the Soviet Union during the Brezhnev era, and actually fell on a per capita basis, the use of grain for animal feed increased nearly threefold, peaking at 125 million tons after the record harvest of 1978.[40] By 1978 the Soviet Union was using more than half of its total grain as livestock feed.

Apparently undaunted by the prospect of such animal feed requirements, the Soviet leadership allowed domestic wage levels to double twice between 1950 and 1970.[41] Containing the dietary demands that accompanied higher income would not be a simple problem, because the rationing of limited supplies through higher state retail prices was soon to prove politically unacceptable. In June 1962, following Khrushchev's decision to raise the retail price of meat by 30 percent, strikes and demonstrations broke out in Northern Caucasia; soldiers, summoned in haste to the town of Novocherkassk, were ordered at one point to restore order by firing directly into crowds of angered citizens marching on local party offices.[42] The official retail price of meat and bread in the Soviet Union has not been raised since 1962; long lines and empty shelves have proved to be a somewhat more acceptable method of rationing scarce food supplies. To encourage production in the socialized sector, of course, state procurement prices must continue to rise, and so the gap between rising procurement prices and fixed retail prices must be filled with an ever-larger retail subsidy.[43]

It was perhaps surprising, given Khrushchev's difficult experience in trying to stay ahead of internal dietary demands, that Leonid Brezhnev, during his first years in power, chose to further stimulate those demands. Even while Brezhnev was busy expanding agriculture's share of new investments to boost food production during the upcoming 1966–70 Eighth Plan, he was increasing his commitment to expanded food consumption. He may have been emboldened to do so, in the short run, by the gratifying recovery of Soviet grain production immediately after the 1963 harvest failure. That recovery was enough to keep GNP growth rates, for the moment, above 5 percent; Soviet consumption goals, overall, were met during the Eighth Plan for the first time ever in planning history, and per capita meat consumption, specifically, increased by a strong 16 percent.[44] A promise of further rapid progress might have seemed entirely possible. Accordingly, Brezhnev proceeded to endorse and publicize an ambitious "scientifically established" meat consumption "norm" for Soviet consumers, set at 82 kilograms per person per year. When compared with prevailing consumption patterns, this norm implied that an additional 40 percent increase in per capita meat consumption would soon be on the way.[45]

Brezhnev also acted in the belief that food consumption opportunities had become critical in obtaining production gains throughout the rest of the Soviet economy. It was in hopes of stimulating such production gains that Brezhnev had originally approved such a generous growth in personal wages. In the absence of high-quality consumer goods, however, these earned wages would begin to go unspent. It was indicative of this problem that money in savings deposits in the Soviet Union increased nearly tenfold between 1960 and 1973.[46] When money wages cannot be readily exchanged for desired goods and services, labor productivity may be harmed rather than helped. Total factor productivity growth rates in the Soviet economy were steeply falling at the time, from an average level of 1.5 percent in the 1960s to only 0.1 percent during the first half of the 1970s.[47] Even GNP growth rates, which had remained above 5 percent during the 1960s, slipped to 4 percent by 1971, and to 1.6 percent in 1972. Brezhnev's early hope that the industrial base of the Soviet economy was sound enough to permit increased emphasis on consumer goods was becoming more dubious. To abandon his consumer goods objectives at this point, however, might compound the productivity problem, through further adverse effects on worker morale.

Brezhnev's determination to continue to push for rapid dietary improvements must have been further strengthened, despite the onset of an economic slowdown, by a sequence of dramatic events in Poland. On the eve of the 1970 Christmas holiday, an ill-timed government decision to remedy food shortages in Poland through an increase in retail prices provoked violent urban riots. Workers seized the shipyards in Szczecin and burned party headquarters in Gdansk, forcing not only a return to lower food prices but also the fall of the Gomulka leadership. Presumably, the lesson was not lost on the leaders of the Soviet Union, where per capita meat consumption at the time was 40 percent below the Polish standard. Widespread civil unrest was still highly unlikely among the traditionally quiescent Soviet workforce, but unsatisfied consumer demands were nonetheless beginning to manifest themselves in other ways, not only in ubiquitous queues, but also in complaints in letters to the press and the emergence of more numerous black and "gray" markets.

Despite the Soviet economic slowdown, Brezhnev therefore took a bold decision to redouble official efforts to satisfy consumer food demands. At the Twenty-Fourth Party Congress in March 1971, citing the need to boost productivity through improved worker morale, Brezhnev set industrial targets for consumer goods higher than for producer goods. The draft directive for the 1971–75 Plan declared that "increasing the people's material and cultural standard of living" was now "the chief task."[48] Higher meat consumption, in particular, was to become the centerpiece of this grand strategy. In February 1971, the government had adopted a landmark decree on the further development of "industrialized" livestock production, to replace more traditional collective farm practices. Fatefully, this decree projected that such expanded operations would require, during the 1971–75 Plan period, a further 40 percent increase in the total supply of animal feed.[49] Because Soviet grain producers were unlikely to be able to expand their own output to meet such a requirement, the clear implication was a willingness on the part of the Soviet leadership to begin regular feedgrain imports.

It is impossible to date precisely this all-important leadership decision to expand domestic livestock herds through an open-ended dependence upon foreign feedgrain supplies. Judging from patterns of Soviet feed use and trade, the decision was probably on its way to being made sometime before 1971. In response to a modest harvest setback in 1965, for example, the Soviet Union took unprecedented pains to avoid the kind of reduction in feedgrain use that had obliged Khrushchev to conduct the distress slaughter of livestock in 1963. Rather than reduce the allotment of grain for feed use in 1965, the Brezhnev leadership *increased* feed use dramatically in that year, drawing down domestic grain stocks, and *importing* as much as necessary, to do so. The significance of this early action was little noticed at the time by outsiders, as the total volume of imports required to sustain domestic feed use in 1965 was actually less than Khrushchev's imports of two years earlier. The new priority assigned to an unbroken increase in feed use in the Soviet Union was also obscured by several years of good weather after 1965, which boosted Soviet grain production once again ahead of domestic feed requirements, permitting a temporary resumption of net grain exports during 1966–70. Despite these resumed exports, evidence could be found that an implicit decision to sustain domestic feed use at all cost, through imports if necessary, had already been taken. For example, even while expanding exports of wheat in 1967, the Soviet Union discontinued all exports of corn to Eastern Europe and began to import feed grain. In 1969, while still a net grain exporter overall, the Soviet Union began to communicate to the U.S. government, through the private trade, its interest in imports of U.S. corn for animal feed on a continuing basis.[50]

Not until 1971, however, would evidence of a policy change become conclusive in actual Soviet trade behavior. Although the Soviet Union had recently enjoyed two years of good weather, it nonetheless reduced its total grain exports and boosted its total imports, emerging as a small net *importer* overall, so as to continue to feed more grain to livestock at home. The yearly feed use of grain in the Soviet Union was by then up to twice the level of 1963, and could be sustained, even in a good year, only through imports. In a bad production year, of course, this new internal feed use priority would produce even more spectacular external trade effects. Indeed, when the Soviet grain harvest next fell significantly short of its own growth trend in 1972, grain imports suddenly surged to an unheard-of level of 22.8 million tons.

Casual observers were stunned by this volume of imports in 1972, and rushed to conclude that Soviet agriculture must have sustained an unprecedented disaster. In fact, the Soviet grain production shortfall in 1972 was rather modest—smaller, in fact, than either the 1963 or the 1965 shortfall. What had changed, since 1963 and 1965, was the total volume of Soviet animal feed requirements, together with the opinion of Soviet leaders that those requirements, buffered by a prudent level of domestic grain stocks, ought never again to be sacrificed. A comparison of domestic grain production, feed use, stock changes, and net imports, in 1963, 1965, and 1972, makes clear this dramatic evolution of food policy priorities toward protection of domestic stocks and feed use, whatever the implied cost in external trade (Table 5).

Soviet leaders were remarkably candid in 1972 when explaining their need for these much larger grain imports to Western officials. At a

Table 5. Soviet response to poor grain harvests

	1963[a]	1965	1972
		(million metric tons)	
Grain production shortfall[b]	−24.6	−12.1	− 8.6
Change in feed use[c]	−11	+16.4	+ 8.7
Estimated change in stock level[d]	+ 3	−14	+ 2
Increase in net grain imports[e]	+12.9	+ 4.9	+24.9

a. All years beginning 1 July.
b. Shortfall from harvest average of preceding three years.
c. Change from feed use average of preceding three years.
d. Change in grain stocks from preceding year.
e. Increase from net import average of preceding three years.
Source: Michael D. Zahn, "Soviet Livestock Feed in Perspective," in U.S. Congress, Joint Economic Committee, *Soviet Economy in a Time of Change*, vol. 2, p. 174.

meeting in Moscow in April 1972 Leonid Brezhnev told Secretary of Agriculture Earl L. Butz, "The Soviet Government [has] publicized its intentions of increasing the protein component in the people's diet by 25 percent, and this goal [can]not be met with domestic production." Butz, eager to develop a market for surplus U.S. grain, claims to have responded with an assurance that Brezhnev would be "absolutely safe" in building up Soviet livestock herds with grain supplies from the United States.[51]

Butz's assurance to Brezhnev of safe access to U.S. grain supplies, coincident with the significant relaxation of diplomatic tensions then under way between the United States and the Soviet Union, suggests that foreign policy calculations were at least a part of the Soviet decision to begin massive grain imports from the West in the 1970s. The bargain prices being offered to the Soviet Union, for U.S. grain in particular in 1972, raise the possibility that grain imports were also suddenly attractive to Soviet leaders from a purely external economic standpoint. For both reasons, larger grain imports from the West might have been momentarily compatible with external Soviet economic and diplomatic objectives. But as those grain imports continued to grow, despite a subsequent decline in détente, and a surge in market prices, their compatibility with external Soviet interests became more difficult to establish. This later period of growth underscores the priority that Soviet officials had come to place upon domestic food policy objectives.

Even prior to détente, the Soviet Union had shown little inhibition against grain purchases from the West. Due to the U.S. shipping restrictions imposed in 1963, two-thirds of these purchases were made in Canada, and most of the rest in Australia, France, and Argentina. Only 5 percent of Soviet wheat and wheat flour imports during the 1960s came from the United States.[52] After 1971, when the Soviet Union did begin to purchase a larger share of its grain imports from the United States, it was the U.S. decision to lift its maritime restrictions, along with a 1971 dollar devaluation (which cheapened all U.S. exports) rather than any *Soviet* diplomatic consideration that made the greater difference.

Because one of the largest early Soviet purchases of U.S. grain happened to come only a few weeks after the May 1972 Moscow summit conference, coincident with numerous other early tokens of U.S.–Soviet détente, the impression could be gained that these grain sales were being driven at one end or the other by diplomatic calculations. In fact, grain purchases were never a part of the formal package of diplomatic accommodations hammered out at the Moscow summit meeting. Bilateral agreements were reached in Moscow on topics ranging from strategic arms, trade consultations, pollution control, medicine, science, technology, and public health, to conduct of naval ships on the high seas—but never on grain. A U.S.–Soviet "grain deal" was in fact one of the few bargains that was *not* reached at the May 1972 summit. Henry Kissinger, among others, would later see nothing but duplicity in the Soviet reluctance to reach an agreement on grain sales at the time.[53] To be sure, when massive Soviet purchases of U.S. grain began, only weeks after the summit meeting, an element of surprise ensured that bargain prices would be obtained. Still, the timing of these purchases is just as well explained by the schedule of Soviet domestic feed use requirements, and by the emerging damage to their own summer grain crop. As this damage became evident, Soviet officials suddenly accepted, at the technical level and without further negotiation, a $750 million three-year U.S. credit offer *which they had earlier rejected.* More important, they began buying grain directly from U.S. companies, *with cash.*[54]

The Soviet Union did manage to capture some remarkable short-run price advantages in 1972. Through a series of separate approaches to competing U.S. grain export firms, the Soviet Union managed for some time to hide the unprecedented size of its total purchase from the market, and was thus able to buy U.S. wheat for as little as $60 a ton. Moreover, even after domestic U.S. wheat prices finally began to climb later in the summer, the price paid by the Soviet Union remained at its fixed low level, due to the careless continuation, by the Department of Agriculture, of a no longer needed export subsidy program. The Soviet Union was thus able to get in and out of the U.S. wheat market in 1972 without experiencing the price effects of its own purchase. Other importers would not be so fortunate. Japan, for example, purchased U.S. wheat later in 1972 for $80 a ton; by early 1973 India (as noted in chapter 2) found that the U.S. export price for wheat had risen to $100 a ton (and was on its way to doubling once again). By any relative standard, the Soviet Union found it a bargain to import U.S. wheat in 1972.

By any absolute standard, however, the purchase was nonetheless burdensome to Soviet foreign economic policy. In 1973, the year in which most of the 1972 purchases were recorded as imports, grain was to account for roughly one-fifth of the total value of Soviet hard currency imports, and was equivalent in value to nearly 30 percent of all of Russia's hard currency exports. To help raise the hard currency needed to purchase grain from the West in 1972, the Soviet Union had to increase its gold sales more than threefold.[55] The massive 1972 Soviet purchase of U.S. wheat, although dubbed a "grain robbery" in the United States, must have presented a very different aspect to Soviet foreign economic policy officials, who had long been accustomed to *earning* rather than *losing* foreign hard currency in the grain trade.

These drawbacks to purchasing grain from the West were compounded after 1972, first due to the higher cost of those purchases, and then due to the decline of détente and the reemergence of significant diplomatic tensions between the Soviet Union and the United States. Both of these factors had emerged as significant at least by 1975.

The Soviet grain harvest in 1975, at 140.1 million tons, was the worst in a decade, 55 million tons below the average of the previous three years. In response, during the year beginning 1 July 1975, the Soviet Union arranged to import a record 26.1 million tons of grain, well above even the 1972 record of 22.8 million tons. Soviet port and transport facilities, which barely had been able to handle the 1972 volume of imports, would now be strained to their limit.[56] But not even 26.1 million tons of imports were enough to make up entirely for the domestic harvest shortfall. Despite determined conservation efforts, a drawdown of domestic grain stocks, and a 5 million ton reduction in continuing Soviet grain exports to Eastern Europe, the feeding of grain to livestock within the Soviet Union had to be reduced by 18 million tons. The unhappy result, for Brezhnev's meat program, was a repetition on a somewhat reduced scale of the distress slaughter that occurred in 1963. Hog inventories fell by 20 percent, poultry by 7 percent, and sheep and goats by 3 percent.[57] It would eventually require three years of recovered feed use, based upon both continued imports and revived domestic production, to repair this heavy damage. But without a record level of grain imports in 1975, the feed use cutback might have been twice as great, and the damage to Brezhnev's meat program would have been even more severe.

The Soviet Union paid a significant commercial and diplomatic price for its record volume of imports in 1975. World grain prices in that year were still abnormally high, so the hard currency cost to the Soviet Union of importing grain after the 1975 harvest failure reached nearly $3 billion, roughly twice the cost of grain imports following the 1972 harvest failure. And once again the Soviet Union had to take a variety of unusual steps to make affordable this purchase of grain from a tightened world market. To increase hard currency earnings the Soviet Union first expanded both the value and the volume of its foreign gold sales. It also increased the total volume of its oil and natural gas exports to foreign hard currency customers, even at the cost of reducing domestic availability.[58] Third, the Soviets financed a part of their more expensive grain imports in 1975 through unprecedented borrowing, a sudden departure from traditional practice that provoked widespread Western concern at the time, as net Soviet external debt increased by $8.5 billion in 1975–76.[59]

There is evidence that the Soviet Union also accepted a fourth kind of economic sacrifice to help finance its much larger grain imports. As import expenditures for grain increased in 1976, hard currency expenditures for the import of other consumer goods declined. A similar reduction in hard currency expenditures for nonfood consumer goods imports had also been noted when grain import costs surged after the bad harvest of 1972. Western analysts were inclined to suspect, from such evidence, that Soviet trade strategists were now favoring internal grain requirements even above other internal consumer goods requirements.[60]

External diplomatic costs were also paid to import grain in 1975.

First, within the Soviet sphere, it had been deemed necessary to reduce grain exports to client states and allied governments, in Eastern Europe and elsewhere. Until 1975, the Brezhnev leadership had tried valiantly to hold onto at least a remnant of the diplomatic and trade balancing gains that Soviet grain exports to fraternal socialist states had provided over the years.[61] Indeed, as late as 1973 the Soviet Union had been in a position to seek diplomatic gains in this fashion, by sharing its grain supplies abroad. Recall that in September 1973 a 2 million ton Soviet "wheat loan" had been employed to court favor with India, which was then having trouble finding available and affordable grain supplies in commercial channels. Indian officials still recall this timely Soviet gesture with undiminished gratitude.[62]

The 1975 harvest failure forced the Soviet Union to scale down such "food diplomacy" programs by a significant margin. Total Soviet grain exports, which had earlier been cut from 6.9 million tons to less than 2 million tons following the bad harvest of 1972, had to be cut from more than 5 million tons to less than 1 million tons in 1975. For the next six years, they would average only 1.7 million tons and would never exceed 3.3 million tons.[63]

A more foreboding diplomatic price was also paid in 1975, when the U.S. government for the first time sought to extract concessions from the Soviet Union in return for continued access to U.S. grain supplies. In late summer 1975, following a round of large Soviet purchases of U.S. grain, the Ford administration responded to domestic concerns about food price inflation by temporarily suspending further grain sales to the Soviet Union. The original intent was not to seek diplomatic leverage over the Soviet Union, but once the sales suspension had been imposed, Secretary of State Henry Kissinger could not resist the temptation to seek concessions in return for a resumption of sales. After negotiating a long-term bilateral agreement to manage future U.S.–Soviet grain trade (this required no concession—the Soviet Union had been seeking such an agreement for a number of years), State Department negotiators in Moscow asked also for an extraordinary arrangement to purchase Soviet oil at a discount price (the hope was to undercut OPEC prices). The Soviet response was a strong negative: Foreign Trade Minister Nikolai Patolichev bluntly told his American counterpart that the Russian people would "starve to death" before they succumbed to such political pressure. He said that he was there to discuss commercial relations, and if the Americans had wanted to discuss politics, they should ask for a meeting with Foreign Minister Andrei Gromyko.[64] While waiting for the United States to lift its sales suspension, the Soviet Union temporarily stepped up the pace of grain purchases from a variety of non-U.S. suppliers, including the European Community, Canada, Argentina, Brazil, Sweden, and Romania. Domestic political pressure in the United States finally forced the Ford administration to relent, and U.S. grain sales to the Soviet Union were soon resumed. Even though the Soviet Union was able to purchase all of the grain that its port and transport facilities could handle in 1975, this first encounter with a U.S. strategy of seeking concessions in return for grain could not have been reassuring. When diplomatic relations with the United States began to deteriorate in the years that followed, the implied diplomatic cost of depending so heavily upon U.S. grain would only increase.

In the face of these growing external economic and diplomatic costs, it was remarkable that Soviet grain imports continued to grow after 1975. (See Table 6.) Why should the Soviet government, once so well practiced in the exercise of "food power," so willingly expose itself in this fashion to the potential food power of others?

First, in strictly commercial terms, the high price of oil prevailing in world markets during the second half of the 1970s allowed the Soviet Union to pay for its much larger grain imports through only slightly larger oil and natural gas exports. Between 1970 and 1978, by simply doubling its hard currency petroleum exports, the Soviet Union was able to gain more than a tenfold increase in hard currency earnings, from $387 million to $5.7 billion. In 1979, with Soviet oil sales still at a modest level of only 1 million barrels a day, export earnings surged still higher, to almost $10 billion in foreign hard currency. This was more than enough to cover not only that year's grain import costs of roughly $4 billion, but also the value of all new imported machinery orders.[65] Even in 1980, oil export revenues remained high enough to cover a still growing grain import bill, leaving the Soviet Union with a small hard currency trade surplus. Because the Soviet Union was a relatively low-cost producer of energy and a relatively high-cost producer of grain, its strategy of trading oil and gas for grain made a great deal of short-run commercial sense.[66]

Hard currency earnings were also boosted, particularly during 1979–80, by an unprecedented increase in the price of gold. In fact, when gold prices first surged above $250 an ounce in 1979, eventually

Table 6. Soviet grain trade, 1965–1983 (million metric tons)

Year[a]	Production	Trade		Net[b]	Feed use	Stock change[c]
		Imports	Exports			
1965	121.1	9.0	5.3	− 3.7	56	−14
1966	171.2	3.9	5.3	+ 1.4	60	+26
1967	147.9	2.3	6.4	+ 4.1	64	− 2
1968	169.5	1.2	7.4	+ 6.2	72	+ 3
1969	162.4	1.8	7.6	+ 5.8	83	−20
1970	186.8	1.3	8.5	+ 7.2	92	− 8
1971	181.2	8.3	6.9	− 1.4	93	+ 2
1972	168.2	22.8	1.8	−21.0	98	+ 2
1973	222.5	11.3	6.1	− 5.2	105	+14
1974	195.7	5.7	5.3	− 0.4	107	−10
1975	140.1	26.1	0.7	−25.4	89	−14
1976	224.0	11.0	3.3	− 7.7	112	+11
1977	196.0	18.9	2.3	−16.6	122	−16
1978	237.0	15.6	2.8	−12.8	125	+19
1979	179.0	31.0	0.8	−30.2	123	−13
1980	189.0	34.8	0.5	−34.3	119	− 2
1981	160.0	46.0	0.5	−45.5	116	− 4
1982	180.0	32.5	0.5	−32.0	117	− 1
1983	195.0	32.9	0.5	−32.4	123	+ 5

a. Year beginning 1 July.
b. Plus sign indicates net exports.
c. Plus sign indicates addition to stocks.
Sources: For 1965–75, U.S. Congress, Joint Economic Committee, *Soviet Economy in a Time of Change*, vol. 2, Table 1, p. 174. For 1976–82, U.S. Department of Agriculture, *Foreign Agriculture Circular*, Grains, FG-14-83, 11 May 1983, p. 5, and SG-12-84, 12 October 1984, p. 7.

to approach $1000 an ounce, the Soviets were able to meet their larger foreign exchange targets with a *declining* volume of foreign gold sales.[67]

Although they scarcely needed it, yet another foreign exchange windfall came to the Soviet Union during the last years of the Brezhnev era, through a sudden expansion of hard currency earnings from arms exports to less-develped countries. After the 1973 Arab–Israeli war, owing both to arms replacement needs and to increased oil earnings among the Arab states in particular, the Soviet Union found itself in a stronger position to export arms for hard currency. Between 1972 and 1978, the value of total Soviet military deliveries to less-developed countries tripled, and estimated hard currency receipts from those deliveries increased more than tenfold to reach $1.6 billion.[68]

For all of these reasons, the Soviet Union's larger volume of expensive grain imports proved easily affordable through the later half of the 1970s and even into the 1980s. Food import costs briefly became problematic in 1981, when a record purchase of 46 million tons of foreign grain at a cost of roughly $8 billion (plus an additional $4 billion in purchases of other agricultural products from abroad) accounted for 40 percent of total Soviet hard currency purchases. The result in that year, despite an expanded volume of oil sales abroad and cutbacks on the import of machinery and other consumer goods, was a troublesome $4 billion hard currency trade deficit. Nevertheless, with its huge economic base and its relatively small foreign hard currency debt (only $11.5 billion at the end of 1981), the Soviet Union was tolerably well positioned to absorb larger foreign economic costs in its newly determined pursuit of dietary improvements at home.

The greatest external challenge to Brezhnev's grain import strategy was to come during the U.S. grain embargo of 1980–81. That challenge was eventually met with relative ease, through a hasty diversification of Soviet trade to non-U.S. suppliers. But the timing of this diversification—which came only after the embargo was announced—reveals how far the Soviet Union had strayed from its earlier habit of seeking external food power.

Why did the Soviet Union wait so long to exercise, through trade diversification, a prudent measure of "defensive" food power? Especially after the brief U.S. grain sales suspension of 1975, which had been accompanied by Kissinger's bold demands for concessions on oil prices, one might expect the Soviet Union to have responded with a reduction of its imports, or at least a lasting diversification of its imports away from the United States. In fact, the Soviet Union did the opposite; it bought more grain than ever before, and bought a larger share of that grain directly from the United States. Between 1973 and 1975, annual Soviet grain imports averaged 13.9 million tons, with purchases from the United States making up 57 percent of the total. Between 1976 and 1978, annual Soviet grain imports averaged 14.6 million tons; purchases from the United States made up 71 percent of the total.[69]

On strictly commercial and logistical terms, it made some sense for the Soviet Union to buy so much of its grain from the United States where export facilities were modern and responsive, prices competitive, and reserve supplies (particularly of corn—a favored animal feed) abundant, year in and year out. But the apparent disregard for the diplomatic exposure associated with its larger grain purchases from the United States, especially after 1975, is nonetheless revealing. The Soviets could have taken any number of foreign policy developments during this period as good reason to lessen their dependence on U.S. grain.

Beginning in 1974, for example, a series of unwelcome U.S. congressional actions had linked "most favored nation" status for the Soviet Union to changes in Soviet emigration policy, and had made that status, in turn, a prerequisite for access to U.S. government credits. When an overall ceiling of $300 million was then placed on Eximbank credits from the United States, the Soviet Union defiantly repudiated its 1972 trade agreement with the United States and began to look elsewhere for credits, and for imports of technology and manufactured goods. Remarkably, it did nothing to diversify imports of grain.

Early in 1976, in an agitated response to Cuba's role in the Angolan civil war, the United States canceled the regular annual session of the U.S.–Soviet Joint Commercial Commission and postponed a number of other bilateral meetings. When Jimmy Carter became president in 1977, he then reconfirmed this growing U.S. tendency toward the use of economic sanctions. First Carter denied an export license for the sale of an advanced Control Data computer to the Soviet Union and in July 1978, to protest dissident trials in the Soviet Union, he denied an export license for a Sperry Univac computer that had been ordered for use at the 1980 Moscow Olympics. In addition, the Carter administration imposed new licensing requirements on exports to the Soviet Union of oil and natural gas equipment. Even then the Soviet Union declined to take any steps to reduce or to diversify its grain trade dependence.

It is important to stress that during this period the five-year "long-term agreement" on grain, signed with the United States in October 1975, did *not* provide the Soviet Union with adequate guarantees of access to large quantities of U.S. grain. The language of that agreement did guarantee, during each year over the period 1976–81, access to at least 8 million tons of U.S. grain, no strings attached. But for purchases above 8 million tons the Soviet Union had first to obtain permission in yearly consultations with U.S. officials. As it turned out, U.S. officials routinely extended permission during each of the first three years of the agreement for total purchases of U.S. grain of up to 15 million tons. But only the first 8 million tons of these permitted sales could have been considered, by the Soviet Union, to be a firm access guarantee.

The willingness to rely on imports of U.S. grain, in apparent disregard of any possible diplomatic cost or risk, was most visible in late 1979, after the first of a damaging sequence of poor domestic grain harvests. With its diplomatic ties to the United States under increasing strain, and only two months away from its own military invasion of Afghanistan, the Soviet Union made plans to import a record quantity of 36 million tons of grain in the upcoming year, including a record 25 million ton purchase directly from the United States.[70] Given the anti-Soviet political drift in Washington and the planning of their own military policies regarding Afghanistan, the Soviet Union might have been expected to place less trust in its access to so much U.S. grain. (The willingness of the United States under the diplomatic circumstances to offer so much grain to the Soviet Union is only slightly less remarkable.)[71]

When the U.S. grain embargo was imposed in January 1980, the Soviet Union was obliged to make a substantial and rapid trade adjustment. Soviet buyers had purchased only about half of their planned imports of 25 million tons of U.S. grain when Soviet troops began moving into Afghanistan in late December 1979, but they accelerated their buying once the invasion was under way; by the time of the embargo announcement they had bought 21.4 million tons of U.S. grain, just short of their planned total. Only a small quantity of this grain (about 5.5 million tons) had actually been shipped, however, so under the terms of the embargo announcement (which allowed them to receive only the 8 million tons they were guaranteed under the long-term agreement) the Soviet Union would be left short of most of the U.S. grain it had already purchased, and as much as 17 million tons of the total quantity of grain that it was originally planning to buy.[72]

This uncomfortable experience—a sudden loss of access to 17 million tons of U.S. grain, significant portions of which had already been purchased—at last inspired a long-overdue "defensive" modification in Soviet grain trade policy. Soviet policy makers took a variety of measures, during and after the embargo, to ensure that U.S. "food power" over the Soviet Union would never again be so great. The Soviet Union moved immediately to diversify its grain purchases away from the United States. The relative ease with which this diversification was accomplished in the short run (ensuring a continued *expansion* of total Soviet grain imports in 1980–81, despite the embargo) is examined in detail in chapter 6. As a long term strategy, this belated trade diversification took form in a series of formal bilateral agreements with non-U.S. suppliers.

Within months of the embargo announcement, the Soviet Union signed an important five-year grain trade agreement with Argentina, which guaranteed yearly access to 4.5 million tons of corn, grain sorghum, and soybeans. A subsequent agreement, negotiated early in 1981, also made available annual quantities of at least 60,000 tons of Argentine beef.[73] Long-term agreements such as these not only ensured access to non-U.S. food supplies; they also encouraged the further production of such supplies. Argentina, which had not previously been assured of foreign markets for such a large portion of its yearly grain surplus, was suddenly in a position to make greater use of its vast potential as a producer of exportable grains. In 1980–81 Argentina increased its acreage devoted to grain by 13 percent, and went on to produce a grain crop nearly 30 percent higher than its production average of the past five years. Argentine wheat and coarse grain exports, which had totaled only 11.4 million tons in 1979–80, nearly doubled, to 19.3 million tons, by 1982–83.[74]

Nor was Argentina the only non-U.S. grain supplier to be courted by the Soviet Union in the wake of the embargo. In May 1981, soon after the lifting of the embargo, the Soviet Union signed an extensive long-term trade agreement with Canada. In this agreement, the first of its kind with Canada in ten years, the Soviet Union was guaranteed access to a minimum of 25 million tons of wheat and barley over the five-year period 1981–85. As with Argentina, Canada would take this agreement as a further incentive to proceed with a long-planned development of its own grain export potential. By 1982–83 Canadian exports of wheat and coarse grains had increased by nearly 50 percent from the 1979–80 level.[75]

Still aggressively pressing this supply diversification strategy, in July 1981 the Soviets signed a five-year food trade agreement with Brazil, ensuring future access to a minimum 2.5 million tons of soybeans, plus a minimum 2.5 million tons of corn, largely in return for Soviet petroleum. Soviet soybean and soybean meal imports would expand during the early 1980s, but U.S. suppliers would initially be shunned in favor of Brazilian, Argentine, and European suppliers, clearly for reasons of foreign policy. Long-term access to European farm products would also become a significant part of the Soviet postembargo import strategy. Late in 1982, the Soviet Union signed a framework agreement with France, agreeing to purchase between 1.5 and 3.0 million tons of French wheat, more than double the quantity purchased in the preceding year.[76] Long-term trade agreements guaranteeing access to smaller quantities of grain and feed were also signed with Thailand (a ten-year pact, ensuring annual purchases of corn, rice, and tapioca), with Hungary (which had been a regular exporter of agricultural products to the Soviet Union even before the embargo), and with India (yearly barter agreements, offering oil in return for rice, corn, and barley, as described in chapter 2).

Actual Soviet purchases of non-U.S. grain after the embargo were in fact well above the total quantities guaranteed under the terms of these new embargo-inspired diversification agreements. Annual Soviet grain purchases from Argentina, for example, reached 16 million tons in a single year in 1981, roughly four times the quantity guaranteed by agreement. But formal agreements were nonetheless a vital source of reassurance to Soviet trade officials, who had always valued predictability in their grain supply relationships, and who wished never again to become so exposed to a sudden exercise of U.S. food trade blackmail. As Deputy Foreign Trade Minister Aleksei Manzhulo later explained to his U.S. counterpart, "You forced us to do it [diversify sources of supply] . . . we are following the proverb 'Don't put all of your eggs in one basket.'"[77]

The Soviet Union remained willing, however, to continue a noteworthy grain trade relationship with the United States. This is not to say that Soviet purchasing agents rushed back to the United States the moment the embargo was lifted in April 1981. Not until the evidence of their own poor harvest had accumulated in late summer did they return to the U.S. market, and even then they played a cool hand, purchasing at first only small quantities, not wishing to appear too eager for U.S. grain—at least not until U.S. officials had agreed in early August to a one-year extension of the soon-to-expire five-year agreement (which guaranteed to the Soviet Union access to at least 8 million tons of wheat and corn yearly). At this point, however, significant grain purchases from the United States were resumed, so that during the subsequent October–September "agreement year" Soviet imports of U.S. grain totaled a significant 13.9 million tons.

Because the Soviet Union was then seeking its largest-yet total volume of grain imports, it had no choice but to resume a larger trade dependence upon the United States. By 1982–83, with a better harvest at home, total Soviet grain imports could be reduced from 46 million tons to 32.5 million tons, so the U.S. share of this smaller import total could be reduced as well. In that year the Soviet Union took from the United States only slightly more than the 6 million tons that they were *obliged* to purchase, under the terms of yet another extension of their long-term agreement. In fact, when President Ronald Reagan offered a firm guarantee of access to as much as 23 million tons of grain on the eve of the November 1982 congressional elections, Soviet commentators ridiculed the gesture, noting accurately that "the plight of the agricultural areas in the United States has drastically worsened the position of the Republican Party in those districts and the President is now seeking to redress the situation at all costs." With a part of its trade successfully diversified away from the United States, the Soviet Union once again enjoyed some bargaining leverage of its own in the world grain market. While Soviet officials chided the United States for having "lost its reputation as a reliable trading partner," market-hungry U.S. exporters began offering the Soviet Union one concession after another—from short-term credits to additional access guarantees—in hopes of winning back a larger share of Soviet business.[78]

The grain embargo experience inspired a significant and successful *diversification* of Soviet imports. Yet it is important to recognize that the embargo did *not* inspire any reduction in the total volume of those imports. Quite the contrary. The total volume of Soviet grain imports, from all sources, not only managed to expand while the embargo was in place; it then continued to expand in the year that followed. Continued Soviet imports of Western grain despite an experience with food trade blackmail is further evidence that foreign policy considerations were not the controlling force behind Soviet grain trade policy during the Brezhnev era. Soviet leaders at times made public reference to the diplomatic risk of importing so much Western grain. In an address to the Central Committee in June 1982, Brezhnev himself referred to the need to "reduce imports from capitalist countries . . . some of which use grain sales as an instrument of political pressure." He returned to this theme in one of his last public speeches, in October 1982, when he reminded high-ranking military and political officials in Moscow of the need to "eliminate in the future the need for grain purchases abroad."[79] If this was an official preference, it is all the more significant that large grain imports were allowed to continue.

To understand Brezhnev's willingness to continue to import large quantities of grains, whatever the associated external economic or diplomatic cost, one must return to the impossible food policy dilemma that Soviet leaders faced at home. Soviet meat production in 1981 stood at 15.2 million tons, only 3 percent above the production average of the preceding Tenth Plan period, and hopelessly short of the 19.5 million ton target for the Eleventh Plan (1981–85).[80] Meat consumption per capita in the Soviet Union had not increased since 1975, when it reached a peak of 57 kilograms. In view of these difficulties, the 1985 goal for meat production was informally modified downward at the Twenty-Sixth Party Congress early in 1981, from 19.5 to 18.2 million tons.[81] Unfortunately, to obtain even this level of meat production by 1985 would require grain-feeding levels at least 20 percent higher than those attained during the earlier five-year plan. Even assuming a miraculous recovery on the production side (for example, *average* grain production by 1985 at the unrealistic target level of 240 million tons) yearly grain import requirements might still fall in the hefty 20–30 million ton range.[82]

Brezhnev explained to the Central Committee in November 1981 that this difficult domestic food situation was now to be viewed "both economically and politically" as "the central problem of the [1981–85] five-year plan."[83] There was little room for retreat, as domestic consumption demands would only grow larger in response to the more generous wage policies that Brezhnev himself had put in place. Average monthly wages of workers and employees in the Soviet Union, which had increased by 16 percent during the Tenth Plan (1975–80), were designated during the Eleventh Plan to go still higher, up an additional 13–16 percent. Estimating the income elasticity of demand for livestock products in the Soviet Union at close to unity, this projected income growth obliged the leadership to hold as close as possible to its ambitious 1985 meat production targets.[84]

Nor was there any escape from further imports on the domestic production side. With the investments already allocated to agriculture making record demands on economic resources, with slower economic growth placing a tighter lid on the future availability of investment resources, and with production returns on agricultural investment low in any case (a ratio of net output to gross investment which was apparently only half that of the United States), simply throwing more money at domestic food problems was not a promising alternative.[85] Improved weather seemed to be the only certain means of securing significant production gains in the short run. Even so, one projection of annual Soviet grain output for 1981–85, based upon "good climate" conditions (comparable to the 1970–74 period) fell 10 million tons short of the planned target, which in turn fell 20–30 million tons short of projected feed use requirements.[86]

Not even a return to good weather could overcome the more serious obstacles to Soviet grain output expansion. Foremost among these, at the end of the Brezhnev era, was a chronic shortage of fertilizers essential to higher crop yields. By 1980 deliveries of fertilizer to the farming sector had increased only moderately to reach 82 million tons, well short of the planned goal of 115 million tons. In a significant admission of failure, this unattained 115 million ton goal was not raised in the follow-up plan for 1985, although grain production targets were. Even in the unlikely event of reaching the 1985 fertilizer goal, therefore, deliveries would still be lagging at least five years behind the rate of expansion once deemed essential.[87]

Significant institutional reform remained the only path of escape. In May 1982, near the end of his tenure, Brezhnev went through the motions of reform, by securing Central Committee approval for the outline of a new "Food Program," promised since October 1980 and earlier touted as a "radical solution" to the nation's food problems.[88] In fact, there appeared nothing at all radical about Brezhnev's proposed reform, the essence of which was to improve coordination among the many separate and poorly integrated units of the Soviet food economy. Brezhnev's plan was to accelerate efforts earlier under way to forge these units into a single vertically integrated "agro-industrial complex," hoping thereby to improve efficiency both "upstream" and "downstream," from "farm to store." This tinkering, in combination with some heightened incentives for private plot production, some revised purchase prices and bonus payments for farm products, and a few modest schemes to encourage farm-level initiative, could hardly be characterized as a "radical" solution. Some aspects of the Food Program that did show promise (rural storage and transport investments, for example, to reduce the huge grain losses incurred in postharvest handling) would be extraordinarily expensive and probably implemented at a slow pace. Nowhere in Brezhnev's Food Program was there a clear remedy to the ills of centrally planned state farming. Brezhnev hastened to observe, while unveiling the details of the Food Program, that nothing in the policy was intended as a repudiation of efforts that had been made before. He described Soviet agricultural policy during the previous seventeen years of his tenure as "a scientific policy, a correct policy, from which we did not depart, nor will depart."[89]

Grain Trade Policy since Brezhnev

Prospects for a more radical overhaul of the Soviet farm economy were not much improved by Brezhnev's passing from the scene in November 1982. In April 1983, Yuri V. Andropov summoned Party officials from across the Soviet Union to an unusual meeting with the Politburo, to lecture them on the extreme urgency of solving the country's food problems. But Andropov, other than placing greater stress on the need for "labor discipline," did little more than to endorse the Food Program left by his predecessor. In May 1983 the failing Andropov then enlarged the authority of Mikhail Gorbachev, Brezhnev's hand-picked party secretary for agriculture, and a principal contributor to the Food Program initiative.[90] Gorbachev would gain even greater visibility upon Andropov's death early in 1984, when he emerged as a strong second in the new leadership hierarchy, behind Konstantin Chernenko, himself an aging and once passed-over Brezhnev protégé. In March 1984 Chernenko and Gorbachev together reaffirmed to the Politburo their insistence that the "agri-industrial amalgamations" envisioned in Brezhnev's Food Program were key factors in improving the output of grain, milk, fruit, vegetables, and most of all, meat.[91]

The inability of Soviet agriculture to respond to such tinkering should have been obvious following the final disappointment of the 1984 grain harvest, when total production fell to an estimated 170 million tons, 70 million tons short of planning targets. With livestock inventories still growing, a massive round of new imports—projected initially at a record level of 50 million tons—would be necessary to sustain feed use. Unable to ignore the magnitude of this latest setback, Chernenko convened a special Central Committee session in October, at which he described the "acute" problem of providing meat supplies now to be "a matter of daily concern." Yet his proposed solution on this occasion—an expensive new irrigation and land reclamation effort—represented no break from the existing habit of wasteful resource commitments. Land reclamation projects since 1966 had already absorbed an estimated $137 billion in scarce investment resources, with dwindling results.[92]

A somewhat more promising means to pursue Soviet meat production objectives at home, without recourse to ever-larger grain imports, would be to consider further modifications in livestock feeding practices. It is one of the curious features of Soviet agriculture, plagued as it is by a shortage of grain, that the standard feed ration provided for livestock contains too much grain, rather than too little. Feed rations containing a smaller measure of imported grains, and a larger measure of home-grown nongrain feed sources (such as silage, feed roots, hay, haylage, oilseed meals, milling by-products, alfalfa, and grass meals) would not only reduce grain import requirements. These altered feed rations would also improve the efficiency (the "feed conversion ratio") of the Soviet livestock industry.[93]

Soviet planners have known, for some time, that their livestock rations have been too heavily loaded with imported grain.[94] Yet before the U.S. grain embargo, Soviet planners had made little progress in dealing with this feed efficiency problem. As late as 1979, the Central Intelligence Agency (CIA) had concluded that an immediate improvement in Soviet feed rations was unlikely.[95] After the embargo, however, the improved use of nongrain feed sources at last began to receive sustained priority. Within a month of the embargo announcement the head of the Soviet Union's grain crop department in the Ministry of Agriculture, Alexander Zholobov, stated that his government would have to "make some changes in our stockraising program." In the "draft guidelines" for the 1981–85 Eleventh Plan published in December 1980, improved fodder production was labeled an "urgent task." Pasture irrigation was promoted, and new incentives were provided to reduce "over-consumption of grain." Total Soviet forage output in 1980 was nearly 10 percent higher than it had been in 1979. By 1984, the Soviet harvest of non-grain feed had increased by 20 percent from the 1980–82 average level.[96]

For the foreseeable future, however, the pursuit of high-priority food policy objectives at home will oblige Soviet leaders to import a heavy volume of foreign grains for animal feed—expending significant quantities of foreign exchange, and experiencing some vulnerability to food trade blackmail in the process. Belatedly, Soviet leaders sought to minimize their diplomatic vulnerability by diverting a part of their trade away from the United States. But beyond such marginal adjustments, they dared not return to their much earlier practice of sacrificing domestic food needs whenever conflicts arose with their external economic or security objectives. Now when such conflicts arose, their external objectives would more likely be sacrificed.

Summary

The presumption that nations seek food power is disconfirmed in recent Soviet grain trade policy. It was a far better guide in the 1930s when Soviet grain exports were promoted, and domestic food needs were sacrificed, in a calculated pursuit of external trade and security objectives. This early Stalinist preference for the pursuit of food power abroad was heavily modified but never completely abandoned by Khrushchev, who simply *added* the pursuit of domestic food policy objectives to the larger policy balance. It was not until the Brezhnev era that the need to *sacrifice* some external needs to pursue food policy objectives at home was at last recognized and accepted. By presiding over the Soviet transformation from a net exporter of grain as late as 1970 to the world's single largest grain importer, Brezhnev was accepting a near total reversal of earlier food policy priorities.

In fairness, perhaps this Soviet abandonment of its earlier "food power" objectives, in pursuit of domestic dietary affluence, is not such a dramatic reversal. Some successful diversification of grain imports, both during and after the 1980–81 U.S. grain embargo, significantly buffered the Soviet Union against a renewed exercise of U.S. food trade blackmail. Also, because of its ready access to foreign hard currency and credits, Soviet foreign economic policy can well enough afford a large volume of grain imports. For that matter, the Soviet Union's abandonment of food power and the new priority it assigns to domestic dietary improvements may reflect nothing more than the nation's emergence as a more secure and prosperous industrial superpower. The Soviet Union is no longer a backward nation, torn by revolution and civil war, struggling to gain security against the menacing designs of various superior industrial neighbors to the West. The Soviet Union of today is an unsurpassed Eurasian superpower which can easily afford to set aside food power as a means to promote its trade and security objectives abroad. With so many other instruments of external influence now at its disposal—from oil and gas exports to thermonuclear weapons—the Soviet inclination to mobilize food trade in pursuit of its external objectives has been reduced. As a mature industrial state, with a large and increasingly affluent urban population, the Soviet Union perhaps recognizes that its future prosperity and security cannot be well served without greater attention to food consumption requirements at home.

4 The United States: Food Power Forgone

When considering U.S. grain trade policies in recent years, there is some evidence that a pursuit of *external* economic and diplomatic objectives may have played a larger role than domestic concerns. A decade-long surge in grain exports between 1972 and 1981 produced remarkable trade policy gains for the United States. Net U.S. agricultural trade, which had been *negative* at one point early in the 1950s and stood at only $1.5 billion as late as 1970, by 1975 soared to $12.6 billion and reached a record $26.7 billion by 1981. Exports of unprocessed grain and feed products were instrumental in these gains—as they grew from only $2.2 billion in 1967 to $18 billion by 1981. These larger export earnings from grain sales abroad could not have been better timed for the United States, helping as they did to compensate for trade and payments difficulties brought on by higher imported energy costs, and by the reduced competitiveness of U.S. industrial products in markets abroad.

External diplomatic and security gains also appeared to be an object of U.S. grain trade policy. In the aftermath of the long, debilitating struggle in Vietnam, U.S. military and diplomatic superiority were no longer self-evident. In this circumstance the inclination to search for some new instrument of foreign policy influence—perhaps even a "food weapon"—would be readily understood.

Despite these appearances, the U.S. has *not* been seeking food power more often of late. The sudden growth in U.S. grain exports noted in the 1970s was not the direct product of an export promotion strategy designed to earn foreign exchange. Policies of grain trade manipulation designed for the pursuit of diplomatic objectives were even less evident. Despite a partial embargo on sales to the Soviet Union in 1980–81, the

United States has manipulated its grain exports in search of diplomatic gains *less often* than at times in the past. Just as India and the Soviet Union have gradually become willing to import grain (including U.S. grain) with little regard for diplomatic appearances, so has the United States gradually become willing to export, with few foreign policy strings attached.

This emerging disconnection between grain trade policy and foreign policy derives in part from an unresolved debate within the U.S. foreign policy community over whether to *promote* the nation's grain exports in search of external *economic* gains, or to *restrict* these exports in search of *diplomatic* leverage. Equally decisive, however, has been the inward-looking character of powerful domestic food and farm policy interests, plus the private and lightly regulated nature of U.S. grain trade institutions.

Grain Exports, Farm Prices, and Foreign Policy before 1933

Before the Great Depression and the first term of Franklin D. Roosevelt's presidency, the U.S. government did not have much that could be called a grain policy, let alone a grain *trade* policy. Direct government involvement and the manipulation of domestic farm prices and production, soon to become commonplace, were as yet unheard of, other than in wartime. Nevertheless, U.S. grain production and exports at times experienced remarkable growth.

U.S. grain began to go abroad in large volume after European industrialization and Britain's decision to repeal its protectionist Corn Laws in 1846. The subsequent expansion of world trade, along with a technological revolution in steam-powered rail and ocean transport, suddenly made cheap U.S. grains competitive in urban European markets. In 1874 the United States replaced Russia as England's principal supplier of wheat, and between 1870 and 1898, the total value of U.S. wheat and flour exports increased threefold, from $68 million to $200 million.[1]

U.S. grain producers, however, were distracted at the time from a full appreciation of the advantages to be gained in these foreign markets. Despite a threefold growth in foreign sales after 1870, wheat prices received by U.S. farmers *fell* by nearly half. The same revolution in technology that had suddenly made larger grain exports possible was also boosting U.S. grain production (wheat production more than doubled between 1870 and 1898), overwhelming both foreign and domestic demand. The value of foreign markets, as a result, went somewhat unappreciated by U.S. grain producers, and political habits not necessarily conducive to export promotion were formed. U.S. grain producers in the West, who might have been expected to press hard for policies of liberal international trade (along with cotton and tobacco producers in the South), instead focused most of their political energy on matters such as internal money policy and the regulation of domestic processing and transport. Grain producers and many Western farmers even gave their support to the McKinley Tariff Act of 1890, believing that they needed tariff protection from exports of Canadian barley.[2]

These confused perceptions of U.S. grain trade interests were compounded after the turn of the century in another unfortunate coincidence. U.S. wheat exports, which had been running above 200 million bushels in 1900, fell to less than 100 million bushels by 1909; they remained at these lower levels until the outbreak of the First World War. At the same time, however, because of high rates of immigration, urbanization, income growth in the United States, and the closing of the Western frontier, domestic supply and demand came into better balance, grain prices increased, and U.S. agriculture entered what is still remembered as its "golden age" of prosperity. The connection between fewer exports and higher grain prices at home was erroneous, but the coincidence reinforced prevailing attitudes of indifference among U.S. producers toward export promotion and liberal trade. Most powerful farm organizations, as a consequence, continued to embrace protectionism.[3]

Not even the dramatic effects of the First World War were enough to convince grain producers of their long-run interest in export promotion. U.S. grain exports burgeoned during the war, but not so much at the insistence of producers.[4] Because of a poor U.S. harvest in 1916, and strong internal demand, grain producers had no surplus stocks available for export, and extraordinary government measures had to be taken to ensure that adequate grain supplies reached allied armies and populations in Europe. Through the establishment of the U.S. Food Administration and the War Trade Board in 1917, the government, out of strategic interest, moved to take unprecedented control over the production, conservation, and export of food. While U.S. consumers suffered directly—per capita food consumption actually declined—grain producers felt pinched as well, because they were denied an opportunity to take full commercial advantage of the surge in foreign demand.[5] These wartime policies were nothing less than a vintage exercise of U.S. food power abroad, accompanied by a measurable sacrifice to both consumer and producer interests at home. Never before or since have such external objectives enjoyed such clear-cut priority.

The traditional misgivings U.S. grain producers harbored toward foreign markets were reinforced after the First World War, when European production recovered and demand for U.S. grain exports evaporated. The painful adjustment that ensued was long remembered by U.S. farmers. Wheat acreage, which had increased by 50 percent during the war, was suddenly far in excess of domestic needs, which had been *falling* in view of the shift away from heavy bread consumption that usually accompanies advanced industrialization. Demand for some feedgrains was also falling, as gas-eating tractors replaced grain-eating horses. Efficient internal combustion engine tractors and harvesting combines—and the widespread introduction of fertilizers and insecticides—simultaneously increased U.S. crop yields, further aggravating the domestic surplus. Wheat prices eventually fell to less than half of the wartime level, corn prices to barely a third of the wartime level, and farm income went into steep decline.

These severe postwar adjustment difficulties triggered a landmark development in the politics of U.S. agriculture—the formation in 1921 of a nationwide federation of agricultural interest groups, the American Farm Bureau Federation. Organized at the same time in Congress was a bipartisan group of farm state legislators which came to be known as the Farm Bloc. Its bipartisan character, aggressive leadership, and estimable size allowed this group to gain unchallenged control over the content of U.S. farm policy. Export promotion was *not* viewed by this group as the most promising means of farm salvation. The Farm Bloc continued, throughout the 1920s, to concentrate most of its political energies on matters such as domestic credit, freight rates, taxation, and regulation of food-trading and food-processing monopolies.[6] Scant attention was paid to U.S. trade policies, which unfortunately presented overseas grain-importing nations with high tariff barriers to the U.S. market, thus dampening foreign demand for U.S. agricultural exports.[7]

The Great Depression

U.S. agriculture, which had been in a depression of its own for nearly a decade after the First World War, was dealt an additional blow by the general economic collapse of the 1930s. Farm prices fell by 56 percent between 1929 and 1932, bottoming out at a level 35 percent below the prewar standard of two decades earlier. A new round of protectionist policies on both sides of the Atlantic further stifled trade, hitting U.S. wheat exports particularly hard. Exports fell from 18.5 percent of total domestic wheat production before 1929 to only 6.7 percent of total production by 1931.[8] So severe was this new agricultural crisis that the Farm Bloc, following the activist lead of the Roosevelt administration, wrote into law unprecedented provisions for direct, continuing federal control over the production and pricing of major farm commodities. These commodity programs were soon to emerge as the determining element behind all U.S. grain export policies.

Export promotion was still not viewed as a feasible solution to the domestic farm crisis. The first inclination, during the early years of the Depression, was to boost farm prices by cutting back on production. Under the original provisions of the 1933 Agricultural Adjustment Act, rental payments were made to farmers who reduced their acreage planted in wheat. Under the influence of such policies, and also in response to low prices, wheat production did decline sharply, by 40 percent between 1931 and 1933. So abrupt was this production adjustment that when a drought was encountered in 1934, federal acreage restrictions had to be eased. The continuation of this drought in 1934–36 obliged the United States to become a temporary substantial *importer* of wheat.[9]

It did not take long, however, for the new domestic commodity programs initiated in 1933 to acquire a lasting bias toward production growth, carried by high price guarantees. At the center of this important shift would be the operation of the "commodity loan" program initiated in October 1933, originally intended to stabilize farm income by buffering producers from extreme fluctuations in farm prices. Under the terms of the program, a farmer could secure a "loan" from the newly created Commodity Credit Corporation (CCC), by pawning his own surplus crop production as collateral at a preset price per bushel (known as a "loan rate"). If free market prices later moved above the loan rate, the farmer had an option to reclaim his produce, sell it for the higher price, pay off the loan, and pocket the difference. If market prices did not increase, he could fulfill his loan obligation by turning over his produce, permanently, to the CCC. The impact of such a program would depend entirely upon the price-per-bushel level at which government loan rates were set. If set above the average price level prevailing in the free market, these guaranteed loan rates would "stabilize prices upward," encouraging surplus production.

The political influence of the Farm Bloc ensured that commodity loan rates would very quickly come to be set at levels too high to permit the domestic market to clear. Loans to corn growers, for example, were first offered in 1933 at 60 percent of the "parity" level. Parity, to begin with, was a highly inflated standard—a measure of farm purchasing power based upon an antiquated ratio of prices paid and received by farmers during the "golden age" of 1910–14. Given the ability of U.S. farmers, through technological innovation, to produce more at lower cost, any such fixed standard was certain to become a stimulus to overproduction—all the more so when legislators eager to boost farm income began to push loan rates even higher. By 1938 corn loan rates had been increased to 70 percent of parity, providing producers with guaranteed prices so high as to overwhelm any parallel efforts to keep total production under control.

This new bias toward surplus production remained partially hidden for a number of years, due to an unusual sequence of developments. The first was the most severe drought in U.S. history, already mentioned, which first struck in 1934 and returned in 1936, holding back grain production despite the high support prices being offered by the CCC. But with the return of favorable weather later in the 1930s production expanded rapidly, so that by 1939 surplus stocks of both wheat and corn on "loan" to the government were beginning to accumulate to troublesome levels. Then came the outbreak of World War II in 1939, which generated not only a U.S. economic recovery, but also a renewed foreign demand for U.S. grain.

World War II and the Marshall Plan

It was fortunate in the short run that U.S. farm programs with a bias toward surplus production were already in place when the Second World War began. Unlike the experience of the First World War, the sudden requirement to produce more food for shipment overseas proved relatively painless. Despite much larger grain exports, per capita U.S. food consumption during the war increased, to reach record levels.[10] Nor were producer interests being slighted in the process, as U.S. farm prices doubled between 1939 and 1945.

As before, U.S. grain was rushed to allied states abroad under a wide-ranging set of ad hoc controls. In June 1942, the Food Requirements Committee was created by the War Production Board to establish wartime food needs for both military and foreign use. The Combined Food Board was also created, to make joint recommendations to the U.S. and British governments on wartime production, transport, and distribution of food worldwide.

In contrast to the First War, however, U.S. foreign policy makers saw to it that foreign demand for U.S. grain would not collapse when hostilities ended. Rather than raising tariffs, terminating all credits and assistance, and calling in all debts as in 1919, the United States after 1945 did quite the opposite—pursuing reciprocal tariff reductions through the General Agreements on Tariffs and Trade and extending foreign assistance in unprecedented quantities, first a $3.7 billion loan to Great Britain in 1946, followed by the Marshall Plan, which provided assistance throughout Europe after 1947. Of the total $12 billion in Marshall Plan aid extended between 1948 and 1950, $4 billion went for food, fertilizer and feed ($1.4 billion went specifically for the purchase of U.S. wheat). This remains the greatest single peacetime exercise of U.S. "food power" abroad; Secretary of State George Marshall stressed at the time that "food is a vital factor in our foreign policy." Meanwhile, the Marshall Plan was of enormous benefit to U.S. grain producers. Between 1948 and 1950, nearly three-fifths of all U.S. farm exports were financed by government grants and loans or took the form of official donations.[11] Thanks to the trade stimulus of these new aid policies, the total volume of U.S. exports of wheat, wheat products, and other grains avoided any decline during the immediate postwar period (Table 7). This strong postwar export performance, promoted and financed by a revolution in U.S. foreign economic policy, helped push domestic farm prices to a new high, a spectacular 110 percent of parity by 1948, a level well *above* existing federal price guarantees.[12]

The years 1949–50 brought a slowdown in export growth; farm prices began to sag, the use of commodity loans increased, and surplus

Table 7.   U.S. grain exports, 1935–1950

Year (average)	Wheat and wheat products (million long tons)	Other grains (million long tons)
1935–39	1.4	1.3
1945–46	10.5	1.3
1946–47	10.7	4.2
1947–48	13.0	2.2
1948–49	13.5	4.3
1949–50	8.0	4.3

Source: Murry R. Benedict, *Farm Policies of the United States: 1790–1950*, p. 501.

stocks in government bins began to accumulate. The Korean War saw a brief commodity boom, relieving the downward pressure on prices somewhat, but the volume of farm exports nonetheless fell rapidly in 1951 and 1952. The dollar value of these exports dropped nearly 30 percent.[13] By 1953, with the Korean War and the Marshall Plan both at an end, there was no longer any foreign policy crisis to absorb the surplus grain production still being encouraged by federal commodity loan programs at home.

The Eisenhower Years

At the base of President Eisenhower's surplus disposal problem lay the high guaranteed domestic prices still offered to U.S. grain producers through commodity loan programs. In the Agriculture Act of 1949, powerful domestic producer interests had opposed any retreat from high prices and pushed support levels for corn and wheat up to 75–90 percent of parity, well above the levels that prevailed before the war.[14] Along the way, they also rejected the so-called Brannan Plan offered by the then secretary of agriculture, which would have compensated farmers through direct payments rather than through commodity loans. This method of direct income support would have saved the government the cost and inconvenience of accumulating surplus stocks, by allowing domestic farm prices to fall and markets to clear. A drop in farm prices would at the same time allow U.S. grains to capture a larger share of the commercial export trade. The plan was rejected by the Farm Bloc because it would have made the generous level of subsidies being offered to producers *more visible to taxpayers*, and hence less secure. Commodity loans tended to conceal subsidies in the form of high market prices and preserved the illusion that surplus production was entirely a consequence of market forces.

For nearly a decade after the Korean War, government officials concerned about surplus grain production fought to lower commodity loan guarantees against the resistance of a bipartisan coalition of farm state legislators. The gains from this battle during the Eisenhower years were disappointing, as federal price guarantees for wheat by 1961 remained as much as 50 percent above the "free market" price that might have prevailed in the absence of a government commodity loan program. For feedgrains, such as corn, support prices remained 20–30 percent above a "free market" level.[15] Farmers took these continuing price supports throughout the 1950s as their incentive to invest in still greater production gains; agricultural productivity growth raced ahead at twice the nonfarm rate. As a consequence, government-owned surplus stocks of wheat and corn continued to swell. By 1961, government-owned stocks of corn were more than twice the level of 1953, and stocks of wheat two and a half times the 1953 level. Total carryover stocks of wheat were equal to more than an entire year's worth of utilization by 1961.

This accumulation of surplus grain stocks at home during the Eisenhower period inspired an innovative series of initiatives to step up the volume of grain exports. As one senior official later described these "surplus disposal" efforts,

> We sold what we could for cash. What we couldn't sell for cash we sold for credit. What we couldn't sell for dollars we sold for foreign currency. What we couldn't get money for we bartered. What we couldn't get anything for we gave away—what we couldn't export by any means we stored. And still the stocks increased.[16]

Grain export promotion efforts in the 1950s were not without effect. By 1960 the total volume of U.S. wheat and coarse grain exports had increased to 29 million tons, roughly twice the earlier peak level reached during the Marshall Plan period. The U.S. share of world grain markets also expanded, as other exporters were then lagging behind the United States in both production gains and export promotion. The U.S. share of world wheat exports, which had sagged from 39 percent in 1949–52 to only 29 percent by 1953–55, recovered and advanced to 45 percent by 1959–61.[17]

Of all the new export promotion devices employed during the 1950s, the most important was the sale of U.S. grain for *foreign currency*, rather than dollars, as authorized under Title I of the 1954 Agricultural Trade Development and Assistance Act, P.L. 480. Over the first three years of the program, 80 percent of all Title I sales went to underdeveloped countries with balance of payment difficulties, countries that probably would not have been significant food importers if hard currency expenditures had been required.[18] Thus, even while these *concessional* U.S. grain exports multiplied significantly (from 3.1 million tons in 1955 to 13.0 million tons in 1957, and then to an average of 10.7 million tons between 1958 and 1960), the U.S. share of world *commercial* grain sales did not appear to suffer. The U.S. share of strictly commercial wheat exports actually increased at the same time, from 10 percent in 1953–55 to 21 percent by 1959–61.[19]

Still, as an instrument of foreign economic policy P.L. 480 proved to be of dubious value. Foreign economic policy officials in the Treasury Department and the Commerce Department had been opposed to P.L. 480 from the start, in the belief that foreign currency sales would eventually become detrimental to hard currency sales.[20] In 1958, when both the volume and the dollar value of U.S. commercial farm exports actually declined, trade officials became aroused. Hard evidence that P.L. 480 sales had replaced commercial sales was still missing, but when the U.S. international balance of payments slipped into deficit in 1958, for the first time since World War II, continued sales of U.S. grain abroad for foreign rather than hard currency fell further out of favor with the U.S. foreign economic policy community.

P.L. 480 grain exports might yet have been justified as an instrument of foreign economic policy if they had succeeded in developing future demand for hard currency sales of U.S. grain in years to come. Supporters and critics alike have attributed to P.L. 480 just this sort of "market development" influence. In fact, much of the P.L. 480 program was poorly suited to market development because of its early emphasis on exports to desperately poor nations (such as India and Pakistan), nations that lacked the international purchasing power to become good commercial food customers. India and Pakistan, which together received almost one-third of all P.L. 480 exports between 1954–76, never joined the ranks of the most important buyers of U.S. commercial farm exports.[21] The program meanwhile ignored significant developing markets in Eastern Europe and the Soviet Union, where commercial grain import demand was soon to skyrocket. The nations of Eastern Europe and the Soviet Union, later to emerge as significant cash customers for U.S. farm exports, were barred under the law from receiving any P.L. 480 Title I sales.

Some of the earliest recipients of P.L. 480 sales later became good customers for U.S. commercial exports—including the Republic of Korea, Taiwan, and a number of OPEC countries. But these nations might well have begun their later cash purchases of U.S. grains as a natural result of their own income growth, even in the absence of P.L. 480. Other early recipient countries, such as Egypt, have yet to graduate from their heavy reliance upon concessional imports of U.S. grains. Some P.L. 480 shipments to nations "fighting communism" produced no market development benefit at all. South Vietnam was the all-time fourth largest recipient of P.L. 480 exports, until it finally fell to North Vietnam in 1975, and receded beyond the range of U.S. commercial market development.

Was the growing P.L. 480 program during the 1950s at least a source of diplomatic influence for the United States? On the surface, any opportunity to arrange sales of surplus grain might have seemed a valuable diplomatic asset. Indeed, the United States had earlier used an ad hoc $50 million food aid pledge to Yugoslavia in 1950 to support Tito's break with Stalin, and had provided food shipments since 1951 as "defense-supporting assistance" to a variety of newly independent developing countries (such as Pakistan).22 The P.L. 480 sales agreements first negotiated in early 1955 were likewise with important security allies, such as Japan and Turkey, in addition to Pakistan and Yugoslavia. It was all the more advantageous that P.L. 480 was at first a relatively inconspicuous aid program, as expenditures were charged to the budget of the CCC, and thus partially hidden from the view of foreign aid critics, easing the sensitive task of extending U.S. aid to nonaligned foreign governments politically unpopular in Congress.23

Such diplomatic advantages were more than counterbalanced, however, by the considerable array of foreign policy drawbacks associated with P.L. 480. From the beginning, recipient country governments were well aware of the significant bargaining leverage that *they* enjoyed, whenever diplomatic discussions turned to the disposal of U.S. surplus farm products. So eager was the United States to arrange P.L. 480 sales that its ability to seek concessions from recipient country governments quite often was reduced to nothing. India, when negotiating its first P.L. 480 agreement in 1956, refused to provide the fundamental assurance demanded at the time, that P.L. 480 imports would not be disruptive to existing patterns of commercial trade.24 Earlier, Colombia had held out for a larger package of *conventional* economic assistance—including irrigation, drainage construction, and deliveries of agricultural machinery and fertilizer—as its *condition* for agreeing to import U.S. surplus food products. Nor were the large reserves of foreign currency generated by the program an unmixed blessing within the recipient country, as they frequently spawned charges of U.S. interference in the management of local economic affairs. Congressional efforts to recycle a portion of these foreign currency funds through loans to private enterprise (known as "Cooley loans") only drew additional complaints from sensitive recipient country governments.25

The largest foreign policy drawback to the early P.L. 480 surplus disposal program was the displeasure it caused among other agricultural exporters, including some important U.S. security allies. During the 1950s, the State Department received official competitor complaints from Canada, Australia, Argentina, New Zealand, Denmark, Mexico, Uruguay, Burma, Italy, and Peru.[26] Small wonder that State Department officials in the Eisenhower administration frequently objected to expanded P.L. 480 sales. So great at one point were the misgivings of the State Department regarding net diplomatic gains that in May 1957 Undersecretary Christian Herter urged that the program be "tapered off" in the coming years, to be replaced where necessary by simple *financial* aid. Shipments of food, in his view, were causing too much "trouble with other countries." As for the alleged diplomatic gains to be had with recipient countries, Herter concluded that these were too often offset; the dumping of U.S. surplus farm products had so displeased local food producers as to give "free ammunition to Communist propagandists." Herter concluded his harsh judgment with a summary view that the State Department "would be better off without P.L. 480 than with it."[27]

In all, these early years of "surplus disposal" through programs such as P.L. 480 were not marked by any convincing exercise of U.S. food power abroad. Perhaps it is in the nature of a surplus that the process of its disposal confers precious few diplomatic or commercial advantages. Not only were such advantages elusive abroad. During the 1950s surplus disposal efforts also fell short of their major objective at home, which was to reverse the growth of expensive government-owned stocks of grain. As a new administration assumed power in 1961, the inclination to experiment with new means of eliminating the domestic grain surplus problem emerged.

The Kennedy–Johnson Years

During the 1960s domestic grain policy underwent adjustments that proved helpful in moving toward an export-led reduction of surplus stocks. But it was the reduction of stocks, and not exports, that remained the first objective. At times during the 1960s the United States undertook grain trade initiatives with more than simply the domestic surplus disposal problem in mind. Even on these occasions, however, the government usually stopped short of consistently pursuing food power abroad.

When the Kennedy administration took office in January 1961, the annual budgetary cost of simply acquiring and storing surplus wheat had expanded to $500 million; the realized cost of the corn program was growing as well, so much so that the Department of Agriculture decided to stop providing annual cost estimates in 1959. By January 1961 feedgrain stocks had grown to such an extent that the storage cost to the government alone, for each additional bushel entering government stocks, began to exceed the value of the grain.[28]

The first instinct of the Kennedy administration was to attack this problem at the production end with a program stronger than a payment-induced acreage reduction scheme. To *pay* farmers not to plant grain was costly; the acreage reduction inducement had to be generous enough to more than offset the *positive* production inducement that was still being provided by high commodity loans. In hopes of limiting grain production at an acceptable cost to taxpayers, Kennedy's Department of Agriculture in 1961 sought congressional approval for strict mandatory production controls. Such controls proved repugnant to farmers, however, who effectively resisted them, first through the Congress in 1961, and then in a direct nationwide "wheat referendum" in May 1963. The Kennedy administration therefore was forced to return to the more costly alternative of using direct cash payments to discourage production.

In its design of payment-induced production controls, however, the Kennedy administration introduced an important innovation, which finally began to uncouple domestic farm income supports from the final export price of U.S. grain. Responding in part to well-timed suggestions from grain export firms, the Department of Agriculture in 1962 gained from Congress the authority to reduce corn loan rates to 50 percent of parity and to support the income of feedgrain producers, when necessary, through direct cash payments. By 1964 domestic wheat subsidies were also modified to permit lower market prices through use of direct cash payments.[29] This simple adjustment in the method of providing income support to domestic grain producers— cash payments rather than high guaranteed domestic prices—eventually provided significant stimulus to commercial grain exports. In the previous decade, since an earlier rejection of this approach in the Brannan Plan defeat of 1949, grain prices had been supported at levels too high to permit export firms to exploit what should have been a U.S.

competitive edge in world grain markets. With U.S. grain export prices held artificially high, other less efficient grain-producing countries (such as Canada, Australia, and Argentina) received an undeserved export incentive. They took full advantage by consciously pricing their grain for export *at or just below the U.S. price*, thereby stealing a share of the export market away from the United States.[30]

Throughout the 1950s, U.S. farmers had given away their competitive edge in this fashion partly out of ignorance and partly due to the inherited mistrust many still felt toward the stability and dependability of foreign markets. Moreover, so long as their representatives in Congress were able to provide them with high and stable price guarantees through domestic farm programs, why should they gamble on their ability to compete abroad? World grain markets were seen by U.S. farmers as a useful dumping ground for the surplus grains acquired by the government, but they were not yet seen as a promising arena for free commercial competition.[31] U.S. agricultural trade policies had long reflected this suspicious attitude toward the commercial gains waiting to be made in the world market. Even while pushing trade liberalization for industry early in the 1950s, the United States had taken the lead in *excluding* agricultural products from the liberalizing rules of the General Agreement on Tariffs and Trade.[32]

By the early 1960s, however, attitudes toward the value of commercial farm exports, and hence toward competitive export pricing, had begun to change. In February 1961 President Kennedy concluded that three consecutive years of U.S. foreign payments deficits in excess of $3 billion required remedial action, and tentatively turned to U.S. agriculture as one industry of "unparalleled efficiency" that might provide a solution to this problem. In 1960, he noticed, the balance of payments on agricultural products had been in net *deficit* by $1.25 billion. Total agricultural exports were still increasing in volume, thanks in part to the continued expansion of the P.L. 480 program, but less than half of these exports were moving in regular commercial channels, returning dollars immediately to the U.S. account. In fiscal year 1959, out of a total of $744 million in U.S. wheat and wheat flour exports, more than 70 percent had moved on a nondollar basis. In March 1961, to remedy this problem Kennedy directed the Department of Agriculture to "intensify" its efforts to expand *dollar sales* of farm products abroad.[33]

It is tempting to conclude from this early initiative that the United States had at last added a significant outward-looking "food power" objective—the repair of its sagging trade and payments balance abroad—to its more traditional pursuit of inward-looking budgetary and farm income objectives. But this early emphasis upon commercial grain export promotion was slow to evolve into a dominant policy strain, as it appeared to raise *diplomatic* costs that might outweigh the possible external *economic* gain.

Friction within the NATO alliance was the diplomatic cost associated with promoting U.S. commercial grain exports in 1961. The member nations of the European Economic Community were just then establishing a highly protectionist Common Agricultural Policy (CAP). Cold War tensions in Europe were intensifying because of the Berlin Crisis; the State Department pleaded with President Kennedy to consider the "broader international political implications" of his agricultural export promotion plan. He soon agreed that the United States could ill afford the division within NATO that a direct challenge to the CAP would entail, so he cautioned the secretary of agriculture *against* an overly aggressive stance on U.S. farm exports. When the CAP for cereals was initiated in 1962, it met little official resistance from the United States. Left unchallenged, the CAP soon began to reduce U.S. grain export opportunities in the European Community, and eventually beyond the community as well.[34]

Beyond Europe there was no such immediate diplomatic inhibition against a U.S. commercial grain export drive. In Japan, for example, the United States went forward with a major offensive to displace Canadian wheat exports, which in 1960 had been outselling U.S. exports two to one. Canadian rail transport subsidies allowed Canadian wheat a price advantage. Hoping to nullify this advantage, the Department of Agriculture began to seek lower freight rates for U.S. grain shipped to the west coast by rail, while the Treasury Department and the State Department began to urge the Japanese government to "buy American." These efforts brought an announcement from the Japanese Food Agency that it would henceforth divide its wheat imports equally between Canada and the United States; by 1963 U.S. wheat sales to Japan had increased 70 percent.[35]

The more lavish use of export subsidies was another means employed to boost commercial sales of U.S. grain abroad. These subsidies, which had been in use on a modest scale since 1949, were paid to U.S. trading companies so as to bring the export price of U.S. grain down to a more competitive level. As a part of its new effort to promote dollar sales of grain abroad, the United States allowed the cost of these subsidies to grow to a record level of $822 million in 1964.

In the years that followed, the need for these export subsidies was diminished, as U.S. domestic price supports were slowly reduced to near world price levels. But by using credits, subsidies, and more competitive export prices, the United States successfully beat back some of its export competitors in what amounted to a minor "international wheat war" during the mid-1960s. Along the way it abandoned completely an earlier practice of "duopolistic" price coordination with Canada.[36]

This commercial export drive was eventually constrained, however, by a different sort of diplomatic complication. The most important "new" market for grain in the 1960s was the Soviet Union, a market that the United States—because of political and diplomatic misgivings—found itself unable to serve. The Kennedy administration, originally hoping to include the communist states in its food export campaign, announced in June 1961 that it would approve export licenses on agricultural commodities destined for the Soviet bloc. For two years, however, public and congressional opposition forced postponement of this plan. Official hopes that farm sales to the Soviet Union might be arranged could not be seriously revived until 1963. Walt W. Rostow, chief of Policy Planning in the State Department, then put forward the view that domestic resistance should no longer be a constraint, in light of the strong U.S. stand taken during the recent 1962 missile crisis and the subsequent signing of a U.S.–Soviet limited nuclear test ban treaty.[37] When the Soviet Union suddenly entered the market for 10 million tons of Western grain in 1963, Rostow and others hoped to capture a sizeable portion of the business. Kennedy learned of Soviet willingness to purchase as much as 4 million tons of U.S. grain, worth an immediate $250 million dollars to the U.S. balance of payments, and decided to endorse the sale.[38]

Unfortunately, this presidential endorsement proved insufficient to persuade Kennedy's domestic political audience. In the end, to escape domestic objections to a Soviet wheat deal, Kennedy was forced to yield to labor demands that half the grain be shipped in U.S. vessels, an expensive proposition for the Soviet Union, and one that quickly dampened their interest.[39] Even so, the grain sale continued to meet determined resistance from Republican partisans opposed to any "trading with the enemy." One notable opponent of the sale was Richard M. Nixon, who argued that a wheat sale to the Soviet Union might turn out to be "the major foreign policy mistake of this Administration, even more serious than fouling up the Bay of Pigs."[40] In the end, such domestic restrictions and inhibitions held the final U.S. sale to less than half of its originally intended size. Comparable sales opportunities were also lost when the Soviet Union returned to the world market for more Western grain in 1965. The Soviet Union found the U.S. shipping restriction still in effect; again they turned primarily to Canada and to Australia to fill their needs. By one estimate at the time, shipping restrictions were costing the United States as much as $100 million annually in lost sales to the Soviet market.[41]

Beset by such difficulties, the commercial grain export drive launched during the Kennedy–Johnson years produced meager results overall. The U.S. share of commercial wheat exports worldwide diminished after 1960, from above 20 percent to a low of 12 percent in 1962, and then after a brief recovery back down to 12 percent in 1964. By the middle of the decade, the United States found its net earnings from farm exports scarcely greater than they had been when the decade began.[42] Later in the decade, as the protective import policies of the European Community began taking full effect, the value of U.S. farm exports went into a further decline. As an effective instrument of foreign economic policy, the U.S. "food weapon" was still hanging fire.

The diplomatic and security concerns that did so much to inhibit U.S. commercial grain exports during the 1960s were themselves no better served at the time. The shipping restrictions adopted in 1963 had eliminated any hope of using grain exports as a flexible bargaining tool in relations with the Soviet Union. Meantime, in most dealings with allies, commercial grain trade issues were a constant diplomatic irritant. World grain markets were so glutted by surplus production, particularly during the later part of the 1960s, that they minimized the diplomatic influence to be gained by any commercial exporter.

Only in the manipulation of its *concessional* grain exports, under the auspices of the continuing P.L. 480 program, could the United States hope to gain a bit of diplomatic food power leverage during the Kennedy–Johnson years. From 1959 forward (in that year P.L. 480 had been named the Food for Peace program), concessional sales began to evolve into more than a vehicle for disposing of a domestic surplus. Conventional U.S. foreign aid programs by then were constrained by closer congressional scrutiny, so the P.L. 480 "food aid" alternative took on a greater diplomatic attraction, even among those State Department officials who had earlier expressed skepticism. President Johnson, looking for additional means of exercising U.S. influence abroad, proposed in 1966 a landmark restructuring of P.L. 480, to eliminate the need for the secretary of agriculture to designate U.S.

food commodities as "surplus" before they could become eligible for use in the program.[43] U.S. grain surpluses were at that time momentarily depleted (due to poor world harvests and the prior expansion of P.L. 480 exports), but the president did not wish to see the P.L. 480 program reduced in scale. Johnson was particularly interested in maintaining his control over P.L. 480 shipments of wheat to India, shipments he was then manipulating in a determined effort to coerce the Indian government into a variety of domestic policy reforms and foreign policy adjustments (see chapter 5).[44]

Other attempts to manipulate food aid to secure diplomatic gains were also plentiful during the Johnson years. The most notable was a termination of P.L. 480 sales to Egypt in 1964, to punish President Nasser for his sharp criticism of U.S. policy in the Congo and for riots in Cairo that had destroyed U.S. property. But the president lost control of this policy when some in Congress eager to take even stronger measures against Nasser fell into a heated conflict with farmers, grain traders, aid advocates, and humanitarian groups, who objected to any termination of food aid to a poor country. What began as a perhaps futile presidential attempt to punish Egypt (Nasser remained defiant throughout), became in the end little more than a counterproductive political squabble at home.[45] P.L. 480 "food aid" could prove doubly difficult to manipulate for coercive purposes, whenever the highly committed domestic "hunger lobby" became involved.

The overall record during the Kennedy–Johnson years gives little evidence that U.S. grain trade policy was consistently used to serve external economic and diplomatic objectives. The pursuit of such divergent external objectives first required an impossible choice between unconditioned export promotion and conditioned export restraint. It also required a practical capacity to manipulate exports which eluded the foreign policy leadership. A more traditional inward-looking objective—finding an affordable way to dispose of grain surpluses and to support domestic farm income—remained, as before, the driving force behind U.S. grain trade policy.

The Nixon–Ford Years

Grain export policies appeared to undergo a shift toward the pursuit of food power after 1969. Food aid programs were conspicuously recast to serve U.S. military and security objectives, first in Southeast Asia and then in the Middle East. Massive grain sales were arranged with the Soviet Union, concurrent with a new policy of détente. And the volume of U.S. commercial grain exports began to expand in a suddenly high-priced world market, partly compensating for an otherwise imperiled U.S. trade and payments balance. What is more, senior policy officials began to talk openly about using the U.S. "food weapon" to match or to blunt the effects of the Arab "oil weapon." U.S. "agripower," in what was to be a coming of age of scarce resources, was widely touted as one means to enhance U.S. influence abroad.

In fact, despite unprecedented *talk* about U.S. food power during the Nixon–Ford years and despite much tighter world grain market conditions, which did momentarily increase the potential for both export earnings and diplomatic leverage, U.S. grain export policies remained, as ever, significantly disconnected from the pursuit of economic or diplomatic advantages abroad. They continued to be driven, as ever, by powerful inward-looking concerns at home. Indeed, owing to the sudden tightening of food markets, an entirely new internal policy concern—domestic food price inflation—emerged as a further constraint against the option of food power.

One means by which U.S. officials did consistently pursue food power after 1969 was through an even more determined effort to manipulate P.L. 480 exports to support military and security objectives. What had earlier been dubbed the "Food for Peace" program was transformed, especially during the final years of the Vietnam struggle, into a "Food for War" program. Congressional support for Southeast Asia aid policies was becoming precarious at best, and so P.L. 480 shipments, particularly after 1972, were seized upon as a "back door" means to keep client governments in that region financially afloat. By 1973, almost half of all U.S. food aid abroad was going to South Vietnam and Cambodia.[46]

When the United States was forced to leave Indochina in defeat, the focus of its diplomatic food aid efforts shifted to the Middle East, where larger P.L. 480 sales were initiated so as to sweeten the terms of peace being mediated by the United States after the 1973 Arab–Israeli war.[47] This diplomatic rerouting of food aid to the Middle East reached its high point after the 1978 Camp David agreements, when Egypt emerged as the single largest foreign recipient of P.L. 480 sales. By 1981, P.L. 480 Title I food aid allocations for Egypt, still largely in the service of diplomatic objectives, were running at roughly five times the level of those for any other recipient nation.[48]

The Nixon–Ford period was also marked by a variety of punitive food aid terminations. Food aid shipments to Bangladesh were on one occasion delayed (as the law then required) to discipline that nation for its decision to sell jute to Cuba. On another occasion credit sales of food to Chile, which had been terminated when Allende came to power, were resumed immediately after his replacement by a more sympathetic military regime in September 1973. But these conspicuous manipulations of food aid eventually provoked strong reactions, especially from those in Congress who wanted the P.L. 480 program to perform only its publicized "food aid" role. The Foreign Assistance Act was therefore amended to require that at least 75 percent of all U.S. food aid go to nations with per capita incomes under $500, placing an effective limitation on P.L. 480 sales to higher-income "foreign policy" recipients such as Israel, Jordan, South Korea, Lebanon, Syria, and Portugal. In 1974 the practice of making foreign currency "counterpart funds" generated from the sale of U.S. food aid available to local governments for defense expenditures was also terminated. Congress then went on to stipulate that food aid could no longer be sent to countries that consistently violated human rights, without guarantees that the benefit from the aid would flow directly to needy people. The cynical use of U.S. food aid to serve diplomatic objectives had thus become something of a self-containing policy by the mid-1970s.[49]

Moreover, by the early 1970s these P.L. 480 grain exports were being eclipsed by an expanded volume of private commercial sales, which proved far more difficult for foreign policy officials to manipulate. P.L. 480 wheat sales did account for 76 percent of all U.S. wheat exports in 1962 and for 39 percent of total exports as late as 1971, but fell to only 13 percent of the total in 1972 and to a mere 4 percent in 1973.[50] Foreign policy considerations were indeed taking over this much smaller U.S. food aid program during the Nixon–Ford years, but food aid was simultaneously losing out in relative importance to commercial grain exports.

In fact, one reason U.S. food aid shipments had been allowed to come so completely under the influence of foreign policy officials was that the Department of Agriculture no longer considered those shipments to be an important part of U.S. grain export policy. Secretary Butz even briefly considered a complete abandonment of the concessional sales program in 1974, when he passed along to the Office of Management and Budget a proposal that included no funding at all for P.L. 480.[51] Food aid shipments were not entirely discontinued in 1974, but P.L. 480 sales slipped to only 0.5 million tons in July–December

1974, less than one-sixth the level of two years earlier. At a time when commercial markets were tight enough to maximize the diplomatic leverage to be gained from food aid abroad, the government was abandoning its P.L. 480 concessional sales program and allowing private commercial sales (over which its foreign policy leaders had much less control) to govern most grain export activity.

The foregoing discussion raises the possibility that a strictly commercial "food power" objective—earning foreign exchange—was at the heart of grain trade policy during the Nixon–Ford years. A logical motive for such a policy would have been the renewed deterioration of the U.S. international trade and payments balance. The trade surplus declined by almost $5 billion between 1964 and 1969, hampered by Vietnam-era inflation at home and a high fixed dollar exchange rate abroad. By 1968, the value of U.S. gold holdings had fallen to $10.9 billion (less than half of the 1957 level), while foreign dollar holdings were up to $31.5 billion (twice the 1957 level). This deepening foreign economic policy crisis had led to the formation, in May 1970, of the Presidential Commission on International Trade and Investment Policy (the Williams Commission), which offered as its chief recommendation that the United States "launch a vigorous export drive for the 1970's." Agricultural products, in which the nation was judged to have a strong international comparative advantage, were recommended as one of the key components in this export drive.[52]

Once more trade analysts had noticed that U.S. farm products were not performing well in commercial markets abroad. U.S. agricultural exports did reach $6.9 billion in 1966, but then began a three-year decline to a level of $5.9 billion. A principal cause of this decline was again the new CAP of the European Community, which was supporting farm prices within the Community at artificially high levels (50–100 percent above world price levels), and protecting these prices with variable import levies.[53] Citing these European Community agricultural policies as an immediate problem, and noting that the anticipated entry of Great Britain into the Community would only compound the damage to U.S. agriculture, the Williams Commission recommended that the United States undertake negotiations at the highest political level, to "immediately and vigorously" assert U.S. agricultural trade interests.[54]

As late as 1970, however, there were still strong diplomatic inhibitions against asking agricultural trade concessions from the Europeans.[55] The U.S. position on agricultural trade throughout the recently completed Kennedy round of multilateral trade negotiations (1962–67) had been one of first asking the Europeans for concessions, but then agreeing to exclude agricultural products from uniform tariff cuts. Though eventually despairing of progress during the Kennedy round, the government had sought an alternative set of grain trade concessions from the Europeans under the terms of the new International Grains Agreement negotiated in 1967 through the London-based International Wheat Council. In this agreement the Europeans were persuaded to join the new Food Aid Convention, designed to expand the concessional element of their grain shipments abroad (thereby lifting a part of the food aid burden from the United States, and permitting an expansion of U.S. commercial exports). A new Wheat Trade Convention, setting a floor on world wheat prices, was also negotiated in 1967, but it proved to be of little value to the United States as it failed to discourage competitors such as France and Australia from the use of export subsidies. When the U.S. world share of commercial wheat exports began to fall from 23 percent to 18 percent by 1968–69, the United States responded by increasing its own wheat export subsidies once more, further undercutting the price floor, and causing the Wheat Trade Convention to collapse in July 1969.[56]

Renewed reliance on sizeable wheat and wheat flour export subsidies was viewed, however, as no more than a costly stopgap solution to the U.S. agricultural export problem. Most officials remained convinced that only a substantial reform of the restrictive trading practices of the European Community would suffice to boost U.S. grain exports. New markets for U.S. grain in the communist world and among the nonindustrial countries were not yet viewed as promising alternatives. The Williams Commission in 1971 had referred to the poor countries as having "never represented a major commercial market for U.S. agricultural exports." In even more dismissive fashion, the Soviet Union was labeled an "intermittent export competitor."[57] U.S. trade policy officials were indeed eager, at this juncture, to use grain exports to better foreign economic advantage, but their efforts at commercial grain export promotion, as late as 1971, were unfruitful and remained narrowly focused on traditional market outlets in the European Community and Japan.[58]

U.S. commercial grain exports suddenly broke out of their decade-long period of stagnation in 1972, and entered a decade-long period of unexpected and unprecedented growth. To the astonishment of all, this growth took place despite the rejection of significant trade policy con-

Table 8.   U.S. exports of wheat and coarse grains, 1961–1984

Marketing year	Exports (million metric tons)	Marketing year	Exports (million metric tons)
1961–62	34.7	1972–73	69.1
1962–63	32.9	1973–74	73.8
1963–64	39.7	1974–75	63.6
1964–65	39.3	1975–76	82.0
1965–66	48.9	1976–77	76.5
1966–67	41.1	1977–78	86.9
1967–68	41.5	1978–79	92.7
1968–69	31.1	1979–80	108.8
1969–70	35.4	1980–81	110.7
1970–71	38.8	1981–82	106.9
1971–72	40.5	1982–83	95.1
		1983–84	94.8

Source: U.S. Department of Agriculture, *Foreign Agriculture Circular*, FG-13-84, October 1984, p. 24.

cessions by the European Community and Japan. Without warning, U.S. commercial grain exports nearly doubled in 1972 alone, and eventually reached a peak level in 1980–81 of roughly three times the level of a decade earlier (Table 8).

This phenomenal export growth generated a much-needed windfall for U.S. trade policy. With real export prices suddenly much higher, total export earnings from grain sales increased even more rapidly than total export volume. Between 1971 and 1973, while U.S. wheat exports were more than doubling in volume, the real export price of each bushel of exported wheat was simultaneously tripling. The agricultural trade balance, as a consequence, increased from a $1.9 billion surplus in 1971 to a $9.3 billion surplus by 1973, and then to a $25 billion surplus by the end of the decade. Earnings from grain sales, specifically, contributed approximately 40 percent to the U.S. farm export total. These export gains were a godsend because the U.S. nonagricultural trade balance, in the meantime, was facing unprecedented difficulty. A small surplus in 1969 had been replaced by a $15 billion deficit in 1973, and then a $50 billion deficit by the end of the decade.[59] The post-1972 grain export surge was thus a major vindication for all who had been arguing for years that the United States had an unexploited competitive advantage in world grain markets. It was not, however, a confirmation of the assumption that significant export growth would require European Community or Japanese trade policy reform.

Grain exports and export earnings surged after 1972 in broad response to an unforeseen tightening of food markets worldwide. World food production experienced a rare 1.6 percent decline in 1972, mainly due to bad weather. This decline included a 35 million ton fall in world grain production (a drop nearly equal to one year's average annual growth).[60] Even while world food production was experiencing this rare setback in 1972, world food consumption was increasing as never before, driven by an economic boom and record income growth in the industrial world, plus high population and income growth rates in the nonindustrial world.[61] The resulting worldwide surge in demand and purchasing power produced a 32 million ton increase in world grain consumption in 1972, to be followed by another 35 million ton increase in world grain consumption in 1973.

Because of its large surplus grain stocks, the United States was uniquely positioned after 1972 to compensate for production shortfalls elsewhere and respond to these larger world consumption demands. U.S. export prices were also suddenly more competitive abroad, owing to significant dollar devaluations late in 1971 and early in 1973. The resulting increase in U.S. grain exports was nonetheless a major surprise to U.S. officials, who had been expecting to encounter continued low prices and sluggish grain export growth, at least through the first half of the 1970s. The private trade community was unprepared as well. Five out of the six major U.S. grain export companies were caught holding a short position in grain futures markets during the critical June–September 1972 period, when exports suddenly began to take off.[62]

It was all the more surprising to U.S. officials that so much of this export growth came from a round of purchases by a single nontraditional customer, the Soviet Union. As late as 1970, the Soviet Union had been a net *exporter* of grain, and at no time before 1971 had the Soviet Union appeared to be a promising sales outlet. When the Soviet Union unexpectedly entered the world market in 1972 for 22.5 million tons of grain imports, U.S. trading companies (whom the Soviet Union approached for two-thirds of these purchases), and U.S. officials (even those few who had been working hard to promote grain sales to the Soviet Union) could not have been more astonished.

The Nixon administration, despite its early emphasis on grain export promotion, had actually been slow to open the U.S. grain market to Soviet purchases. In June of 1969, despite pleadings from the secretary of agriculture, who had learned from private traders that the Soviet Union desired to begin modest purchases of U.S. grain on a continuing basis, President Nixon decided not to remove the restrictive shipping requirement imposed by Kennedy in 1963.[63] He did not change his mind until late May 1971, following a breakthrough in the ongoing Strategic Arms Limitation Talks (SALT). Three weeks after this SALT breakthrough, on 10 June 1971, Nixon announced an end to the requirement that half of all U.S. grain sales to the Soviet Union be shipped on U.S. vessels.[64] Elaborate efforts were made at the same time to appease the International Longshoremen's Association, which had long insisted upon its shipping preference.[65] In addition to the gathering momentum of détente, foreign economic policy considerations also reinforced this critical decision. For the first time in recent history, the United States was running an overall deficit on its current trade account, and the dollar, still overvalued at a fixed rate of exchange, was under intense pressure.[66] A desired commercial reward was soon realized from this policy change when the Soviet Union went forward, in October 1971, with a significant purchase of more than 3 million tons of U.S. feedgrains.[67]

Some have speculated that not only these first Soviet grain purchases late in 1971 but also the much larger purchases made in 1972 were part of a covert official design to reward the Soviet Union for its earlier concessions on strategic arms.[68] But the volume of grain purchased by the Soviet Union in 1972, far out of proportion to amounts officially anticipated by the United States, makes this a dubious argument. If officials had been using the prospect of such sales to reach a better foreign policy bargain with the Soviet Union, as alleged, they surely would have monitored those sales more closely and surely would have sought a more substantial quid pro quo.

Despite its considerable interest in promoting grain sales to the Soviet Union in 1971–72, the U.S. foreign policy leadership had been remarkably inattentive to the bargaining possibilities that these sales could provide. After playing a key role in the lifting of U.S. shipping restrictions in 1971, Henry Kissinger had withdrawn from the problem by designating the Department of Agriculture as "lead agency" in subsequently negotiating credit terms with the Soviet Union. The Department of Agriculture, which was insensitive to foreign policy questions and persisted in viewing those credit terms as the essence of the grain sale problem, kept the National Security Council staff informed of the negotiations only in general terms. At one point Kissinger did delay a trip by Secretary of Agriculture Butz to Moscow, to ensure, as he later claimed, that "trade follow political progress and not precede it."[69] But this was a futile gesture. As it turned out, the Soviet Union had little interest in credit. They could now purchase as much grain as they might need for cash directly from private U.S. grain export companies, without prior approval; it was not even required, at the time, that private companies notify the U.S. government in timely fashion after arranging such sales. Official U.S. bargaining leverage had thus already been lost.

The degree to which the government permitted its foreign grain sales to be arranged in this way, by private traders acting significantly beyond the control of the policy community, was symptomatic of its indifference at the time to food power. The United States had no institutional equivalent to the Canadian Wheat Board or the Australian Wheat Board, which had sole authority in those countries to arrange grain exports and could thereby enforce an occasional diplomatic restraint on trade. U.S. grain producers and exporters had long resisted such restraining institutions, out of habit, ideology, and self-interest. The spectacular growth of U.S. grain exports during the 1970s, in contrast to the sluggish growth of Canadian and Australian exports, appeared to vindicate this preference. Amid the controversy that followed large sales to the Soviet Union in 1972, export reporting requirements were tightened, and a variety of ad hoc export controls were put in place, but legislative proposals to create a U.S. grain marketing board or to give equivalent powers to the existing CCC, were routinely defeated in the Congress. The unusual leeway given to the private trade cost the United States whatever diplomatic food power advantage it might otherwise have enjoyed over the Soviet Union in 1972.[70]

Commercial advantages were lost as well in 1972, when inattentive Department of Agriculture officials carelessly continued to cheapen U.S. grain sales to the Soviet Union with generous export subsidies, even after higher world market prices had rendered those subsidies commercially unnecessary. The Department of Agriculture, still viewing its mission as the disposal of a U.S. grain surplus, subsidized U.S. wheat sales to the Soviet Union in 1972 by as much as 47 cents a bushel, at a cost to the U.S. Treasury of more than $300 million.[71]

This puzzling disinclination on the part of the United States to seek food power over the Soviet Union may also be explained by the inward-looking political concerns of the Nixon administration. Going into the 1972 election, farm state Republican candidates were understandably eager for some upward movement in farm prices and farm income. U.S. grain carry-over stocks were larger than they had been at any time since the mid-1960s; farmers were suffering from the lowest grain prices in five years. Because additional acreage cutbacks would be costly and unpopular, export expansion was seen as one of the few remaining means to firm domestic prices. So single-minded and widespread was this official desire to reduce surplus stocks and to strengthen domestic farm prices in 1972 that serious thoughts of placing conditions on exports did not arise. As Kissinger later explained, "the Soviet purchase of grain in our markets was seen as a domestic matter, an element of our agricultural policy."[72]

All this was soon to change. The magnitude of the Soviet purchase and its perceived impact on world markets and on the U.S. food economy meant that a very different mix of policy concerns—both foreign and domestic—soon came into play. Foreign policy leaders, for their part, belatedly realized the unprecedented degree of trade leverage that might be available from the continued tightening of world grain markets. Intelligence reporting on foreign grain import needs was therefore upgraded, and monitoring of private U.S. grain sales abroad was improved. But even at this point, foreign policy officials were unable to embark upon a concerted pursuit of food power. One inhibition was their own inability to choose between economic and diplomatic food power objectives. A second inhibition could be traced to an even more restrictive mix of domestic policy constraints.

Official desires to expand U.S. commercial grain sales during the period after 1972, partly to help pay for more expensive foreign oil, constantly offset any parallel search for diplomatic gains through threatened export restraint. Early thoughts of using a food export embargo to force the OPEC countries to lower oil prices were thus replaced by determined efforts to balance trade accounts through a further *increase* in U.S. grain exports to oil producers. This expansion of commercial sales, in turn, further reduced the share of U.S. grain exports going abroad through the more easily manipulated P.L. 480 "food aid" program.

Nevertheless, foreign policy officials seeking diplomatic gains did make several tentative efforts, after 1972, to gain greater control over commercial exports. Kissinger, from 1972 onward, sought to ensure that all commercial grain sales to the Soviet Union in particular would be treated "as foreign policy matters and subjected to interagency monitoring."[73] It was at his insistence that the State Department gained full representation on the Food Deputies Group, the interagency committee most heavily involved in making grain export policy. But this interagency committee proved singularly unresponsive to those with foreign policy concerns, as it was chaired by a representative of the Council of Economic Advisers and designed primarily to balance *domestic producer and consumer interests*. When the Food Deputies Group acted in 1974 to discourage larger grain sales to the Soviet Union, its motive was to protect domestic consumers from a further increase in food prices at home, and so it paid little heed to the diplomatic consequences abroad, which were, if anything, adverse to Kissinger's interest at the moment in détente. Even when the Department of Agriculture was able to win approval early in 1975 for a renewed expansion of sales to the Soviet Union, diplomatic calculations remained a secondary concern.[74]

Only during one brief interlude, between August and October 1975, was Secretary of State Kissinger able to exercise effective control over the pace and the volume of U.S. grain sales to the Soviet Union, and even then it was a renewed fear of domestic price inflation that gave him his opening. Kissinger made himself a member of the newest interagency coordinating body for grain trade policy, the Economic Policy Board Executive Committee, and secured from the Department of Agriculture (in July 1975) an agreement not to promote additional grain sales to the Soviet Union without Economic Policy Board review.[75] He saw his opportunity to condition those sales on his own objectives in August, when consumer advocates and labor leaders pressured the administration to guard against higher domestic food prices by placing a "voluntary" suspension on additional Soviet sales. Kissinger at this point proposed to ask for cheap Soviet oil sales to the United States, below OPEC prices, as a condition for lifting of the new U.S. sales suspension. Undersecretary of State for Economic Affairs Charles W. Robinson was designated to lead a team to Moscow to negotiate this grain-for-oil agreement.

Because the State Department was almost alone in the government in its desire for placing "cheap oil" conditions upon renewed grain sales to the Soviet Union, its dominant position in the policy-making process was short-lived. The Soviet Union firmly resisted any concessions on oil in the Moscow negotiations, and Robinson's "food power" efforts quickly bogged down. Domestic U.S. grain producers and exporters meanwhile began to register vigorous complaints over the continuing sales suspension. The Executive Committee of the American Farm Bureau Federation, the largest general farm organization in the nation, which had objected to the sales suspension originally as a "cave in" to organized labor, now objected to the lead role of the State Department in the Moscow negotiations. These visible objections by U.S. farmers only strengthened the Soviet will to resist, and by mid-October President Ford felt obliged to call home his negotiators and terminate the sales suspension. The negotiations had produced a five-year agreement with the Soviets to govern grain trade relations (the Soviet Union had long been seeking precisely such an agreement), but no concessions had been extracted on discount sales of oil.

This State Department attempt in 1975 to take control over grain export policy ultimately served to strengthen the greater control being exercised by domestic interest groups. Not that those groups were always in agreement over the preferred direction of policy: domestic consumer groups were making strong demands for export restraint, to the considerable frustration of producers and traders, who were now less powerful on balance than in previous decades. The U.S. farm population was not only declining in size (from 25 percent of the total population in the 1930s to 15 percent by 1950, and to less than 5 percent by the 1970s). Rural political representation was also being reduced, especially after 1964, by court-ordered "redistricting" of state legislatures. Rural districts, which had constituted 83 percent of an absolute majority of the House of Representatives as late as 1966, fell to only 60 percent of a majority by 1973.[76] It was in that year, for the first time, that farm state legislators found it necessary to join in a coalition with backers of organized labor and consumer interests, in order to pass a farm bill (significantly titled the "Agriculture and Consumer Protection Act").

When domestic food prices began a sudden rise in 1973, this new balance of domestic political forces shifted even further in the direction of serving consumer demands. During the first six months of 1973, the index of consumer prices for food rose by 15 percent, and food prices became a major battleground for those concerned about serious across-the-board domestic inflation. President Nixon, anxious to strengthen his domestic political position amid the early round of 1973 Watergate disclosures, decided to veer sharply in the direction of responding to consumer sentiments. He announced that "in allocating the products of America's farms between markets abroad and those in the United States, we must put the American consumer first."[77] The Commerce Department gave substance to this new policy by declaring a temporary suspension on all U.S. exports of soybeans, for which prices had recently tripled, owing in part to stronger foreign demand.

By yielding to domestic consumer demands for a soybean export suspension, U.S. officials not only overrode the preference of U.S. farmers, they also caused grave if unwitting damage to their commercial and diplomatic interests abroad. Nothing could have been further from an ideal pursuit of food power. The export suspension decision was taken without consulting Japan, an important soybean customer and an important security ally. The State Department would have raised strong objections to the sales suspension on foreign policy grounds, but was not even included in the decision-making process.[78]

Consumer interests continued to override producer interests at key points in 1974 and 1975, when grain exports to the Soviet Union were twice placed under restraint—informally late in 1974 and then explicitly after August 1975, as previously noted. Once again, as with the 1973 soybean embargo, these export restrictions were undertaken with little regard for the interests of U.S. foreign policy. It was George Meany, president of the AFL-CIO and an opponent of the Kissinger–Ford policy of détente, who had managed to dictate the original terms of the temporary 1975 export suspension. Acting as a self-designated defender of domestic consumer interests, he had gained his momentary victory through negotiations with the Labor Department and the president's Council of Economic Advisers. Again, both the State Department and the Department of Agriculture had been temporarily preempted.

When Kissinger's subsequent attempt to extend this 1975 sales suspension proved futile, however, it became the producers' turn to mount a power play of their own. By threatening credibly to abandon the Republican party in the upcoming presidential elections, Midwestern grain producers not only forced President Ford to lift the suspension and concede to the Soviet Union a five-year grain agreement (which guaranteed minimum annual access to 8 million tons of U.S. wheat and corn). By demonstrating their political interest and influence on this occasion, the grain producers also managed to trigger a competition between the two major party candidates to promise them even larger favors. In his search for a means to gain rural support during the January 1976 Iowa party caucuses, Democratic candidate Jimmy Carter made a point of promising that if he were elected there would be "no more grain embargoes." Ford countered by selecting an outspoken champion of grain state interests, Senator Robert Dole of Kansas, as his running mate.

Carter's narrow victory did not put an end to the renewed assertiveness of domestic grain producers, who turned in 1977 to their friends in Congress (including Dole) to further protect themselves from domestic consumer demands for grain export controls. They inserted into the 1977 Food and Agriculture Act a new provision (Section 1002), which required the secretary of agriculture to move commodity loan rates all the way up to 90 percent of parity in the event of any future export suspension undertaken for reasons of tight domestic food supplies.[79] Using this so-called embargo insurance provision to good effect in the years that followed, they were able to pressure trade policy officials to make as much U.S. grain available to the Soviet Union as it wished to buy, often several times the amount guaranteed in the new long-term agreement.

The newly negotiated U.S.–Soviet long-term agreement might have otherwise given consumer groups—or perhaps even foreign policy leaders—a formal opportunity to impose restrictions or to place conditions on large sales to the Soviet Union, as it specified that *official U.S. approval* would be required for annual Soviet purchases of more than 8 million tons.[80] But with U.S. producers now fully aroused to protect their Soviet market and with the Department of Agriculture serving as lead agency in the twice-yearly trade consultations with Soviet officials as prescribed, the agreement began to function as a device for one-way *export promotion.* On a routine basis after 1975, U.S. officials extended to the Soviet Union permission to purchase quantities of grain far above the 8 million ton guarantee contained in the agreement. From the very first year of the agreement Department of Agriculture officials began to offer to the Soviet Union, no questions asked, yearly access to at least 15 million tons of U.S. wheat and corn.[81]

These offers were made, once again, with little regard for the larger drift of U.S.–Soviet relations. Détente was now in decline. In August 1977 President Carter issued a presidential directive (PD 18) which specified that the United States should now condition its economic ties with the Soviet Union on progress in larger diplomatic and strategic dealings. But only months later State Department and National Security Council officials learned from the newspapers about a new unconditional Department of Agriculture offer of 15 million tons of U.S. grain to the Soviet Union.[82] The U.S. food weapon, as usual, was going unused.

It now seems remarkable that grain sales to the Soviet Union remained such an overriding policy concern throughout the decade of the 1970s. The new Soviet market was a significant source of growth for

U.S. commercial grain exports during that decade, but hardly the only source of growth. Even during the first year of large Soviet sales in 1972–73, they accounted for only about 20 percent of the $5 billion rise then taking place in total U.S. farm exports.[83] Over the entire decade of the 1970s, growth in Soviet grain imports accounted for about one-third of total growth in world trade. In fact, the *nonindustrial developing countries* were the more important source of commercial trade expansion, accounting during this period for 55 percent of total growth. The OPEC nations, flush with foreign exchange, tripled their grain imports between 1970 and 1980, while upper- and middle-income developing countries, such as Korea and Taiwan, saw their grain imports more than double. Even some of the low-income countries, on occasion, became attractive commercial outlets for U.S. grain during the boom years of the 1970s. India, in 1975, was the largest single overseas cash customer for U.S. wheat.[84]

Despite the larger commercial importance of these non-Soviet markets, the domestic political debate in the United States continued to revolve around the supercharged issue of sales to the Soviet Union. Producers, who erroneously had come to associate their newfound prosperity almost entirely with Soviet sales, were now determined to retain their access to the Soviet market, whatever the cost perceived by U.S. consumers, and whatever the growing complications for U.S. foreign policy. Consumers, meantime, believed that sales to the Soviet Union were the key stimulus to domestic food price inflation (an equally erroneous assessment) and had become equally determined to restrict such sales, whatever the larger diplomatic or commercial cost. In the midst of this polarized domestic political debate, there was little room for those in the foreign policy community who entertained various dreams about "food power" ever to gain the upper hand. Some officials talked a great deal about the exercise of food power during the Nixon–Ford years, but they were frustrated by the continuing need of their government to respond, as though it had no other priority, to shifting patterns of producer and consumer demands at home.

The Carter Years

Few would have guessed that President Jimmy Carter, elected on a promise of "no more embargoes," would be the one to break from prevailing habits and finally interrupt U.S. grain exports to the Soviet Union for reasons directly tied to foreign policy. Even after Carter's own 1977 directive specifying that U.S. economic resources be put to use in bargaining with the Soviet Union, and even after his subsequent suspension of various high-technology exports to the Soviet Union, Carter was disposed to treat grain exports as a special case, effectively insulating grain trade policy from diplomacy. Foreign policy officials on Carter's National Security Council began to monitor grain sales to the Soviet Union more closely in 1978, but as late as 1979 they remained unwilling to challenge those sales. The volume of U.S. grain sales to the Soviet Union therefore continued to grow even as détente fell into decline.

The expectation that Carter would permit these expanding grain sales to continue was strongly reinforced until the moment of the Soviet invasion of Afghanistan in December 1979. As late as October 1979, the Soviet Union had been offered access in the coming year to an unprecedented total of 25 million tons of U.S. grain, a quantity half again as large as the massive sales of 1972. This offer was unconditional and remarkably one-sided, as it was unaccompanied by any firm Soviet assurance as to how much grain above the 6 million ton long-term minimum they actually intended to purchase. More important, this record grain offer for 1979–80 was made at a time of rising conflict with the Soviet Union over the controversial presence of a "combat brigade" of Soviet troops in Cuba. At the very moment the Department of Agriculture was offering a huge quantity of U.S. grain, Secretary of Defense Harold Brown was announcing a halt on U.S. sales of advanced computer technology, in explicit retaliation for the military policies of the Soviet Union in Cuba. Senior officials tried to explain away this seeming contradiction by arguing that the president still viewed grain embargoes as "bad policy that would hurt the U.S. economy." U.S. farmers and traders thus were given assurances, even at this late date, that grain sales to the Soviet Union would be allowed to continue "on their individual merits."[85] The Soviet Union, judging from its continued complacency, was no doubt assured as well.

Carter's grain embargo, announced on 4 January 1980 on the heels of the Soviet invasion of Afghanistan, was a surprising policy departure. The embargo is discussed in full in chapter 6; for our purposes here, it is important to note that the decision was an anomaly for Carter, who had never used a comparable food trade sanction against any other country (not even against Iran during the fifteen-month embassy hostage crisis). As one element of consistency, to be sure, the embargo was never more than partial in its design (8 million tons of grain sales to the Soviet Union each year were exempted), and was never implemented in more than a half-hearted fashion. Nonetheless, it provoked sufficient additional outrage from U.S. grain producers to weaken both the long-term ability and the inclination of future presidents to repeat the exercise.

Just as the brief sales suspension of 1975 had prompted a 1977 legislative "insurance" clause against any future export interruption caused by consumer complaints at home, so did the 1980–81 grain embargo motivate a parallel congressional initiative, to insure producers against future export interruptions occasioned by *foreign policy* concerns. In 1981, farm state representatives added Section 1204 to that year's Agriculture Act, specifying that producers be compensated at 100 percent of parity in the event of any new export suspension that singled out agricultural products for reasons of national security or foreign policy.[86] This was a potent requirement. Had the government imposed a selective grain embargo against the Soviet Union in the aftermath of the 1981 martial law crisis in Poland, this legislative provision would have immediately required additional farm budget outlays estimated as high as $3 billion.[87] The authors of this remarkable 1981 provision admitted that their purpose was not so much to provide compensation to farmers in the event of another embargo as it was to make selective food embargoes too expensive for the government ever again to contemplate.

These efforts by U.S. grain producers to insure against any repeat of the grain embargo experience would have had a strong constraining effect even if President Carter had remained in the White House after 1981, and even if U.S. commercial grain exports had continued to expand. Carter's replacement by Ronald Reagan and the decline in U.S. commercial grain exports that began in 1981 offered more cause for domestic producer interests to tighten their grip on grain export policy, practically eliminating all leeway enjoyed by foreign policy officials to seek external food power objectives.

The Reagan Years: Food Power in Eclipse

Any inclination that Ronald Reagan might have had to manipulate U.S. grain exports in search of diplomatic gains was counterbalanced first by his own 1980 antiembargo campaign promise to domestic producers, and second by the deepening economic distress that had overtaken U.S. farmers soon after the beginning of his term in office.

During Reagan's first term, as a consequence, the United States conspicuously abandoned any further pursuit of diplomatic food power, and worked instead to promote U.S. commercial grain exports to all paying customers abroad, including the Soviet Union, with no diplomatic strings attached.

President Reagan signaled where his priorities would lie when he fulfilled in April 1981 his campaign pledge to terminate the Soviet grain embargo, despite strong objections from Secretary of State Alexander Haig, who argued that such a move would be misunderstood by Soviet leaders as a sign of weakness in the new administration. Reagan's other foreign policy advisers, including the secretary of defense, the ambassador to the United Nations, the U.S. trade representative, and the National Security adviser, seconded Haig's objections. But Secretary of Agriculture John Block, at Reagan's first Cabinet meeting, reminded the president of his pledge to lift the embargo, and soon was able to prevail, with strong support from domestic political advisers in the White House. As Haig later recalled, lifting of the embargo in the end was "viewed almost exclusively as a domestic issue."[88]

Once it had been established, Reagan's habit of divorcing grain sales policy from foreign policy was to continue, despite repeated efforts (by Secretary Haig in particular) to revive the pursuit of "food power." On the day the embargo was lifted, when Haig publicly warned the Soviet Union that any provocation in Poland would cause a renewed grain embargo, White House spokesmen contradicted him immediately, describing such a response as just "one of many options" open to the president. Still Haig persisted; in August 1981 he sought to gain State Department control over the process of negotiating a new long-term grain trade agreement with the Soviet Union (the original five-year agreement was due to expire in October). Once again he was rebuffed, as the president reaffirmed his intention not to make future grain sales to the Soviet Union hostage to foreign policy concerns. U.S. Trade Representative William Brock, rather than Haig, was put in charge of the negotiations; a one-year extension of the agreement was promptly arranged, with no foreign policy conditions mentioned. The United States had suspended all other high-level diplomatic contacts with Soviet officials in the summer of 1981, but was making an exception for grain. Grain sales would move according to their own logic, conspicuously detached from the rest of U.S. foreign policy. Grain export policy was now planned by Reagan's Cabinet council on food and agriculture, where Haig's State Department had earlier been denied participation.[89]

Even the declaration of martial law in Poland in December 1981 was insufficient to alter U.S. policy on wide-open grain sales to the Soviet Union. Earlier, in October, the Department of Agriculture had offered to the Soviet Union a hefty 23 million tons of U.S. grain during the first extension year of the long-term agreement, 15 million tons more than the terms of the agreement itself required, and nearly as much as the notorious 25 million ton offer that had been extended in October 1979, on the eve of the Afghanistan invasion. Despite the imposition of martial law in Poland, this substantial offer of grain was not revoked. In response to the Polish crisis a variety of other economic sanctions were imposed on the Soviet Union—including suspension of Soviet Aeroflot service to U.S. airports, closing of the Soviet Purchasing Commission in the United States, and denial of new or renewed licenses for export of oil and gas equipment, electronic equipment, computers, and other high-technology materials. Conspicuously missing from this list of sanctions was a renewed grain embargo. President Reagan did briefly postpone what were as yet unscheduled negotiations to draft an entirely new long-term grain agreement, but later in 1982 he allowed the old agreement to be extended a second time for one year, without any Soviet concessions on Poland; still later he permitted the negotiations on a new agreement to begin in April 1983, even though martial law had at that time not yet been lifted.[90]

Reagan's decision to continue to promote grain sales to the Soviet Union in 1982–83 was more than a little disconnected from the rest of his foreign policy. It actually did significant damage to that policy, as it stirred resentment among allied governments, who were being pressured at the time to discontinue their own sales of technology and equipment for use in the Soviet construction of a Siberian natural gas pipeline. Reagan's one effort to explain this double standard to resentful French and German allies was less than persuasive. He tried to argue that building the natural gas pipeline would eventually *earn* valuable hard currency for the Soviet Union, while he characterized the U.S. grain sales as a damaging *drain* on the Soviet foreign exchange position. Both the Europeans and the Soviet Union were aware, however, that domestic agricultural problems had been Reagan's decisive consideration. U.S. farm income and farm exports were then falling sharply, and in October 1982, only two weeks before congressional elections, Reagan had once more extended to the Soviet Union an offer to purchase in the year ahead yet another 23 million tons of grain. This time, playing to his anxious domestic farm audience, Reagan promised that any Soviet purchases made by the end of November would be delivered, no questions asked, whatever the course of events in Poland.

Reagan offered this extraordinary foreign trade assurance under intense domestic pressure. Late in 1982 the Senate had already passed a more formal provision of its own, a so-called contract sanctity provision, which would *require* that the president permit agricultural shipments already contracted to continue, even during a declared embargo. President Reagan had been seeking in every other area to *increase* his executive authority to manipulate trade for foreign plicy purposes, so he was formally opposed to this legislation; nevertheless he signed it into law in January 1983.[91]

One more constraint on the exercise of food power against the Soviet Union was set in place in August 1983, when a newly completed U.S.–USSR long term grain trade agreement was signed in Moscow. This agreement, negotiated under intense domestic pressure from export-conscious U.S. producer lobbies, raised the minimum Soviet access guarantee 50 percent. Previously assured at least 8 million tons of U.S. wheat and corn a year without prior consultation, the Soviet Union was now guaranteed, through 1988, at least 12 million tons yearly.

The remarkable control farm interests had come to exercise on behalf of unrestricted grain exports was not enough to bring the Soviet Union completely back into the U.S. market. The Soviet Union was still determined to diversify its imports away from the United States, and when the total volume of its import needs momentarily declined in 1982–83, U.S. sales fell despite Reagan's best promotional efforts. Sales in the "agreement" year that began October 1982 fell to 6.2 million tons, from the previous year's level of 13.9 million tons. The U.S. share of Soviet grain imports, above 70 percent before the grain embargo, by 1983 dropped to less than 30 percent. When Soviet grain imports from all sources increased sharply in 1984, U.S. sales experienced a strong recovery. But by then producer interests had managed to create even larger inhibitions against the use of food power. Both major party candidates in the 1984 presidential election were pressured to disavow the future use of a selective grain embargo against the Soviet Union. The agricultural plank of the Republican party platform stated it was "unalterably opposed to the use of embargoes of grain or other agricultural products as a tool of foreign policy."

If not consonant with U.S. diplomatic strategy, perhaps the steps made by the Reagan administration to promote U.S. commercial grain exports after 1981 were part of a purely economic food power strategy, designed to secure external economic objectives. A few months after Reagan took office, as if to endorse such a strategy, a cable stressing the vital foreign economic policy contribution made by U.S. farm exports was sent to all diplomatic and consular posts abroad:

> [A]gricultural exports are one of the most dynamic elements of our trade. The U.S. has a large agricultural trade surplus (expected to reach $30 billion in [fiscal year 1981]) which is crucial to our balance of payments. Agricultural exports should bring in $47 billion in 1981, accounting for about 20 percent of total U.S. export revenues. Our agricultural exports pay for roughly half of our oil imports. . . . This administration intends to maintain and strengthen the position of the U.S. as the world's leading agricultural exporter. The State and Agriculture Departments, together with the Office of the U.S. Trade Representative, will work together closely toward this end. The effort to promote agricultural exports is one of major importance for the U.S.[92]

However persuasive this external economic rationale, it would never actually dominate the larger food policy-making process. In fact, a narrow search for affordable ways to increase farm income at home determined the content of grain trade policy.

The domestic farm economy was hit during Reagan's first years in office by an unanticipated combination of stressful circumstances. Record production and the onset of a recession depressed farm prices, just as high energy costs and record real interest rates were pushing up farm operating costs. Net farm income, which had been forecast to rise in 1981, instead fell by roughly 40 percent. High interest rates also hurt farm exports, as they led to a major increase in the exchange rate of the dollar against foreign currencies (a 14 percent appreciation in 1981 alone), which now made U.S. grain less attractive to customers abroad. As a consequence, the U.S. share of world grain exports, which had been growing for a decade, began to decline. Total trade volume declined as well, owing to a world recession and a severe global credit squeeze. As a result by 1982 the total dollar value of U.S. grain and feed exports had plummeted a devastating 20 percent.[93]

U.S. domestic farm income growth had come to depend heavily upon continued export growth. In the past decade the share of U.S. farm market returns gained from exports had increased from 15 percent to 25 percent. One out of every three acres of U.S. cropland now produced for export. Wheat producers exported almost two-thirds of their total production, and thus felt particularly exposed to changes in marketing conditions abroad. One-third of all corn production was sold overseas. Farmers who had capitalized themselves to export during the growth years of the 1970s now were convinced of their need for expanding export outlets.[94] They insisted that the Reagan administration launch a major export promotion campaign in an effort to restore domestic farm income.

The elements of this export promotion campaign eventually came to include more generous trade incentives—including an increase in direct government export credits, and export credit guarantees, as well as "blended credits" to produce below-market interest rates for foreign grain customers—plus an intensification of trade pressure against the European Community, which was using unprecedented export subsidies of its own to dump surplus wheat into markets in China and Latin America that were coveted by U.S. producers. Upon failing to win from the European Community any negotiated concessions on export subsidies, early in 1983 the United States took an even stronger measure, subsidizing a sale of 1 million tons of wheat flour to Egypt (a principal European Community market) at prices well below the regular U.S. export price. Farm state legislators applauded, and asked for a still tougher U.S. stance in what had become an escalating farm trade war with the European Community.[95]

Unfortunately, efforts to rescue U.S. domestic farm income by dumping surplus grain products into saturated markets abroad carried a measurable diplomatic cost. Far from fashioning the sort of grain export policy that might pay foreign policy dividends, the United States was once more seeking export outlets for its domestic grain surplus in ways that would only compromise its larger diplomatic objectives. Nor was the damage confined to U.S.–European relations; the United States began in 1981 to use diplomatic muscle and lavish financial inducements to persuade some of its smaller allies (such as South Korea and the Philippines) to purchase more U.S. wheat, calling forth formal complaints from allied wheat exporters such as Australia. Rather than manipulating its commercial food trade to serve diplomacy, as advocates of food power might prescribe, the United States was now manipulating its diplomatic ties and foreign economic policies in the service of domestic farm income, harming its relations with other allied exporting states in the process.

An even larger drawback attended these grain export promotion efforts, because the key to successful export promotion—competitive commodity pricing—could not be made a part of U.S. domestic farm policy. Producer interests, pushing hard in 1980 and 1981, had managed to secure much higher domestic commodity loan rates and target prices for U.S. grain products. When the unexpected world recession then took hold and foreign demand went into a slump, these now unrealistic domestic support levels made the competitive export pricing of U.S. farm products that much more difficult. By July 1983 even the chief economist at the Department of Agriculture was willing to admit that "our fear of indexing our way out of world markets has become a reality."[96]

Nor did reducing domestic commodity loan rates and relying more heavily upon direct cash payments to farmers, as in the 1960s, offer the Reagan administration an easy way out of the export promotion dilemma. With annual federal budget deficits exceeding $150 billion by 1983–84, additional out-of-budget spending for farm subsidies became unthinkable. Mandatory federal farm subsidy outlays had already tripled as the recession had taken hold in 1982, and in 1983 they doubled once more to reach a record $22 billion, a level of outlays greater than total U.S. net farm income. Any heavier reliance on direct cash payments, as a means to permit a lowering of export prices, was thus an unacceptable short-run political option.[97]

Faced with this intractable mix of domestic political and budgetary constraints in 1983, the Reagan administration opted for a desperate expedient to support farm income—enticing grain producers into massive acreage reductions by paying them not in cash but "in kind," with surplus commodities then being held in government storage. This new payment in kind (PIK) program was made sufficiently attractive to farmers so that wide participation was enlisted; planted acreage in wheat and corn fell as a consequence by about 25 percent. Even before U.S. grain markets were subsequently disrupted by a late summer drought, PIK had proved a useful device to reduce government surplus stocks and to shore up net farm income (primarily through input cost reductions), while minimizing short-run budgetary costs. But by boosting farm prices and by idling such a large share of U.S. farm capacity, PIK unwittingly further damaged commercial grain export prospects. Grain export competitors, taking maximum advantage of the artificially high world grain prices that the PIK program was now helping to maintain, reacted to U.S. restraint by expanding their acreage planted in grains in 1983. With foreign production now expanding to replace production cutbacks in the United States, further reductions in the U.S. share of world grain exports were in prospect.

It was largely an inward-looking preoccupation with farm prices, farm income, and budget deficits, therefore, that shaped (and in some ways inhibited) the grain export policies of the Reagan administration. The precise combination of inward-looking concerns had changed dramatically from the preceding decade, when domestic consumer pressures had at times directly constrained exports. Nor was this new mix of domestic concerns identical to that which had prevailed during earlier periods of abundance, in the 1950s and 1960s. Domestic farm interests now were so heavily dependent upon foreign commercial markets that they harped continuously upon the task of export promotion. Unfortunately they did not yet fully comprehend the constraint on exports which their own high domestic crop loan rates in combination with high dollar exchange rates had come to imply. They found it much easier to scapegoat the policies of the European Community and Carter's still-despised 1980–81 grain embargo. By using so much of their political influence to insure against any repeat of that embargo, and at times also to browbeat the Europeans, they certainly placed tighter limits on U.S. diplomatic food power options abroad. But by refusing, meanwhile, to surrender their high domestic grain price guarantees, they unintentionally restrained export growth, thereby limiting their own income gains and reducing official options to make purely commercial food power gains abroad as well.

Summary

U.S. grain trade policies in this century seldom have been subordinated to the pursuit of foreign diplomatic or economic objectives. More often they have been driven by a changing mix of internal political requirements and inward-looking policy concerns. Frequently these domestic concerns favor export promotion, but at times they actually constrain export growth. At least since the Marshall Plan, U.S. grain trade policies seldom have been designed or implemented consciously for the purpose of producing an international "food power" benefit.

Even when such food power designs do arise, domestic concerns hamper the result. For years, until the 1970s, occasional grain export promotion policies adopted at the insistence of foreign economic policy leaders were hobbled by high domestic loan rates (as well as by various diplomatic obstructions), and thus produced meager results. When commercial grain exports did expand rapidly during the 1970s to the tremendous advantage of U.S. foreign economic policy, it was scarcely the result of a conscious policy design. Most of the growth came from unforeseen market conditions or unexpected market growth in the Soviet bloc and in the Third World, and despite failed U.S. efforts in traditional markets to negotiate international agricultural trade policy reforms. The foreign policy community struggled during the 1970s to catch up with these events, to secure in this tightened world grain market a measure of diplomatic food power abroad, but again with scant success. While foreign policy officials remained torn over the difficult choice between seeking diplomatic or commercial food power, domestic policy officials were under new pressure to fashion export policies in direct response to inward-looking complaints from food consumers. The result, particularly in the conduct of U.S. grain trade with the Soviet Union, was constantly frustrating to diplomatic strategy. During the peak years of détente, U.S. grains sales to the Soviet Union had to be awkwardly interrupted several times, at the insistence of domestic consumers. Then, as détente declined after 1975, grain sales to the Soviet Union were more heavily promoted in response to the revived influence of domestic producers. The anomaly of the 1980–81 U.S. grain embargo actually reinforced this long-term trend away from foreign policy influence over the conduct of U.S. grain trade policy, as the disappointing foreign policy results of that embargo, along with a further political backlash from angered U.S. grain producers, led to a new round of legislative restrictions on foreign policy-inspired food trade manipulations.

The presumption that nations pursue food power is a poor guide to understanding the recent grain trade behavior of the United States. Parallel to patterns previously noted in India and in the Soviet Union, U.S. grain trade policy has become significantly divorced from the conduct of foreign policy. As with India and the Soviet Union, this disconnection even appears to have grown more pronounced in recent years. In contrast to the earlier record of both World Wars and the Marshall Plan, and also in contrast to the early years of the P.L. 480 program, almost all U.S. grain exports go abroad today in the form of private commercial sales, which are only lightly regulated and hence quite removed from direct diplomatic control. Except during the brief period of the 1980–81 grain embargo, these commercial exports have been made available to all paying customers abroad, diplomatic friend and foe alike, in considerable disregard for diplomatic gains or appearances.

The reasons nations choose *not* to pursue food power differ. In India, a switch from large "food aid" programs to commercial food imports helped to reduce that nation's diplomatic sensitivity to food trade questions; in the Soviet Union, the top Party leaders were concerned with enrichment of domestic consumer diets. In the United States, it was the enduring political need to placate well-organized domestic producers, and at times consumers, that made the pursuit of food power difficult. In each case, internal forces and inward-looking objectives so dominated the conduct of food policy at home as to restrict the freedom of foreign policy leaders to shape food trade policy abroad.

5 Testing Food Power: U.S. Food Aid to India 1965–1967

It has been shown that India, the Soviet Union, and the United States have not often attempted to exercise food power. There are noteworthy exceptions, however. This chapter and the next review two instances in which the United States broke from its usual habits and sought to gain a food power advantage over India in 1965–67, and over the Soviet Union in 1980–81. Did the United States, as the food-exporting country, gain the advantage on these occasions, as proponents of the "food power presumption" would predict?

President Lyndon Johnson's exceptional attempt in 1965–67 to use food power against India, is in no way typical of the larger pattern of U.S. grain trade policy, or of U.S.–Indian grain trade and food aid relations. Never before or since was India the target of such a determined U.S. food power exercise. Never before or since had India been such a vulnerable food power target; in 1965 and again in 1966, India experienced scanty monsoons and severe drought nationwide, so that the need for imported foodgrains reached an all-time high. Because of foreign exchange constraints, India could not afford to purchase these grains from commercial suppliers; it had no choice but to seek a larger volume of concessional P.L. 480 wheat shipments from the United States. But U.S. officials were just then noticing a momentary shrinkage of their own domestic wheat reserves, having already sent so much to India. They were looking for ways to begin cutting back on concessional grain exports. With India momentarily caught in this vulnerable condition, President Johnson could not resist putting U.S. "food power" to the test.

Johnson's response to India's much larger wheat import needs was to put food aid shipments on what he called a "short tether." He allowed the volume of P.L. 480 wheat shipments to grow but refused to release those shipments on more than a short-term basis, pending his personal month-by-month assessment of India's willingness to comply with a changing variety of demands. Most of those demands were focused on the reform of India's own internal agricultural policies, in India's own supposed long-term interest. But Johnson also pursued a more self-serving food power objective, by linking monthly food aid shipments to changes in Indian foreign policy, specifically to less vocal Indian criticism of U.S. war policy in Vietnam.

Because this is an unusual case, in which the United States enjoyed so many exceptional advantages over India, it is of limited value in supporting *positive* generalizations about the success of food power. Yet such an unusual case may help advance negative generalizations. If the food weapon should fail to produce a full range of advantages under circumstances so well suited to success, then it is likely to prove even less advantageous when employed in more ordinary circumstances.

U.S. Food Power Potential

India's dependence on concessional grain shipments from the United States had become critical even before 1965. That need was intensified by two consecutive years of severe drought. In 1965–66 Indian foodgrain production plunged to 72 million tons, a disastrous 19 percent below the harvest of the previous year. Ninety-one districts in seven separate states recorded harvests at only 25–40 percent of normal levels. The next year's foodgrain harvest was hardly better at 76 million tons, and in the impoverished states of Eastern Uttar Pradesh and Bihar, the effects were even more severe. It was in response to this emergency that P.L. 480 wheat imports increased to 6.35 million tons in 1965, and to a record 8.06 million tons in 1966. In 1967, with the effects of the drought still lingering, food aid imports from the United States remained at a substantial 5.96 million tons.[1] This urgent and unprecedented expansion of U.S. food aid shipments briefly transformed India into the largest wheat-importing country in the world.

It is true that India's wheat imports, even during this severe crisis, never satisfied more than a modest 8–10 percent of total national foodgrain consumption. But such calculations greatly understate the *political* significance of these food shipments. P.L. 480 wheat imports in 1965 provided directly for nearly 60 percent of total *public* foodgrain distribution through India's subsidized fair price shops.[2] Recall that by 1965 India's public foodgrain distribution system had become that nation's most important domestic food policy instrument. It was the principal means by which the central government sought to moderate prices and to guarantee minimum supplies for politically powerful urban groups, in times of short supply. The drought required that public foodgrain distribution be expanded, to compensate for the shortage of high-quality free market supplies.

When the drought first struck in 1965, India was in a particularly weak position to expand public foodgrain distribution; government foodgrain stocks stood at their lowest level in six years. Without imports from the United States, the Food Corporation of India would have been forced to reduce its public distribution of subsidized foodgrains by *more than half*. Apart from the grim cost to human life, such measures would have brought a crescendo of urban violence, looting, and political disorder, perhaps sufficient to topple the Congress party government from its otherwise secure position. As India's minister of agriculture later recalled, this was "a frightening situation . . . one of the most critical that we had ever faced in the country as far as food was concerned." The U.S. ambassador in New Delhi noted, "Even the delay of a few days in ship departures from American ports was reflected in the most tragic terms in [India's] drought-ridden areas."[3] If the United States was ever in a position to exercise food power over India, this was surely the time.

It is important to note that India was *not* well positioned in 1965–67 to meet its vast food import needs though commercial purchases from non-U.S. suppliers. The same drought that had devastated India's foodgrain production had also cut into the production of cash export crops—such as cotton and jute. As a consequence, Indian planners estimated in 1965 that during the upcoming planning period total export earnings were likely to fall about 24 percent short of the nation's "maintenance imports" and debt service obligations. And even then there would be no foreign exchange to cover planned import expenditures for new projects. To finance such projects it was calculated that the annual level of foreign assistance receipts would have to increase from an average $1.1 billion during the previous planning period, to an average $1.7 billion during the next five years.[4] There was, unfortunately, little assurance that such aid would be forthcoming. After India's September 1965 war with Pakistan, a costly venture on its own terms, additional U.S. financial aid had been temporarily suspended. Because of this crisis in external financing in 1965, India was forced to request $200 million from the IMF, while approaching the World Bank with a request to reschedule at least $125 million of the nation's foreign debts due in 1966. Paying out foreign exchange to import food at this juncture was understandably daunting to the Indian government. If purchased in the word market, through normal commercial channels, India's P.L. 480 food grain imports in 1965 alone would have cost more than $400 million.[5] Without the concessional terms available through the P.L. 480 food aid program, India would not have been able to import the sustained volume of foodgrains that it required.[6]

While India's dependence on U.S. food was reaching an all-time high in 1965–67, U.S. dependence upon India, as an outlet for surplus grain, was noticeably in decline. In 1956, to be sure, the United States had been quite anxious to expand P.L. 480 wheat shipments to India. But since 1961, U.S. wheat stocks had fallen, from a 38.4 million ton high to only 22.2 million tons by 1965.[7] Large P.L. 480 wheat shipments to India had played a significant role in this much-desired reduction of U.S. surplus grain stocks, and many officials in the Department of Agriculture still viewed such shipments as highly beneficial.[8] By 1966, however, when India's food needs were reaching their peak, the eagerness of the United States to export its surplus wheat on a concessional basis was notably dwindling. The July 1966 crop report in the United States indicated that production would fall so sharply that U.S. wheat available for P.L. 480 export would have to be considered in "tight supply." Secretary of Agriculture Orville Freeman, who happened to be visiting India at the time, warned his hosts that the United States *also* "had suffered a drought" and was "no longer in the same surplus position."[9]

Lyndon Johnson's 1965–67 "short-tether" food power strategy against India was therefore initiated at a time of maximum U.S. advantage in the food trade relations between the two countries. Any interruption of U.S. food aid to India during this unusual period would have damaged the Indian food economy far more than ever before, while damaging U.S. food trade interests scarcely at all. The potential leverage available to the United States was therefore as great as any food exporter could hope to enjoy.

Objectives and Tactics

India's potential vulnerability to U.S. food power did not go unnoticed in Washington, and various proposals to take advantage were quick to surface. Not long after the onset of drought conditions in India, in the summer of 1965, Secretary of Agriculture Orville Freeman sent a memorandum to President Johnson restating his belief that food aid should be used as a "lever" for Indian economic development. Freeman advised that the upcoming negotiation of a new P.L. 480 agreement was an opportunity to induce India to "take steps which they would not take on their own in improving their food situation."[10] By August, tactics for implementing Freeman's advice were being prepared in the Department of Agriculture. It was suggested that there be no *explicit* threat of a food aid suspension. A more subtle technique was proposed, that the United States discontinue its customary practice of authorizing food aid to India on a long-term multiyear basis. Instead, the United States should "agree to supply food aid to India through a series of short-run extensions of our present P.L. 480 agreement. . . . [I]t would be made crystal clear to the [Government of India] that agricultural performance would weigh heavily in determining the terms of future food assistance."[11] This Department of Agriculture proposal to authorize food aid shipments to India on a short-term or "short-tether" basis, was seized upon eagerly by President Johnson.[12] In fact, Johnson had already been toying with the use of food power against India, but for reasons distinctly unrelated to Indian farm policy. Earlier in the spring the president had already gone out of his way to delay the approval of a new P.L. 480 agreement, to express his growing annoyance with Prime Minister Shastri, on the occasion of a minor diplomatic misunderstanding. Shastri had been humiliated when Johnson abruptly canceled his scheduled state visit to Washington on the dubious excuse of an overload of presidential business. Shastri had felt obliged to counter with a mild criticism of the deepening U.S. military involvement in Vietnam. Johnson bridled at this criticism and delayed the new food aid agreement, to indicate to the Indians that he would "not allow himself to become a target" for what he viewed as "slander."[13]

From the start, then, Lyndon Johnson was inclined to manipulate food aid to India for purposes that went far beyond Orville Freeman's objective of prompting agricultural policy reforms within India. Even so, Freeman's objectives were initially at the heart of the short-tether exercise. The need for a radical change in Indian agricultural policy had been acknowledged at least since the publication in 1959 of an influential Ford Foundation study, which faulted the Indian government for having failed to make adequate public investments in agriculture, and for failing to provide adequate price incentives to agricultural producers. On a visit to India in 1964, Orville Freeman was distressed by general lack of progress in agriculture, and found that such recommended changes had not been incorporated into India's Third Five-Year Plan. He blamed ineffective U.S. policy, and concluded that large quantities of food aid dumped on the Indian market had only added to the "unfavorable price relationship" that constrained Indian farmers.[14]

When Freeman's proposed corrective, the so-called short-tether policy, was formally adopted by the president in fall 1965, the specific reform measures to be asked of India were never elaborated in public. But they were spelled out privately, in some detail. In return for U.S. food aid, India would be asked to increase its acreage under irrigation, and step up fertilizer production, not only through a better use of existing plant capacity, but also through an expansion of capacity, based upon an increased use of *private* capital, foreign as well as domestic. At least two additional economic policy conditions—a more vigorous family planning policy, and a devaluation of the rupee—were later added to this original list of food power demands.

These specific demands were made known to the Indian government in autumn 1965, in a manner that was at first neatly calculated to maximize the chances of Indian compliance. Freeman had become aware that his Indian counterpart, Agriculture Minister Chidambara Subramaniam, was doing his best inside the Indian government to advance the agricultural policy reforms Freeman favored. Hoping to use Subramaniam's position to best advantage, Freeman arranged a series of private meetings late in November 1965, when both were attending a United Nations Food and Agriculture Organization conference in Rome. At these meetings U.S. conditions for continued food aid shipments to India were made clear. The intention was to make the most of Subramaniam's considerable influence; he was to return to India "armed with a package of promises and penalties," which he could use as he thought best against opponents of reform within the Indian government.[15] As Freeman later recalled. "We had them over a barrel and we squeezed them, but he [Subramaniam] didn't object very much to being squeezed. . . . He had a pretty wide mandate, and he seemed fairly confident that if this did not leak that he could get it through the Cabinet and get it through the Parliament."[16]

Subramaniam's memory of the November 1965 meetings in Rome is somewhat different.[17] But within a week of his return to New Delhi, he reported to Parliament that adequate P.L. 480 shipments were now an "uncertain" prospect—in part due to dwindling surplus stocks of grain in the United States. He made no *public* mention of the conditions Freeman had spelled out in Rome, but discussed those conditions privately with Prime Minister Shastri and quickly secured permission to place a significant package of agricultural reforms before the full Cabinet.

Until that time, Subramaniam had not been willing to risk such a full Cabinet debate on agricultural policy reform, fearing that any adverse outcome would be "difficult to reverse." He knew he would face strong opposition from the Planning Commission, which remained more eager to push forward with industrialization and was suspicious, on ideological grounds, of any proposed modernization of agriculture that might at first enrich only bigger farmers, thus aggravating social inequities. And he also faced opposition from Finance Minister T. T. Krishnamachari, who objected to the use of scarce foreign exchange to import the new seed varieties and fertilizers that would be necessary to the success of Subramaniam's strategy.[18] It is therefore significant that Subramaniam was able to secure a landmark decision from the full Cabinet on 6 December to incorporate his proposed package of agricultural reforms into the upcoming Fourth Five-Year Plan.[19] These reforms included not only the import of new high-yielding varieties of seeds, improved price incentives to producers, and a concentration of expensive inputs in irrigated areas, but also a less widely publicized decision; namely, to provide concessions to private foreign companies contemplating investments in India's fertilizer industry. Any foreign company signing a contract before 31 March 1967 would be allowed greater freedom to set its own prices and manage distribution.[20]

The U.S. response to Subramaniam's initial success within the Indian Cabinet was suitably swift and supportive. Freeman notified Johnson, who welcomed India's actions as "the first important direct result of our new policy." Recalls Johnson, "[W]ith that strong Indian commitment in hand, I gave Secretary Freeman instructions in a telephone call on the morning of December 11. Move the wheat, I told him."[21] Accordingly, a much-needed consignment of 1.5 million tons of P.L. 480 wheat was released for immediate shipment to India.

In India, the coincidence of the U.S. decision to authorize new P.L. 480 assistance immediately following the Cabinet decision to adopt a sweeping plan for agricultural policy reform could hardly go unnoticed, and by mid-December the Indian press was carrying reports from Washington that described the process by which Subramaniam had secured U.S. "approval" for his reform package. These reports confirmed that the United States was now using a slowdown in approval of food aid shipments as a "tool," to modify Indian agricultural policy. But in India Subramaniam denied that any compromising strings had been attached to P.L. 480 wheat shipments. He insisted in public that "we shall try [to ensure] that those strings are not attached," and rejected as "fantastic nonsense" opposition charges that India had yielded to pressure from Washington.[22]

Subramaniam was for a time successful in denying the existence of a U.S. food power exercise directed against Indian agricultural policy, in part because most Indians suspected at the time that the strongest U.S. pressures were more likely being brought to bear on Indian foreign policy. Only recently, in reaction to India's September 1965 war with Pakistan, the United States had terminated all military and economic aid (except food aid) to both countries. India felt doubly resentful of this indiscriminate aid cutoff, as Pakistan had launched the war, using military arms supplied largely by the United States. In the context of this larger economic and military aid suspension, the purpose of Johnson's short-tether policy on food aid was thus easily misunderstood. In October 1965, Secretary of State Dean Rusk had to provide clarification to the embassy in New Delhi:

> The decision to extend food shipments for only thirty days has nothing RPT [repeat] nothing to do with Kashmir and is not RPT not to be construed in any way as political leverage to force India into a political settlement with Pakistan. It is based on evidence available to the highest authority that a longer term extension, or a new agreement on P.L. 480, should not be undertaken until such time as the [U.S. government] has convincing evidence of the [Government of India's] determination to put its food house in order.[23]

Ambassador Bowles continued to doubt that agriculture was at the heart of Johnson's short-tether policy; he had witnessed several attempts by Johnson earlier in 1965 to manipulate economic aid for diplomatic purposes.[24] And to be sure, as time went on Johnson's diplomatic purposes did tend to displace Freeman's agricultural reform purposes. All of the early suspicion in India, that Johnson was using food power to force a change in India's foreign policy, nonetheless proved beneficial to Subramaniam. It focused political and press concern on foreign policy questions, distracting those in the Indian opposition who might have otherwise noticed and objected to the link that

had been forged between U.S. food aid shipments and Indian concessions on agricultural policy.[25]

Prospects for continued success appeared to brighten when Subramaniam's influence within the Indian government continued to rise.
On 31 December 1965, Krishnamachari resigned from his position as
finance minister, and was replaced by Sachindra Chaudhuri, who was
known to be receptive to Western advice and was a strong proponent
of currency devaluation. Then, at Tashkent in January 1966, Prime
Minister Shastri suffered a fatal heart attack. His successor, Indira
Gandhi, was not at first confident in her own handling of agricultural
policy and strengthened Subramaniam's position by appointing him
full member of the Planning Commission. As he later recalled, "Mrs.
Gandhi gave me much greater support and I was able to go forward
with much greater freedom after January, 1966."[26] The enormous
food power potential of the United States over India thus appeared,
through a combination of careful strategy and advantageous circumstance, to be on its way to full realization. In the end, many of the
economic reform objectives of Lyndon Johnson's short-tether policy
were achieved, but some of the difficulties encountered from 1966
onward illustrate the limits of food aid coercion, even under circumstances "most likely" to ensure total success.

Domestic Objections in the United States

The food power advantage enjoyed over India in 1965–67 might well
have been lost within the U.S. domestic arena had it not been for a
unique exercise of direct presidential control. Lyndon Johnson insisted
personally that a short-tether policy on food aid to India remain in
effect, even after India's second harvest failure in 1966, despite growing objections in his own administration. With the threat of an Indian
famine looming by 1966, a group of senior officials within the Johnson
administration and many influential members of Congress had begun
to advocate terminating the food power exercise, but with no success.
As Johnson later recalled, "I stood almost alone, with only a few
concurring advisors, in this fight to slow the pace of U.S. assistance. . . . This was one of the most difficult and lonely struggles of my
Presidency."[27] According to one official, "[The short-tether] policy
was probably as uniquely the President's personal achievement as any
that emerged during his administration. For weeks, he held out almost

alone against the urgings of all his advisors, and later against a shrill press."[28]

How did Johnson manage, against such opposition, to protect his food power policy from failure and collapse at home? The first key to his success lay in the prior care which Johnson had taken to strengthen his own role in the economic assistance process. Johnson's long experience in manipulating Congress, through timely allocations of project money to key members, had driven him instinctively to seek tight White House control over the parallel allocation of economic assistance, including food aid, abroad. Here, in an otherwise unfamiliar diplomatic world, Lyndon Johnson had felt at home. Johnson had insisted that all new aid program loans in excess of $5 million, and all new project loans greater than $10 million, be submitted for direct presidential review and approval. In addition, Johnson had specified that the Agency for International Development (AID) submit to the president all new aid commitments "which involved special foreign policy issues."[29] Johnson's determination to monitor all new food aid commitments abroad was especially keen. New P.L. 480 commitments earlier had been made through a middle-level Interagency Staff Committee chaired by an official of the Department of Agriculture and composed of career bureaucrats. In 1965, Johnson was asked to approve a new Executive Order that would have diminished the role of the Department of Agriculture on this committee, and move all responsibility for P.L. 480 to a newly created "War on Hunger" office within AID. But upon considering such a draft order, Johnson decided instead that all new P.L. 480 agreements, with the ten largest recipient countries, henceforth must be cleared by him personally.[30]

Secretary of Agriculture Orville Freeman was at first a willing supporter of this procedural change, wishing to avoid the alternative of an unwanted extension of AID or State Department authority, and Freeman was remarkably successful throughout 1965 in influencing the White House in its new discretionary control over P.L. 480. His department not only provided conceptual and operational support for the short-tether policy toward India, it also took the lead in redesigning U.S. food aid policies elsewhere, better to advance Freeman's personal interest in Third World agricultural policy reform. In this regard, the Department of Agriculture was responsible for drafting the "Food for Freedom" proposal, submitted to Congress in February 1966, which mandated a "particular emphasis on assistance to those countries that are determined to improve their own agricultural production." This revised act nonetheless confirmed that the ultimate judgment on such matters would now be made by the president. Section 109 of the act empowered the president to terminate any P.L. 480 agreement "whenever the President finds that such a [self-help] program is not being adequately developed."[31] This further enhancement of presidential control over P.L. 480 food aid proved, in the end, a frustration to Freeman. By late 1966, Freeman was persuaded that Indian agricultural reforms were advancing enough to merit a more generous U.S. assistance commitment, but he had no means, at that point, to recover control from the president and terminate the short-tether policy.

Internal opposition to Lyndon Johnson's short-tether policy was also slow to build because neither Johnson nor the Indian government at first called much attention to the policy. The Indian government was understandably reluctant to admit that it was being pressured by the United States, and Johnson had decided not to admit in public that pressure was being applied. For most of the first year of the policy, in fact, Johnson succeeded remarkably well in giving the impression to his domestic political audience that he was doing everything within his power to rush U.S. food aid to India, presenting himself to Congress and to the press as the foremost advocate of massive new wheat shipments to meet India's rapidly growing emergency food requirements. In the aftermath of a state visit to Washington by Indira Gandhi in March 1966, Johnson sent a special message to Congress to gain its endorsement of expanded food relief shipments, in language that gave an artful impression of presidential impatience.[32] While posing in public as a champion of accelerated food aid, Johnson was gaining time to pursue his short-tether policy in private.

Johnson's effort to maintain this deceptive public appearance continued at least through July 1966. In response to a request from Ambassador Bowles that he go beyond "vague assurances" and provide to the Indian government "the specific amounts and dates when the grain would be shipped," Johnson called a bipartisan group of thirty senators to the White House, where he invoked the special responsibility of the United States to carry its share of the world's food burdens, and put the question to them—would the Senate support a massive program of food shipments to India? Although Senate resistance had never been a problem, he insisted upon a unanimous endorsement. On the following day he repeated the exercise before some sixty members of the House of Representatives. But as Bowles recalls, "With a favorable Congressional response to his appeal, we assumed the President would instruct the State Department, AID, and the Department of Agriculture to proceed with the grain shipments. Instead, he embarked upon a foot-dragging performance that I still fail to understand."[33] Although the excuse was becoming increasingly transparent, Johnson continued to stall on the argument that he needed more time to "win the necessary support from Congress."[34]

Then came India's second monsoon and crop failure in 1966, which brought the specter of a widespread famine. During the autumn months, when it began to appear that further food aid delays could mean tragedy, Johnson's domestic audience for the first time became genuinely alarmed. Indian officials at this point also began to warn of the danger, as they were unable to proceed with the advance planning that their elaborate public distribution and rationing system required. In late November, Subramaniam himself forecast that without a prompt U.S. approval of India's latest 2 million ton food aid request, the pipeline would run dry by mid-January. Prime Minister Gandhi also abandoned her silence and stated in public that the delay in U.S. food aid commitments was a growing source of concern.[35] The U.S. aid community took the cue and voiced its concerns to the press, which led promptly to a spate of editorial comments sharply critical of the president. On 29 November the *New York Times* denounced the short-tether policy as "a serious error," and rejected White House explanations about the need for further study of India's needs. On 11 December the *Washington Post* commented, "There are good reasons for a firm American policy that, in the long run, will assist India in resolving its recurrent food difficulties. But people sometimes starve to death in the short run and India is on the brink of famine." Johnson recalls this period as one in which he weathered a "heavy propaganda barrage," waged by Indians and by "Americans who considered themselves India's best friends. . . . In the press and at Washington cocktail parties I was pictured as a heartless man willing to let innocent people starve."[36]

In order to maintain his freeze on new food aid commitments, Johnson at this point also had to overcome objections from senior officials within his own administration. The State Department, which had sent a memorandum to the White House in September outlining India's significant progress in meeting the president's reform demands, favored immediate release of the 2 million tons then under consideration. AID administrator William Gaud also recommended approval of the 2 million ton shipment, arguing that "neither the withholding of aid or food supplies nor the public criticism of Indian performance can possibly improve Indian performance in the agricultural sector before the national elections in February [1967]." By early November 1966, even Freeman was advising the president not to delay on the next 2 million ton food aid shipment, which he described as "the minimum necessary allocation to avoid breaking the pipeline."[37]

Johnson, however, would not be moved. He retreated to yet another tactic of delay, dispatching two separate study teams to India—one consisting of agricultural experts from the Department of Agriculture and the other composed of members of Congress, led by Congressman Robert Poage, chairman of the House agriculture committee. The Department of Agriculture team reported promptly that India's food needs had been, if anything, understated. And the congressional inspection team, upon returning to Washington, recommended that at least 1.8 million tons of additional food aid shipments be authorized, on an interim basis, to cover anticipated needs in February, March, and April 1967.[38] These reports forced Johnson to act in mid-December 1966, but his action was to approve only *half* of the aid level that the congressional study mission had recommended: a mere 0.9 million tons of wheat and other grains, no more than enough to keep the pipeline in operation. As Johnson explained later, "I kept the 'short tether' on. No one would starve because of our policies. India would receive the grain it needed, but on a month-by-month basis rather than a year-to-year basis."[39]

By early 1967, with the food crisis in India entering what was to become its most desperate interlude—the wait for the spring wheat harvest—the heavy pressure on Johnson to call off his food power exercise continued to build. Johnson again was able to relieve this pressure, employing yet another tactic of delay. On 15 January 1967, he sent Undersecretary of State for Political Affairs Eugene Rostow on a special round-the-world mission to coax other wealthy food surplus countries into joining the United States in providing food relief to India. This "burden-sharing" requirement promptly became Johnson's favored means to explain the continuing slowdown in new U.S. food aid commitments. In late December 1966, Johnson had asked World Bank President George Woods to join in persuading other nations to extend food aid to India; at a meeting sponsored by the Bank in Paris early in 1967, Rostow was in fact able to win approval from Britain, France, Germany, Japan, and the Scandinavian countries for a "cooperative plan" to share the food aid effort. But in the launching of this cooperative plan, Johnson only found yet another opportunity to delay, by way of seeking one more round of congressional approval. Even with that approval in hand, Johnson then placed additional conditions upon new U.S. food aid to India, arbitrarily stipulating at one point that they be matched on a strict 50–50 basis by the other Western industrialized powers.[40]

Lyndon Johnson's grip on India was not relaxed even when India's own domestic food supply was mercifully replenished in 1967, after a welcome return of good weather. With the benefit of an excellent monsoon season, India enjoyed a record 95 million ton foodgrain harvest in 1967–68, 21.4 million tons more than the drought-reduced harvest of the preceding year. Prices fell, public grain distribution requirements were eased, and import needs eventually declined. India's moment of extreme vulnerability to U.S. food power was finally at an end. Yet even in the final months of his presidency, Johnson still looked for ways to exercise food power over India. In a curious turn of events in the spring of 1968, it suddenly became in the U.S. interest to *expand* its food aid shipments; wheat production was up, farm prices were down. Accordingly, the Department of Agriculture and the State Department approached the Indian government to suggest that India take *more* P.L. 480 wheat than it had already requested. After much discussion, the Indian government agreed to request an additional 2–3 million tons of wheat. Then, after the Indians had rebuilt their ration and distribution plans around the expectation of these larger U.S. wheat shipments, Johnson stepped in once more, refusing to authorize the food shipments according to the anticipated schedule. Indian planners had expected the additional shipments in September, but weeks went by without the necessary presidential action; by October India actually faced the prospect of another food crisis. Johnson was again overruling both the State Department and the Department of Agriculture, but this time on the grounds that any further action on food aid to India should await the outcome of the U.S. elections and the installation of a new president and Congress in 1969.[41] Not until early November, after yet another change of heart, did Johnson suddenly approve shipment of the much-needed supplies.

In the United States, where political or governmental opposition can so easily inhibit this sort of food power exercise, Lyndon Johnson never lost his grip. Against considerable odds, he managed for more than two years to hold India under a nearly constant threat of food aid denial. He did so by expanding the powers of his office over the entire concessional food sales process and by making full use of his own considerable political skills and personal energies. National Security Adviser Walt W. Rostow later recalled that Johnson "knew the dates of shipments from American ports of grain required for timely arrival in Calcutta and the state of Indian grain stocks. He personally guided the negotiation of each tranche of food aid."[42]

Unfortunately, this obsessive personal involvement, which allowed Johnson to overrule and intimidate his domestic critics, had a cost. As his personal involvement grew, Johnson began to turn the short-tether policy into a personal crusade. The original objectives of Indian agricultural policy reform came to be obscured by Johnson's many other concerns, including his growing concerns in the foreign policy realm. As a means to achieve such foreign policy purposes, the U.S. food weapon would prove a disappointment.

Response of the International Food Aid Community

In the international food aid arena, India found little relief from Johnson's threatened food aid denials. The magnitude of India's needs in 1965–67 meant that no other concessional food aid supplier could be found to step in. Johnson's short-tether policy had been designed with this lack of alternative suppliers in mind; in fact, as already noted, it became one of the stated objectives of the policy to *create* such alternative suppliers. Johnson eventually made a successful effort to encourage non-U.S. aid alternatives, but in a way that intensified the coercive pressure on India.

When India's first crop failure struck in 1965, the United States was India's only available source of large-scale food assistance. The United States was not by any means the world's only source of *commercial* grain exports at the time, but it was close to being the world's only source of *concessional* food aid. Of all the food aid being given through multilateral and bilateral channels at the time, 96 percent came from the United States, and during the preceding year P.L. 480 Title I shipments had accounted for 98 percent of India's total concessional foodgrain imports.[43]

In the mid-1960s, with its surplus grain stocks momentarily in decline and facing the need to repair its sagging foreign commercial trade balance, the United States was anxious to reduce its long-term food aid commitments. If the government could coax smaller grain producers and exporters into exporting a share of their normal commercial sales on a concessional basis to nations such as India, added room might be made for U.S. commercial exports to expand. At the very least, the U.S. food aid burden would be reduced. By late 1966 and early 1967, Johnson's short-tether policy for India was being implemented with this trade expansion purpose partly in mind.

Johnson had launched his burden-sharing initiative in December 1965, but in a manner apparently calculated to *increase* the pressure on India. Johnson wanted India to take the lead in the search for other donors, despite the added discomfort this would create for India, which did not relish "marring the reputation it has been trying [to] promote for sound economic planning and performance, by having to go to prospective donors with begging bowl in hand."[44] While India was busy making such requests, Johnson would have one more reason to go slow on his own P.L. 480 commitments.

The foreign response to India's first obligatory round of food aid requests was indeed disappointing. As of early April 1966, only $150 million worth of non-U.S. commodity aid had been promised to India, most of it in the form of a 1 million ton gift of wheat from one country, Canada. Thirteen nations were at this point only "considering" a contribution, thirty-three had not answered India's request, and forty-three others had answered that they had no food aid available.[45]

India's second monsoon failure in 1966 intensified the pressure on non-U.S. foreign suppliers to accept a larger share of the food aid burden, as they now risked appearing partly responsible for a significant Indian famine. Johnson, of course, did not hesitate to use the clear and present danger of a food calamity in India to coerce as many nations as possible into providing aid. As other donors continued to drag their feet, India's resentment toward Johnson turned to anger.

India had focused its non-U.S. aid requests primarily on Canada, Australia, France, the Soviet Union, Mexico, and Argentina. There was a limit to the grain Canada could provide directly to India, due to logistical constraints at its west coast grain terminals, so it was restricted to arranging small exports of third-country rice, purchased from Thailand and Burma, or bartered from Egypt. Australia could provide only a 150,000 ton wheat gift, plus a smaller quantity of grains on a deferred payment basis. France informed the Indian government that it could only provide wheat "on the usual commercial terms," and the Soviet Union, although the world's single largest producer of wheat, refused at first even to answer India's requests for aid. The

Soviet wheat harvest of 1966 had been adequate (30 million tons above the harvest of the last year, and nearly three times the size of the entire U.S. wheat crop in 1966), but at least until late December 1966 the Soviet Union was not eager to make any food aid available to India. They finally agreed, just before the end of the year, to provide India with a modest gift of 200,000 tons of wheat, to be delivered in January 1967.[46]

Johnson declined to accept as adequate these meager contributions from others, and set as his objective no less than a 50–50 matching arrangement between U.S. food aid to India and food aid contributions from non-U.S. sources. His preferred method was to leave the task of requesting the aid entirely up to India. The United States offered to India its "good offices" around the world, as an intermediate means to search for alternative aid suppliers, but continued to rely most upon the short tether on new U.S. aid to pressure others into action.[47]

Only with the dispatch of the round-the-world Rostow mission in mid-January 1967 did the United States at last intervene in earnest to help India seek food aid from other donors. Rostow's efforts, in coordination with those of the World Bank, bore fruit in April 1967, when Canada, Japan, and the European Community members of the ten-nation Aid-to-India Consortium pledged to match an upcoming 3 million ton U.S. food aid shipment. Canada, specifically, was persuaded to increase its scheduled assistance to India by yet another 100,000 tons. Johnson would later claim that these concessions, made to assist India, were the basis for a more general principle of food aid "burden sharing," endorsed in the 1967 Food Aid Convention, a significant multilateral pledge of aid that was added to the International Wheat Agreement later that year.[48]

Whatever Johnson's final success in coaxing more food aid for India out of others, the pressure on India was scarcely reduced in the process. Within India, however, this pressure did not always produce the intended result.

Impact on India

No matter how sustained a coercive food power tactic may be inside the exporting country or in the international food-trading system, it may still fall short of its potential due to a malfunction in the political or economic system of the target country. If the real or threatened denial of imports is inadequate or inappropriate to produce the intended effect within the target country, an exporter's coercive advantage from food power may not be fully realized.

In the case of Lyndon Johnson's short-tether policy, the threatened interruption of U.S. food aid shipments was at first followed by a significant number of compliant Indian policy actions. The December 1965 Cabinet decision had gone a long way to meet U.S. demands for specific agricultural policy reforms, including new public investments in farming, the use of new seed varieties, price guarantees for producers, increased fertilizer application, and enlargement of foreign as well as domestic private sector participation in India's fertilizer industry. These were not the only steps taken by the Indian government in compliance with U.S. suggestions and demands. Additional concessions on fertilizer policy were then made in April 1966, when the Indian government agreed to permit majority shareholding for foreign investors and to make a portion of the large U.S.-owned reserve of Indian currency (generated by P.L. 480 sales) available to U.S. companies considering such investments.[49] These new fertilizer concessions, which were immediately seen to have been taken under U.S. and World Bank pressure, were criticized by a number of senior members of Prime Minister Gandhi's own Congress party as "dishonorable" and "humiliating."[50] Charging the prime minister with a complete "sell-out," one former Congress party deputy finance minister warned that these new concessions, designed to attract private foreign capital, would "cut at the root" of a long-standing national policy.[51]

Nor did India's concessions stop with its agricultural and fertilizer policies. New foreign private investment opportunities were also offered in petroleum, delicensing proceeded in a number of industries, and a major new commitment was made to family planning, through creation of a separate Department of Family Planning in the Ministry of Health. In June 1966 came the most dramatic step of all: the Indian government announced its decision to devalue the rupee—by 36.5 percent.[52] This remarkable string of 1966 reforms undertaken by the Gandhi government, in combination with those initiated by the Shastri government the previous December, placed India in near-total compliance with the original agricultural and economic policy reforms demanded by President Johnson's short-tether policy.

Some of these reform initiatives, including the devaluation, had been particularly awkward for India. The Indian government had hesitated on devaluation until late in May, when it learned that continued IMF credits, World Bank help, aid through the Aid-to-India Consortium, and economic assistance from the United States (including food assistance) would require such action. When the devaluation was finally announced, opposition leaders swiftly attacked the government for having "yielded to pressure from Washington."[53] Former Finance Minister Krishnamachari warned of "economic slavery" to the United States.[54] Indian officials tried their best to deny, in public, that U.S. pressure had been responsible, and U.S. officials tactfully tried their best to support these official Indian denials, as when Ambassador Bowles denied that the United States had even "mentioned" devaluation.[55] But the announcement, only ten days after India's devaluation, that the United States was at last unfreezing economic aid left little doubt of a prior arrangement.[56] Even while Prime Minister Gandhi tried to offer new assurances to the opposition that the government would "rather starve than sell our national honor," the evidence that the United States had exercised an advantage over her government, at least in part derived from "food power," was becoming irrefutable. Agriculture Minister Subramaniam thus came under heavy fire for having yielded too much, and was finally forced to concede in public what all had suspected: that Indian economic policy had been operating under a tight and explicit U.S. food power constraint. When a spokesman for the opposition demanded that he make no further concessions to the United States on fertilizer policy, he replied in all candor, "I do not think we are in a position to take that attitude."[57]

Nevertheless, the appearance of such extensive U.S. food power in this instance can be deceiving. First, it was not simply U.S. food power that was forcing the Indian government to consider reforms. Second, some of the Indian agricultural and economic policy reforms suggested by the United States were never taken; some of the reforms that were taken were never fully implemented; and most important, many of the reforms taken during the short-tether period probably would have been taken anyhow. Third, the short-tether demands that were placed on India *beyond* the agricultural and economic policy realm—particularly those in the diplomatic realm—were rejected entirely.

It has already been noted that the U.S. short tether in 1965–67 was only one part of a more general Western strategy of economic pressure on India. During this period India required financial assistance (from the United States, the Aid-to-India Consortium chaired by the World Bank, and the IMF), almost as much as it needed its concessional P.L. 480 food shipments. Indian planners estimated in 1965 that to finance the upcoming Fourth Plan, foreign assistance from these various sources would have to increase to an unprecedented annual level of $1.7 billion.[58] When new economic aid from the United States was suspended after the war with Pakistan, India was in a weak position to refuse any new Western aid proposal, even when difficult conditions were attached. Such conditions *were* attached, and in most respects were parallel to those surrounding the continuation of U.S. food aid. The specific requirement that India attract more foreign private capital to its fertilizer industry, as well as the requirement that it devalue its currency, were conditions attached specifically to new credits from the IMF, to new loans from the World Bank, and also to a full resumption of regular bilateral economic aid from the United States. Devaluation, in particular, was the major condition attached not only to $187 million in new IMF credits in 1966, but also to an Aid-to-India Consortium promise of $900 million worth of new project aid.[59] Alongside such financial inducements, the continuation of U.S. food assistance was no doubt a large concern, as the value of food aid alone represented almost two-thirds of total aid supplied to India at the time. But India's parallel need for direct financial assistance to sustain its development efforts in other areas was of comparable urgency; therefore, to attribute India's economic policy reforms in 1965–66 to U.S. food power alone misses the fact that other powerful means of Western economic coercion were at work.

Those doubting the extent of U.S. food power over India also note that some of the economic reforms demanded were never taken, or were never seriously implemented. In the agricultural policy area, specifically, India refused to eliminate entirely its "food zones," which had been criticized by U.S. advisers for their price-weakening effects in states that could have been producing larger surpluses.[60] Among those concessions never fully implemented, India's imports of modern agricultural supplies (such as fertilizer, pesticides, and machinery) were expanded, from a mere 3 percent of total imports in 1965–66 to more than 10 percent of total imports by 1968–69. But the absolute level of expenditures for such imports was in the end only about one half of what had earlier been demanded by India's own Food and Agriculture Ministry. The implementation of India's 1966 currency devaluation also left much to be desired. Indian officials remained so wedded to their predevaluation trading preferences that even before the year had ended they had begun to use other bureaucratic instruments of economic control to continue acting on those preferences.[61] Rather than doing their best to make the devaluation work, many Indians came to view it as an "imported evil," and took every opportunity to frustrate its success.

There is also a deeper reason to question the extent of U.S. leverage over India in 1965–67. A significant number of India's apparent "concessions" were reforms that already had been decided upon, or would likely have been taken anyway. Agriculture Minister Subramaniam already had launched an effective program to modernize Indian agriculture *well before the short-tether policy was set in place.*

Subramaniam himself argues that his original November 1965 Rome agreement with Orville Freeman consisted of nothing more than U.S. endorsement of "steps we had already taken and that we proposed to take." He criticizes Lyndon Johnson for seeking to take credit for reforms already under way:

> Johnson always had a sense of self-importance. If anything good or important was happening in the world, it should be a Johnson initiative. . . . He reiterated in speeches that India should adopt this new technology. . . . These speeches gave ammunition to those who were attacking me on the grounds that I was following American advice and American technology. We had already announced and had taken all these steps and I had to tell people that President Johnson was telling us nothing new, and that we had already launched a programme of this kind.[62]

Ambassador Bowles concurred, at the time, with this radically different assessment of the actual leverage exercised by the short-tether policy. In early November 1965, when that policy was first being communicated to the Indian government, Bowles cabled the State Department to express his confusion and to request clarification. It was Bowles's view, at that time, that suddenly conditioning U.S. food aid on agricultural policy reforms would only "mystify" the Indian government, because a significant schedule of such reforms had *just recently been undertaken.*[63] Indeed, it was in June 1964, shortly after he became agriculture minister, that Subramaniam successfully launched—*without pressure from the U.S. government*—his first broad series of initiatives in the area of agricultural policy reform. It is true that he was in close contact with experts from the World Bank, the Department of Agriculture, AID, the Rockefeller Foundation, and the Ford Foundation, but he was not yet operating under any threat of a food aid suspension. More than a year before any explicit application of U.S.

food power, he had succeeded in providing a 15 percent increase in incentive prices offered to Indian wheat producers, and had then ensured that these incentive prices would be maintained from one season to the next, by persuading the government in January 1965 to create the Agricultural Prices Commission.[64] To provide the means for offering these higher prices to producers, he had also secured a Cabinet decision, in July 1964, to establish a public foodgrain-trading corporation (the Food Corporation of India), which was designed to rely less upon compulsory procurement and more upon competitive prices to acquire public stocks. Even India's willingness to seek private foreign investment in fertilizer production predated the short-tether policy. Negotiations with a large international fertilizer concern for a joint venture to set up five large fertilizer factories in India began late in 1964.[65] And Subramaniam's own comprehensive agricultural strategy had been spelled out in detail to the Indian Development Council by January 1965. The strategy had already been presented to Parliament, in the form of a seventy-one-page report in April, six months before the meeting with Freeman in Rome.[66] In late summer 1965, with Johnson's short-tether policy just beginning to take shape in Washington, Subramaniam was already well along in arguing his case for reforms before the Indian Planning Commission.

Whether or not Subramaniam would have prevailed over doubters in the Planning Commission and the Finance Ministry, without the added incentive that Johnson's policy may have initially provided, must remain a matter for speculation. Subramaniam did appear to gain from the short-tether conditions at the time of his success in the Cabinet in early December, so we may question some of his later assertions that the policy was a hindrance. It remains plausible, however, that even at the December Cabinet meeting the threat of a U.S. food aid cutoff was not the key consideration. No less important had been the sudden termination of all U.S. economic and military aid (*except* P.L. 480) after the war with Pakistan. This unfriendly U.S. action had momentarily boosted the stature of any Cabinet minister who could claim to be promoting schemes of economic "self-reliance" for India. Subramaniam's new agricultural strategy, then before the government, held out the tantalizing prospect that a crash program of agricultural modernization, despite some short term input dependence, might lead to foodgrain "self-sufficiency" for India within five years.[67] The war-related experience of an actual U.S. economic and military aid cutoff, as much as any threat of a future food aid suspension, was perhaps Subramaniam's strongest tactical asset in the Cabinet.

In the end, there were simply too many forces working in combination to allow confident judgment of what happened or did not happen in India due to "food power." L. K. Jha, the former Indian ambassador to the United States, later characterized the exercise of influence as a dubious one of "leaning against open doors."[68]

One of the doors that was *not* open in India, against which Johnson leaned hard but without success, was Indian foreign policy. Johnson's efforts to use food power to alter Indian diplomatic conduct met repeated frustration. Here, political dynamics within India ensured that food power would fail to produce concessions similar to those that had been won in Indian agricultural policy and economic planning.

The incapacity of U.S. food power to alter the conduct of Indian foreign policy was foreseen from the start by Ambassador Bowles, who was best positioned, in New Delhi, to appreciate India's likely reaction. Bowles had warned as early as August 1965 that any manipulation of U.S. economic assistance "to pressure the Indians to adopt a foreign policy which they believe to be contrary to their national interests" would fail. Bowles went on to explain that such manipulations would in fact backfire; they would "make us sitting ducks in India for the Soviet propaganda machine, the Indian Communists, and the Krishna Menons."[69] When Johnson ignored this advice and sought to use his short-tether policy as a means to force diplomatic concessions out of India, he ran into precisely these sorts of difficulties.

Some U.S. demands for Indian foreign policy change failed because they were pursued in half-hearted fashion. Briefly in the spring of 1966, Johnson sought to extract from India a pledge to restrict its military spending, but this condition was quickly dropped when it became clear that the Indians would not comply.[70] Other U.S. foreign policy demands that might have been made were prudently avoided. In 1966 the United States altered its P.L. 480 legislation to permit food aid to go to countries trading with communist states (as long as the goods being traded were "nonstrategic" in nature), so that India could continue its jute exports to Cuba. It had been considered unlikely that India would agree to terminate these exports.[71]

The one foreign policy demand that consistently accompanied Johnson's policy was an insistence that India soften its public criticism of U.S. military actions in Vietnam. Johnson, whose personal sensitivity on the subject was well known, could not abide critical comment on Vietnam from India, a beneficiary of so much U.S. food aid. As Ambassador Bowles recalled, after every public criticism of U.S. Vietnam policy in New Delhi, "Cables from Washington burned with comments about 'those ungrateful Indians,' and the shipments of wheat were further delayed."[72]

But if Johnson's purpose was to tone down India's public criticism of U.S. foreign policy, he scarcely could have done worse than to threaten a termination of food aid. By 1966, U.S. food aid delays had already raised the specter of "foreign interference" in India's domestic agricultural and economic policies, placing the Indian government in a compromising position at home. Already under criticism for having capitulated to the U.S. government in the domestic arena, Indian officials were that much less willing to consider concessions in the conduct of their foreign policy. Indeed, to deflect the domestic policy criticism that had already been aroused, they felt a compensating need to publicly *defy* the United States on questions of foreign policy. India's criticism of U.S. policy in Vietnam was to some extent a *product* of the short-tether policy.[73] It was in some ways surprising that Johnson did not understand this.

The greatest misunderstanding emerged after a state visit by Prime Minister Indira Gandhi to the Soviet Union in July 1966.[74] At the conclusion of that visit, she signed a joint communiqué, cleverly drafted by the Soviet Union in cooperation with a low-ranking member of the Indian delegation, which contained language highly critical of the United States. The communiqué condemned the "aggressive actions of the imperialist and other reactionary forces," a phrase Indian diplomats had never before used and one that President Johnson was not about to let pass.[75] India's recent agricultural and economic policy concessions, including the dramatic rupee devaluation of the month before, were suddenly discounted in the president's mind, and new U.S. food aid commitments would now be further delayed for diplomatic reasons, to punish India for its careless insult.

Already under massive domestic criticism for having "sold out" to the United States on the devaluation, Prime Minister Gandhi could not afford, at this point, to retreat on the issue of Vietnam. Facing the prospect of national elections early in 1967 and under constant pressure from the left, she decided instead to become even more outspoken in her criticism of the United States. In October 1966, she repeated her earlier call for an end to U.S. bombing in Vietnam, but now in a joint statement with President Tito of Yugoslavia and President Nasser of Egypt; this occurred precisely when Johnson was seeking international support for his war policies from Asian leaders assembled in the Philippines.[76] Predictably, Johnson responded with a further delay in new food aid commitments. Just as predictably, this conspicuous new delay placed even greater pressure on Indira Gandhi to demonstrate her independence from Washington. As Bowles had earlier predicted, procommunist newspapers were by now stirring up heightened fears within India of "dictation by the State Department," and V. K. Krishna Menon, a former left-wing Congress party leader known for his antagonistic views toward the United States, had launched a new political campaign, largely based on the charge that the prime minister was likely to abandon the nation's self-respect and independence in her efforts to secure U.S. wheat.[77]

The negative reaction in India to Lyndon Johnson's short-tether policy at this point became so intense as to threaten some of the domestic agricultural policy reforms the policy had earlier helped to encourage. Agriculture Minister Subramaniam, in particular, found his credibility exhausted, as fears of Johnson's larger motives began to spread through the Indian political system. Johnson, for his part, inadvertently helped to compromise Subramaniam, by paying such little regard to appearances. On one unfortunate occasion, earlier in 1966, Subramaniam had been summoned by Johnson to make a special trip from New Delhi to be present for a dramatic press conference, at the LBJ ranch in Texas, at which the president intended to announce his latest decision on the next consignment of food aid to India. It was painfully obvious at that press conference that Subramaniam had no advance knowledge of what the president's decision would be. The humiliating circumstances of the announcement "made Subramaniam look like an American puppet and weakened him further at home."[78] By the end of the year, opposition leaders in Parliament were calling for his resignation or impeachment. He progressively lost his former position of influence within the Cabinet, and was eventually defeated—along with a number of other high-level Congress party leaders—in the national elections held early the next year.[79]

In retrospect, Johnson's short-tether policy would have provided the United States with a more satisfying sort of food power advantage over India if it had not been kept in place so long, and if its purposes had been consistently restricted to the realm of agricultural policy reforms within India. By continuing to hold the short tether in place, even after

India's politically difficult currency devaluation, Johnson managed to compromise the very officials in India that the policy was originally intended to strengthen. Also, when he finally began conditioning food aid shipments on India's foreign policy actions, Johnson placed himself in a spiral of self-defeating diplomatic conflict. The greater his determination to prevail in this conflict, and the more he sought to use "food power" to that end, the more troublesome became India's diplomatic defiance.

Indeed, Indian diplomatic defiance of the United States became one of the more long-standing legacies of the short-tether episode. Throughout 1967 India continued to take actions designed to underscore its foreign policy distance from the United States. In June, India used its seat on the United Nations Security Council, which it had gained the previous fall with Israeli support, to criticize Israel, a close U.S. ally, on the occasion of the Six-Day War in the Middle East. Indira Gandhi also sent birthday greetings to Ho Chi Minh, leader of North Vietnam, and later in the year made a show of attending the fiftieth anniversary celebrations of the Russian Revolution in Moscow.[80] Even with Johnson's passing from power, Indian officials were slow to forgive and loath to forget the short-tether experience. The reputation of the United States suffered permanent damage in India from Johnson's decision to wield food power in India's hour of greatest need.

What are the lessons that can be drawn? The short-tether experience does confirm that under select circumstances a substantial short-run food power advantage can be gained by an exporting country. But the experience also raises doubts about the extent and duration of such an advantage. Lyndon Johnson was originally successful in his use of food power to persuade the Indian government to adopt a variety of internal agricultural and economic policy reforms. This initial success was made possible, however, by an extraordinary combination of favorable circumstances. If India's short-term food import requirements had not been so high, if U.S. surplus grain stocks had not been in decline, if India's development plans and her foreign exchange position had not been in such jeopardy, if Western financial institutions had not joined in the exercise of economic pressure against India, if a full complement of parallel U.S. economic pressures had not been employed, if other food-producing nations had not been so reluctant at the time to replace U.S. food aid shipments, if Lyndon Johnson had not been so determined to employ the full measure of his own personal power to maintain the credible threat of a food aid denial, and if key officials within the Indian government had not already embarked upon the exact program of reform that Johnson had demanded—there is little assurance that the food power policy would have yielded a measurable advantage.

Moreover, despite this combination of exceptionally favorable circumstances, the food power advantage enjoyed by the United States was not enough to produce total compliance with U.S. economic reform demands; it certainly was not sufficient to produce any visible gains for the United States in the diplomatic realm. Rather than yielding in the foreign policy area, the Indian government became markedly more defiant, and the position of those within the Indian government who had been most sympathetic to the United States was eventually weakened. Under the best possible circumstances, therefore, food power was able to produce only a limited range of advantages for the exporting country.

The limited advantage available to an exporter, by means of threatening food aid denial to a poor and dependent nonindustrial country such as India, is one example of the uncertain value of the food weapon. That dubious value is even more obvious in the case that follows, a case of suspended commercial grain sales to a more powerful U.S. food customer, the Soviet Union.

6 Testing Food Power: Embargo on U.S. Grain to the Soviet Union 1980–1981

We now turn to President Carter's attempt to use food power against the Soviet Union in the 1980s. The unhappy experience of the 1980–81 grain embargo helps to refine our understanding of the limited range of foreign policy advantages available to exporters from the use of a real or threatened food export interruption. Lyndon Johnson's *threatened* suspension of *concessional* food assistance to a *poor* importing country (India) was difficult enough for him to manipulate to advantage. Jimmy Carter would learn that the external gains available from an *actual* suspension of *commercial* food sales to a *rich* importing country (the Soviet Union) were close to nonexistent.

When President Carter decided to embargo grain sales to the Soviet Union in January 1980, following the Soviet military invasion of Afghanistan, the potential U.S. food power advantage appeared to be at an all-time high. In the year just ended, Soviet grain production had fallen 21 percent below planning targets, and 25 percent below the record harvest of the preceding year. To compensate for this harvest setback the Soviet Union was making plans to import a record volume of grain, about *twice* the import volume of the last year. And roughly 70 percent of these foreign grain purchases were expected to be made in the United States. Between July 1979 and June 1980, the Soviet Union was expected to import nearly twice as much grain from the United States as it had during the previous twelve-month period, and *more than twice* the volume taken from the United States during the year of the so-called Great Grain Robbery in 1972–73.[1] Without such expanded total grain imports in 1979–80, the feed use of grains within the Soviet Union (and hence meat production) would have to be reduced sharply. As in the case of President Johnson's short-tether policy, Carter's grain embargo policy was initiated at a time of peak potential leverage. If the United States would ever be in a position to exercise food power over the Soviet Union, this would be the time.

Yet not even the modest sorts of gains made by Lyndon Johnson were realized by Jimmy Carter. Carter, unlike Johnson, met frustration at all points in the food power process. Carter confronted the impossible political task of designing an embargo policy that would appear to punish the Soviet Union without also appearing to harm powerful U.S. farm and grain export interests. He was even more frustrated by his inability to secure support for the embargo from other grain exporters around the world. In the end the embargo produced neither the intended effect on the Soviet livestock sector, nor the desired Soviet policy response. How could such an apparent food power advantage have failed to materialize?

U.S. Food Power Potential

As noted in chapter 3, the Soviet Union had allowed itself to become heavily dependent upon imported grain to sustain a steady expansion of livestock herds and hence domestic meat production. Even in 1978– 79, a year that produced a record domestic grain harvest of 237 million tons, the Soviet Union still felt obliged to import more than 15 million tons of grain. Moreover, nearly three-quarters of these foreign grain purchases were made in the United States. When Soviet domestic grain production fell to only 179 million tons in 1979, it was not surprising to see this significant import dependence grow even larger. Brezhnev announced in late September 1979, as the full magnitude of the harvest setback became clear, that livestock inventories should nonetheless be maintained; monthly grain import volumes began to grow.[2] Soon thereafter, the Department of Agriculture forecast that total Soviet grain imports during the 1979–80 July–June year would *more than double* to an unprecedented 34 million tons, close to the presumed limit of what Soviet port and transport facilities could at that time handle.[3]

It was also predicted that the largest share of these anticipated Soviet grain imports, perhaps more than 70 percent, would be purchased from the United States. We may recall that the Soviet Union, despite the decline of détente, had as yet neglected to diversify its grain import dependence away from the United States. In October 1979, only two months before the Afghanistan invasion, U.S. officials had approved a record 25 million tons of grain sales to the Soviet Union and Soviet officials had given every indication of planning their anticipated purchases on the basis of that offer, as they began to sign numerous contracts with private U.S. suppliers.[4] Believing that the United States was unlikely to use food power in an offensive mode, the Soviet Union took no precautions to seek food power in a "defensive" mode. They still favored U.S. grain, especially corn, as an imported livestock feed. They appreciated the competitive prices, the greater convenience, and the proven reliability of U.S. shipments, which could be arranged in bulk with the eager cooperation of U.S.-based private companies.

The anticipated Soviet purchase of 25 million tons of U.S. grain represented only a modest share of total Soviet grain consumption (equal to 231 million tons during the preceding year). But the contribution of grain imports to total consumption was an inadequate measure of Soviet vulnerability to the U.S. food weapon. Soviet grain imports (much like Indian grain imports) performed a discrete and politically sensitive function, making them more valuable than a simple ratio of imports to total consumption might imply. Soviet grain imports were used, almost exclusively, to sustain livestock.[5] The Soviet Union was expected to feed about 128 million tons of grain to livestock during 1979–80 and its anticipated total imports of 34 million tons of foreign grain made up a significant 27 percent of this feed use total. U.S. grain, specifically, was expected to contribute roughly 22 percent to this feed total.[6]

To be sure, this significant Soviet grain trade dependence was counterbalanced by some degree of U.S. grain trade dependence upon the Soviet Union. But U.S. dependence upon continued sales to the Soviet Union was *much less* significant. The share of total U.S. grain exports going to the Soviet Union in calendar year 1979 stood at only 16 percent for wheat and 21.2 percent for corn. As Secretary of Agriculture Bob Bergland explained, "the Soviet Union is not and never has been our most significant export customer."[7] Indeed, because of the anticipated availability of rapidly expanding grain export opportunities in Mexico and in China, the Department of Agriculture could project, at the time of the embargo announcement, that total U.S. grain sales abroad would enjoy uninterrupted growth in 1980, despite the partial suspension of sales to the Soviet Union. Bergland expected total wheat and feedgrain exports to increase, despite the embargo, from 93 million tons to 99 million tons (from $11.4 billion to $14.5 billion) during the 1979–80 fiscal year.

By several criteria, therefore, the grain trade relationship between the United States and the Soviet Union in January 1980 was marked by unusual asymmetry. Never before—and perhaps never again—would the United States be so well positioned to test its presumed food power advantage. Precisely because of this favorable context, the failure in practice of President Carter's grain embargo takes on telling significance.

Objectives and Tactics

From the outset, Carter's grain embargo was marked by strategic confusion and tactical improvisation. In contrast to Lyndon Johnson's short-tether policy, Carter's embargo did not benefit from a period of informed bureaucratic preparation and consideration, nor could its implementation be favored by the same sort of official discretion and public distraction. President Carter was obliged to make his embargo decision quickly and in full public view, in the immediate aftermath of a dramatic and largely unanticipated external provocation, the December 1979 Soviet military invasion of the neutral nation of Afghanistan. Carter, who characterized this Soviet move as potentially "the greatest threat to world peace since World War II," explained at the time that his purpose in responding with a grain embargo was to demonstrate that such provocative Soviet military action could not be made "with impunity."[8] But behind the superficial clarity of this explanation lay a considerable degree of confusion.

The official confusion that hampered Carter's grain embargo policy was symptomatic of a larger problem in U.S. foreign policy toward the Soviet Union: top officials had become deeply divided over the continuing value of détente. But much of the confusion was directly attributable to the troublesome logic of "food power" itself. For an embargo to produce the intended effect on the Soviet Union, at least some sacrifice would have to be asked of U.S. grain producers or of grain-exporting allies. These sacrifices were small by any economic calculation, but they proved politically difficult to command at home, and diplomatically impossible to coax from abroad. In the process of implementing his grain embargo decision, President Carter was tempted to pull his punches in hopes of minimizing these domestic and alliance sacrifices.

Nor was the president's original grain embargo decision a model of well-prepared or well-informed policy making. Soviet military threats to Afghanistan had been a source of presidential concern since May 1979, but the U.S. response had been at first only to "admonish" the Soviets against any direct intervention.[9] It was not until 10 December with Soviet troops massing on the Afghan border that the White House finally initiated a detailed review of presidential options in the event of such an intervention. And only when the invasion began, on Christmas Eve, did these White House discussions finally produce a range of specific policy options, which could be formally considered by the National Security Council. At this initial stage, the two "extreme" options (doing nothing, or responding with military action) were immediately set aside. A third option—to impose economic and cultural exchange sanctions—was selected as the most suitable immediate response.[10]

Both the State Department and the National Security Council had by this time drawn up a list of possible sanctions—numbering some forty in all.[11] Carter recalls, "[A]n analysis of possible sanctions revealed that [a grain embargo] was the only one which would significantly affect the Soviet economy."[12] He quickly came to favor such an embargo on grain sales, despite "strenuous objections" and "strong opposition" from a number of his key policy advisers, including Vice-President Walter Mondale, Stuart Eizenstat, and Jody Powell. As the president noted at the time, he wanted his economic sanctions against the Soviet Union "to go the maximum degree." He wrote in his diary, "This is the most serious international development that has occurred since I have been President and, unless the Soviets recognize that it has been counterproductive for them, we will face additional serious problems with invasions or subversion in the future."[13]

Curiously enough, the president was not pressured by his hard-line foreign policy advisers on the National Security Council to impose a grain embargo on the Soviet Union. Zbigniew Brzezinski, Carter's special assistant for National Security Affairs, was concerned about future relations with the Soviet Union, and argued less vociferously for punitive economic measures than did the State Department. At an initial National Security Council session on Afghanistan sanctions on 30 December it was Secretary of State Cyrus Vance who took the lead in advocating a deep cut in U.S. grain sales.[14] Anticipating the president's decision, however, Brzezinski had by then already asked the CIA to prepare an estimate of the potential impact of a grain embargo on the Soviet Union.

It is of some interest that Brzezinski did not at first seek a parallel impact estimate from the Department of Agriculture.[15] Former Defense Secretary Harold Brown later expressed the prevailing attitude of the foreign policy community on Department of Agriculture estimates: "[The Department] was speaking for farmers, so their numbers might have an unconscious bias."[16] To have asked the Department of Agriculture for an early estimate would also have increased the risk of a damaging information leak to the farm community or to private trade groups, possibly producing panic sales in commodity futures markets or a preemptive storm of domestic political protest. Just the same, top agriculture officials had become aware that a grain embargo was under White House consideration, and promptly initiated their own independent examination of its potential impact on the Soviet Union. This study, initiated on 31 December, concluded that a U.S. grain embargo might be a major inconvenience to the Soviet Union but probably would not inflict serious damage. It anticipated that a U.S. embargo, on all sales above the annual 8 million tons guaranteed to the Soviets under the terms of the 1975 long-term agreement, would produce in 1980 no more than a 1–3 percent drop in Soviet meat production. Agriculture Secretary Bergland provided this assessment to Vice-President Mondale on the evening of 2 January and to the Cabinet on 3 January. This was not enough, however, to discourage the president, who reached his own decision to impose a grain embargo on the afternoon of 2 January.[17]

Carter had made his decision on the basis of a far more optimistic damage estimate, prepared in haste by CIA. Working from a variety of mistaken assumptions (including an assumption that the United States would *not* provide the 8 million tons guaranteed to the Soviet Union by the 1975 long-term agreement), the CIA predicted a reduction in Soviet meat output as high as 20 percent. It was with this misleading estimate in hand that President Carter decided to go forward. By March 1980, these CIA estimates of the impact of the embargo were adjusted sharply downward (to a mere 2–3 percent reduction range, in tacit agreement with the Department of Agriculture) but by then the president was firmly committed to his embargo decision.[18]

In fact, Carter might have gone ahead with his decision even without an exaggerated CIA estimate of the impact on Soviet meat production. President Carter was under heavy pressure at the time to demonstrate to his domestic audience a capacity for "strength" and "leadership." The continuing Soviet arms buildup, a sequence of unanswered Soviet bloc military actions in Angola, Ethiopia, Yemen, and Kampuchea, a furor earlier in the fall over the presence of a Soviet "combat brigade" in Cuba, and, finally, the humiliation of the November embassy seizure in Teheran—all of these events had combined by the end of 1979 to produce public demands for stronger presidential action to defend vital U.S. interests abroad.[19] Had the president in this context allowed a record volume of U.S. grain sales to the Soviet Union to continue after the Afghanistan invasion, election-year challengers in both parties would have found an easy target for attack. With the Iowa Democratic party caucuses less than a month away, the president's political dilemma was that much more difficult. With Iowa in mind, White House Press Secretary Jody Powell had sent Carter a memorandum advising him against the embargo. Still, had Carter hesitated to embargo grain exports on the eve of the Iowa caucuses, his critics would have charged that he was weakening U.S. foreign policy at a moment of crisis, in a self-serving attempt to solicit the votes of a few Iowa corn growers.

As one further domestic political incentive to act, the International Longshoremen's Association was beginning to contemplate a direct "food power" action of its own, in the form of a preemptive refusal to load any more U.S. grain on ships bound for the Soviet Union. Anticipating such an action, Carter understandably wanted to be seen taking the lead rather than following. For any one of these reasons, an embargo announcement actually held out some short-run domestic political attractions to the president, apart from its uncertain long-run impact on Soviet meat production.

Harming Soviet meat production was not, in any event, Carter's only concern, as evidenced by his last-minute decision to *exempt* from the embargo the 8 million tons of wheat and corn promised to the Soviet Union for each October–September year under the terms of the 1975 long-term agreement. Although this agreement had been concluded under very different diplomatic circumstances and by a Republican administration, Carter was persuaded by legal advisers not to violate its terms to avoid weakening the credibility of other such executive agreements. Credibility with U.S. farmers, who valued the 1975 agreement as their principal guarantee of minimum sales to the Soviet Union, was also a concern. Whatever his motives, by continuing these guaranteed sales Carter diminished in several ways the chance that the embargo would result in substantial punitive damage to the Soviet Union.

The direct consequence of meeting this annual 8 million ton commitment was to ensure that the Soviet Union would be able to import, during the sixteen-month period of the embargo, about 10.5 million tons of U.S. grain that might have otherwise been denied. The first 2.5 million tons of these guaranteed imports were especially vital, as they arrived between January and April 1980, just when Soviet import needs were acute, before the peak availability of non-U.S. new crop exports from the southern hemisphere and before the beginning of the summer grain harvest in the Soviet Union.[20] The second 8 million ton portion then became available to the Soviet Union beginning 1 October 1980, at an equally critical juncture. The Soviet Union by then had suffered the misfortune of a second bad grain harvest, had drawn down its own internal stocks nearly to exhaustion, and had already purchased most of the uncommitted supplies of non-U.S. grain available on the world market. Without this second installment of 8 million tons of guaranteed grain supplies from the United States, Soviet live-stock inventories would have been far more difficult to sustain through the winter of 1980–81.

Honoring the long-term sales agreement also weakened the embargo in a less direct way. With 8 million tons of U.S. grain still being sold to the Soviet Union every twelve months, U.S. officials found it far more difficult to persuade other exporters to exercise restraint. Why should allies agree to sell any less to the Soviet Union than the alliance leader? The continued annual sale of 8 million tons of U.S. grain to the Soviet Union also complicated the task of explaining the president's action at home. The Longshoremen's Union, among others, was not satisfied with a "partial" sales suspension, and sought for a time to discontinue all further grain shipments to the Soviet Union by means of a cargo-loading boycott, which began five days after the president's grain embargo announcement.

From the start, therefore, President Carter found himself torn between too many objectives, and as a consequence pulling too many punches, in the design of his grain embargo strategy. Unwilling to violate the terms of an existing executive agreement, eager to seize upon the embargo in part for appearance sake, and ambivalent about his own larger foreign policy purposes, Carter selected food power tactics that might have seemed expedient in the short run but were ill-suited to provide substantial foreign policy advantages in the long run. It did not take long for the embargo policy to begin breaking down at several vital points in the food power process.

Domestic Objections in the United States

It could be argued that the grain embargo failed most conspicuously within the domestic political system; President Ronald Reagan lifted the embargo in April 1981, apparently in fulfillment of a 1980 campaign promise to U.S. grain producers. In doing so he denied the embargo an opportunity to produce some possible punitive effects later in 1981, after the expiration of the 1975 long-term guarantee and after yet a third sequential harvest setback in the Soviet Union.

In fact, the termination of the embargo in April 1981 was not necessary for the continued expansion of Soviet grain imports that year or for the survival of Soviet livestock herds. By the time it was finally lifted at home the embargo had lost its effectiveness abroad. The Soviet Union already had gained access to sufficient quantities of non-U.S. grains to guarantee a continued expansion of its total grain imports, even if the U.S. embargo had remained in place. Indeed, knowledge that the embargo was crumbling abroad was one of the more powerful arguments for finally ending it. Compared to the more short-lived export suspension of 1975, which President Ford was forced to discontinue after only a few months, the 1980–81 grain embargo probably deserves credit for surviving *as long as it did,* in the face of growing domestic opposition.

Carter's embargo policy endured because the president's legal authority to suspend grain exports (for reasons of "foreign policy" or "national security") was unambiguous, under the provisions of the 1979 Export Administration Act.[21] The mood of the Congress in January 1980 was one of approval and deference in any case. Senator Adlai E. Stevenson convened hearings on the embargo on 22 January, the first day of the new congressional session, and found the tentative mood of those present to be one of bipartisan acceptance.

This initial absence of congressional criticism may be traced, in part, to an element of surprise. Grain producers, by 1980, were well practiced at opposing embargoes undertaken for domestic economic policy reasons, but not those undertaken for national security or foreign policy reasons. After President Ford's 1975 grain export suspension, which was triggered by food price inflation at home, U.S. producers inserted an "embargo insurance" provision into the 1977 Food and Agriculture Act guaranteeing them a generous federal crop loan rate at 90 percent of parity in the event of any future export suspension undertaken for reasons of tight domestic supplies. This provision had generated a false sense of security among farmers; it did nothing to protect them from an embargo undertaken for reasons of national security or foreign policy.22

Beyond the question of legal authority and congressional endorsement, President Carter also enjoyed a broad base of domestic popular support for his embargo decision. Even the general farm organizations at first withheld criticism, not wishing to appear unpatriotic. The American Farm Bureau Federation endorsed the embargo at its annual convention in mid-January, and the National Farmers Union said it would not criticize the action so long as the administration took necessary actions to protect farmers who might be hurt. Initial domestic criticism came almost entirely from presidential candidates jockeying for a stronger showing in the Iowa caucuses, scheduled for 21 January. All of the president's challengers in Iowa, Republicans and Democrats alike, with the exception of Congressman John B. Anderson, came out against the embargo. But Carter's strong two-to-one victory over Kennedy in the Iowa caucuses, along with Anderson's better-than-expected showing, confounded these early embargo critics, and put the issue to rest for some months to come. It was clear that the embassy seizure in Teheran and the Soviet invasion of Afghanistan had triggered a temporary surge of popular support for the White House. Grain producers and traders who were privately opposed to the embargo were forced to await a more opportune moment to challenge the president's policy.

Rather than seeking to terminate the embargo outright, domestic grain producers and trading companies had to be content, at first, to seek compensation for the effects of the embargo. In this they succeeded remarkably well. Secretary Bergland had warned President Carter that farm support for the embargo would collapse without special measures to support commodity prices and to protect those traders holding embargoed export contracts. Analysts in the White House and the Department of Agriculture had calculated that without any compensatory steps, the embargo might produce a decline of about 15 cents per bushel in corn and other feedgrain prices received by U.S. farmers, and a 25 cent decline in wheat and soybean prices, resulting in a $3 billion reduction in farm income overall, as well as substantial financial losses to those private trading companies with whom the Soviet Union had contracted to purchase wheat and corn.23 Carter promised Bergland, Mondale, and other embargo critics that he would "do whatever was necessary to maintain grain prices and to compensate the farmers for any loss."24 Congress, as it turned out, would accept nothing less. At an early round of hearings, House Agriculture Committee Chairman Thomas Foley had said, "The practical question isn't whether the President's action should have been taken, but what is necessary to protect farmers."[25] Bills to aid producers, ranging from lavish emergency loan programs to plans for increasing commodity loan rates to 90 percent of parity, surfaced immediately. In order to forestall such troublesome legislation, as well as to maintain support for the embargo, the administration improvised its own set of costly protective and compensatory actions.

First, to avert a panic sale of grain futures contracts, a two-day suspension of all futures trading in grains and oilseeds was announced. Prices still dropped sharply when futures markets were reopened but recovered within a few weeks as other compensatory measures took hold.

Second, to minimize financial losses to export companies, the CCC offered to purchase all grain, in excess of the 8 million tons minimum, which had already been contracted for shipment to the Soviet Union at the time of the embargo announcement. Under the terms of an extraordinary "exporter's agreement" (first concluded in the immediate aftermath of the embargo announcement and formally approved in mid-February by a dozen private exporting firms), the CCC proceeded to assume outstanding contracts for a total of 4.3 million tons of wheat and 8.9 million tons of corn, as well as 1.2 million tons of soybeans and soybean products.[26] In part because of a severe late-summer drought in 1980, the CCC eventually was able to "retender" into the domestic market all such contracts at weighted average prices (for wheat and corn) *above* the preembargo level.[27]

Third, the CCC also used open market purchases to support farm prices for wheat and corn. Between January and June 1980, in purchases made either from county grain elevators or directly from farmers, the CCC bought approximately 4 million tons of corn and an equivalent amount of wheat. At one point in April, wheat was purchased at 20–40 cents per bushel above the cash market price.

Fourth, the Department of Agriculture undertook a considerable expansion of the "farmer-held" grain reserve, announcing an increase in loan levels and waiving first-year interest costs to attract wider participation in the reserve, and increasing release and call prices to move these reserve supplies farther away from the open market.

Next, in late July the president announced, as an additional price support measure, a further increase in reserve release and call prices, and in commodity loan rates for wheat, soybeans, and foodgrains.

Finally, the administration announced a program to encourage, through tax incentives, loans, and loan guarantees, an expansion of "gasohol" production, as one more means to tighten the domestic market for grains. Grain exports to customers other than the Soviet Union were also more actively promoted, through an expansion of the CCC's Commercial Risk Assurance Program.

The combined cost of these protective domestic measures was estimated at $3.4 billion for fiscal year 1980. The Government Accounting Office in a report issued upon termination of the embargo in 1981 concluded that some of these measures had been expensive, excessive, and unnecessary.[28] But U.S. grain producers held a different view on the matter, and made themselves increasingly difficult to satisfy.

A panic sale of grain futures contracts had been successfully averted in the immediate aftermath of the embargo announcement, but average prices received by farmers for wheat, corn, and soybeans nonetheless declined between February and April 1980, causing measurable hardship to those farmers then holding crops. In part this decline was set off by the prospect of a record world grain harvest early in 1980, but distressed U.S. farmers found it politically more convenient to blame the president's embargo. This three-month price decline dramatically reversed when bad weather arrived in June (average prices received by U.S. farmers for wheat, corn, and soybeans rose throughout the prolonged summer drought of 1980), but it was too late for Carter: patience with the embargo on the part of producers was now exhausted. The American Farm Bureau Federation withdrew its formal support in April, charging that the administration had failed in its promise to protect farmers from adverse price effects. Support within the administration had also begun to weaken; in May, Secretary Bergland sent a private memorandum to the president recommending an end to the embargo.[29] Bergland cited the lack of cooperation by other grain exporters abroad, but his chief concern was the heavy criticism his department was now encountering from farm groups at home.

The first of several congressional efforts to force an actual termination of the embargo came when Republican Senator Robert Dole introduced legislation to that effect in June, with bipartisan support from three other cosponsors on the Senate agriculture committee. Dole argued that the embargo was "falling apart and should be ended before damage gets beyond repair."[30] This legislation went nowhere, but it helped to trigger a more fateful political decision by Republican presidential candidate Ronald Reagan. On 3 July Reagan characterized the embargo as having "hobbled American farmers," and promised, if elected, "to fully assess our national security and foreign policy and agricultural trade needs to determine how best to terminate yet another of the inequitable and ineffective policies of the Carter administration."[31]

Carter was not moved by such pressures. While speaking to a "town meeting" rally in Merced, California, on the day after the Reagan statement, he said, "I'm not going to lift the farm restraints on the Soviet Union in the foreseeable future. . . . I believe it's important for our nation to make sacrifices, if necessary, in order to stop aggression overseas." Carter went on to place a previously unstated condition upon termination of the embargo—that the Soviet Union "make some tangible move" to remove its troops from Afghanistan. Still later, at the Democratic National Convention in August, Carter tried to ridicule Reagan's opposition to the embargo alongside his less than forceful position on the Olympic boycott: "He [Reagan] does not seem to know what to do with the Russians," said Carter. "He is not sure if he wants to feed them, play with them, or fight with them."[32]

Carter had good reason to believe that the domestic opposition to his embargo was unlikely to spread far. In late July the House of Representatives had turned back several attempts by Midwestern members to legislate an end to the embargo, by decisive votes of 267 to 149, 279 to 135, and 414 to 1. Then in early August, the administration had been able to counter its critics with a well-crafted report prepared in the Department of Agriculture, detailing the many problems then facing Soviet livestock producers and attributing these problems "at least in part" to the U.S. grain sales suspension. This attribution was widely quoted and repeated, at times out of context, by supporters of the president when the Senate finally debated the embargo in September.[33] It had become clear that the Soviet Union was suffering its second bad grain harvest in a row, and those who had doubted the success of the embargo until then were momentarily persuaded that it might at last produce results. With U.S. grain prices reaching a new high (due to the summer drought and record grain exports to non-Soviet customers), the plea of a few farm state legislators to lift the embargo now seemed much less compelling.[34]

Until the November election, President Carter was never in any immediate danger of being forced by his domestic critics into a termination of the embargo. Illinois Senator Adlai E. Stevenson captured the mood of many legislators at the time, in his belief that a forced end to the embargo would only "humiliate the nation and embarrass its President." Stevenson lamented the damage he saw being done by the embargo to Illinois grain producers, and he questioned its effectiveness as a means to punish the Soviet Union, but he nonetheless argued against forcing its termination: "[O]ne mistake does not deserve another."[35]

Jimmy Carter was swamped in the November election, losing to Ronald Reagan in all but six of the fifty states. Farmers and traders were jubilant, expecting that president-elect Reagan would immediately reaffirm his pledge to terminate the embargo. Even then they met frustration, however, as Reagan began to grow evasive, describing the embargo as something worthy of "a great deal of study." And once in office he appeared to stall, delaying his final decision to lift the embargo until 24 April 1981. For a period of three months as president, Reagan decided, in effect, to keep the Carter embargo in place.

Fear of aggravating domestic food price inflation was one reason for his delay in lifting the embargo. Chicago grain analysts had predicted in January that an end to the embargo could lead to a new surge in wheat, corn, and meat prices in addition to the 12–15 percent increase already forecast for 1981. It was more for reasons of foreign policy that Reagan moved so slowly on the embargo issue, however. With Soviet military forces poised for a possible move into Poland early in 1981, and with the new president being urged by Secretary of State Haig to strike an uncompromising posture toward the Soviet Union, an immediate termination of the embargo, without Soviet concessions, was at first judged unwise.[36]

Whatever thoughts Reagan had of seeking some concession from the Soviet Union in return for lifting the grain embargo were in the end never pursued, as the best Reagan could manage was to delay the termination until April, gaining three months' time in which to send "signals" in all other areas that the thrust of his policy toward the Soviet Union would be one of firmness after all. Even this was a noteworthy achievement, given the intensity of farm state feelings. Reagan finally yielded, not only to fulfill his campaign pledge but to gain support from farm state congressmen for his cost-conscious domestic spending policies. At least three Republicans on the Senate budget committee who had earlier voted to defeat the president's budget proposal switched their votes immediately after the embargo was lifted.[37]

In all, it is noteworthy that powerful domestic grain producers and traders, firmly opposed to the embargo, were unable for *sixteen months* to bring it to an end. Had Jimmy Carter won his bid for reelection, the embargo might have continued indefinitely. As with Johnson's short-tether experience, the impression could be gained that a determined president seeking to exercise food power can successfully manage even a commercial embargo policy, within the domestic political arena, at tolerable political cost.

In fact, this would be a mistaken impression. One reason the embargo survived as long as it did at home was that it had long since collapsed abroad, thereby opening up wider options for U.S. exporters. When allied grain exporters declined to support the embargo, and began to redirect a larger share of their own grain sales to the Soviet Union, they initiated a dramatic shift in world grain trade patterns, which in turn ensured an abundance of alternative export opportunities, at least in the short run, for U.S. producers and exporters. If U.S. allies abroad had provided greater support for the embargo (if they had *not* shifted a larger share of their own exports toward the Soviet Union) these alternative export opportunities for U.S. grain producers might not have opened up, and domestic political resistance to the embargo might have developed much sooner, and to greater effect.

Response of the International Food-Trading System

When the grain embargo was lifted in April 1981, it is significant that purchasing agents from the Soviet Union did not immediately rush in to exploit their renewed access to the U.S. market. They had by then managed to fill all of their existing grain import needs from non-U.S. suppliers. From the Soviet vantage point, the embargo had lost its bite at least a year earlier, as soon as a number of other Western exporters had begun to supply grain. It was within the international grain-trading system, where it proved impossible for the United States to control alternative sources of supply, that the embargo met its downfall.

In the process of making the embargo decision, U.S. officials spent remarkably little time considering the probability that other Western suppliers would step in to meet Soviet grain import needs. Statements made at the time betray an unusual degree of official confusion on this matter. While briefing the press before the president's 4 January 1980 embargo announcement, White House Press Secretary Jody Powell was asked whether the U.S. embargo would be supported by other exporters. "Yes for the EC [European Community], Canada and Australia," Powell replied. When asked directly if Argentina would cooperate, Powell stated erroneously, "They don't count for these products."[38] Carter's announcement speech was likewise confused and misleading in its references to other grain exporters. The president offered a brief but hopeful statement on allied cooperation: "After consultation with other principal grain-exporting nations, I am confident that they will not replace these quantities of grain by additional shipments on their own part to the Soviet Union."[39] In fact, Carter was in no position to offer such reassurances, as high-level consultations had not yet been undertaken.[40] About a week before his speech the State Department did instruct U.S. embassies to inform foreign ministries of the economic sanctions—including a grain embargo—which were then under consideration in Washington, to ascertain the likelihood of international support. But such low-level inquiries had produced little response. Not until the evening of 4 January were direct contacts sought on the specific question of a grain embargo. And these contacts were also undertaken at a low level—by the associate administrator of the Department of Agriculture's Foreign Agriculture Service. The secretary of agriculture and his principal deputies busied themselves notifying *domestic* farm leaders and grain traders, another indication of the inward-looking preoccupation of most U.S. participants in the embargo process.

Undertaken at the last minute by low-level officials, the consultations with other exporters probably did more harm than good. Among those officials who could be contacted on short notice in Europe, Canada, and Australia, none responded with an immediate commitment to cooperate. Efforts to reach ranking officials in Argentina failed entirely; the leaders of the junta in Buenos Aires learned about the grain embargo in the newspaper the next morning.

Obviously, there was a practical limit to the range of consultations that could have preceded an embargo announcement. An element of surprise was necessary to ensure maximum advantage over the Soviet Union, and also to preempt political opposition and to avoid premature disruption of commercial markets at home. Even so, the consultations undertaken with other grain-exporting countries were too little as well as too late. Prior notification at the head-of-state level might not have been enough to obtain the full cooperation of other exporters, but without this diplomatic courtesy the likelihood of full cooperation was nil from the start. This failure to take steps that might have improved the success of the embargo abroad suggests that a central purpose of the embargo was to satisfy, with largely symbolic sanctions policies, a restless political audience at home.

Belatedly, after the embargo decision had been publicly announced, a more energetic effort was initiated to secure the cooperation of other Western grain-exporting nations. On 6 January Secretary of Agriculture Bergland called for a meeting of sub-Cabinet-level officials from the European Community, Canada, Australia, and Argentina. On the eve of this meeting, officials from Canada, Australia, and the European Community came forward with a series of public statements interpreted by the White House as promises of support. Prime Minister Joe Clark of Canada was particularly forthright, stating on 11 January that his Cabinet had decided "It will not be business as usual [with the Soviet Union]. . . . No quantity [of Canadian grain] above the normal and traditional amounts will be sent."[41] Clark recognized that passing up the new Soviet sales opportunities that had been created by the embargo would be costly to Canadian grain producers, and went so far as to promise them financial compensation. The European Community commission in Brussels offered its formal support, agreeing not to undertake larger-than-normal sales of cereals from Europe. Britain wanted the European Community to go further by restricting sales of butter, meat, and sugar as well as grain, but France, the major European food exporter, argued that food trade sanctions should not go beyond those of the United States. Still, the French gave an early impression of supporting the embargo on grain. President Giscard d'Estaing explained, "The Soviets have broken the principles of détente. The actions of the United States as a superpower are justified. France will not substitute embargoed items, and will make no grain sales."[42] Similar public assurances were received from Australia.

In Buenos Aires on 10 January the military government of Jorge Rafaél Videla had issued an eleven-paragraph communiqué announcing plans to send a representative to the meeting, scheduled for 12 January in Washington. But it warned it would not participate "in decisions or punitive actions that have been adopted without our prior intervention or that come from decision-making centers not of our country."[43] With this troublesome Argentine statement as its prelude, the meeting in Washington led to a confusing, ultimately disappointing result. Undersecretary of Agriculture Dale Hathaway, after chairing the meeting, announced that "there was general agreement these governments would not directly or indirectly replace the grain the United States would have shipped to the Soviet Union." Hathaway even quoted a statement written by the Argentine representative subscribing to this viewpoint. Upon its being monitored in Buenos Aires, however, this statement was promptly denied; four days later, on 16 January the Argentine minister of agriculture stated outright that his country would not participate in the U.S. embargo.[44]

Argentina's critical decision not to support the embargo was based on a good deal more than its displeasure over not having been consulted. First, Argentina was understandably constrained by the much larger relative dependence of its economy on grain exports. Argentina could not as easily afford to play "stop and go" with its commercial grain exports, which accounted for about 30 percent of total export earnings, compared with only 8 percent of total export earnings for the United States. And at the time of the embargo announcement, roughly 15 percent of Argentina's grain exports had been going to the Soviet Union. Total Argentine trade with the Soviet Union in 1979 had reached $470 million, so this was not a market to be lightly sacrificed.[45]

Argentina had a diplomatic as well as a commercial interest in the continued expansion of its trade ties with the Soviet Union in 1980. Despite conspicuous ideological differences, these two regimes found they had a common cause in resisting U.S. human rights policies. President Carter had repeatedly annoyed the Argentine leadership with his disparaging references to its human rights record (which he judged "abominable"), and so the junta felt little obligation to do favors for Washington.

The greatest enticement for Argentine grain exporters was simply the higher price that Soviet purchasing agents were suddenly willing to pay. In the short run, Argentina could not respond to these enticements by expanding the *total volume* of its grain exports, as it carried no reserves and its maturing crop was just then suffering from a significant drought (which would eventually reduce total production from the preceding year's level by more than 40 percent). In 1980, in fact, total Argentine grain exports actually fell by nearly half.[46] Nevertheless, Argentina could be persuaded, by these generous price offerings, to redirect a substantial portion of its reduced grain exports away from traditional customers and toward the Soviet Union. The Soviet

Union wasted no time in offering such prices. A high-level Soviet trade mission—led by Viktor Pershin, the director of Exportkhleb—visited Buenos Aires at the end of January and contracted for grain deliveries directly with Argentine grain cooperatives at prices well above those offered by Argentina's traditional foreign customers. At a time when Argentine wheat normally would have been priced $4 to $10 per ton *below* U.S. wheat, the price in Buenos Aires suddenly moved up to more than $23 per ton *above* the U.S. export price. By late April, due to Soviet price premiums, corn prices in Buenos Aires had risen to about $150 per ton (compared with U.S. corn at $112 per ton), and Argentine grain sorghum was selling for export at $145 per ton (compared with the U.S. export price of $117 per ton).[47]

The Argentine government tried to argue that its high-priced sales to the Soviet Union were simply the result of "free market competition." It was true that the junta had lifted Peronist controls on grain prices some years earlier and was no longer playing such a dominant role in the control of grain exports, but Argentina's response to the high prices offered by Exportkhleb was nonetheless a conscious policy choice by the junta. At the time of Pershin's visit to Buenos Aires the Argentine government negotiated a formal agreement with the Soviet Union to ensure sales of at least 4.5 million tons of corn, sorghum, and soybeans in 1980, in addition to the 1.6 million tons of wheat that had already been sold. These officially guaranteed sales covered no less than 75 percent of all Argentine corn then available for export.

By June 1980, the premiums offered by the Soviet Union for Argentine corn reached their peak level, at 83 cents per bushel, pushing prices 30 percent above the U.S. export price. Thereafter, with the Soviet Union's own summer harvest soon to begin, with an additional 8 million tons of U.S. grain scheduled to be available after 1 October, and with a permanent redirection of Argentine trade accomplished, Soviet purchasing agents felt less need to pay such exorbitant prices. Argentina now wanted its larger Soviet sales to continue, even at a lower price, because its traditional customers had begun to fill their needs elsewhere—primarily from the United States. After full recovery of Argentine grain production in 1981, total exports to the Soviet Union thus continued to increase, to more than 40 percent above the 1980 level.

In fact, both Argentina and the Soviet Union were eager to maintain this expanded volume of trade, with or without an eventual termination of the U.S. embargo. During a visit to Argentina by Vice-Minister of Foreign Trade Alexei Manzhula in April 1980, the two governments concluded a *long-term* bilateral grain trade agreement (signed in July) ensuring for the next five years annual exports to the Soviet Union of at least 4 million tons of feedgrains, and 0.5 million tons of soybeans.[48] For a nation such as Argentina, as yet lacking in the means to store large quantities of grain between harvests, a five-year guarantee of annual exports at this level was just the incentive needed by producers to go full-speed ahead with expanded production. And it was precisely this further expansion of Argentine grain production and sales to the Soviet Union that did so much to blunt the impact of the U.S. embargo during its second winter season early in 1981, after the Soviet Union's second poor harvest. While harvesting a bumper grain crop between January and June 1981, Argentina shipped an unprecedented 8.5 million tons directly to the Soviet Union. This was more than *twice* the export level of the January–June 1980 period, and nearly *ten times* the preembargo shipment rate.[49] Knowledge that these vastly expanded Argentine grain shipments would be available during the first six months of 1981 was important to Soviet planners, who had exhausted their own reserve stocks, who were just then depleting their latest 8 million ton allotment from the United States, and who therefore might otherwise have been forced into deeper livestock feed cutbacks. It was because the Soviet Union enjoyed access to so much Argentine grain during the early months of 1981 that it felt no need to make any additional purchases from the United States when the embargo was finally lifted in April. Significant Soviet purchases of U.S. grain were not resumed until late summer 1981, when large shipments from Argentina had been completed, and when the Soviet Union had become aware of its *third* consecutive bad harvest.

During the sixteen-month period of the embargo between January 1980 and April 1981, Argentina exported 11.1 million tons of grain to the Soviet Union. These exports were more than a minor or isolated blow to the embargo, because Argentina's success in taking commercial advantage of the embargo inspired others to follow suit. The grain export policies of Australia, Canada, and the European Community never became so damaging as those of Argentina, but each of these nations would be inspired to reduce its own support for the embargo in due course.

Among this group of allied grain exporters, Australia showed the least restraint. Australia could not claim to be so heavily dependent upon its foreign grain sales as Argentina, as grains made up only about

13 percent of its total export earnings. Nor was Australia traditionally a heavy supplier of grain to the Soviet Union. During the last two complete marketing years before the embargo, Australian grain exports to the Soviet Union had averaged annually only 0.2 million tons (less than 3 percent of Australia's total grain exports). When Australia proceeded to increase these exports severalfold in 1980 and 1981 while the U.S. grain embargo was in place, it was clearly rejecting U.S. requests that it hold sales within "normal and traditional" bounds.

During the first calendar year of the embargo, grain shipments from Australia to the Soviet Union rose from the 1979 level of 1.2 million tons to an unprecedented level of 4.3 million tons. Australian officials could point out that most of these expanded grain shipments had been contracted before President Carter's surprise embargo announcement, a fortunate coincidence that was used to maximum advantage. During the first months of 1980, simply by refusing to cancel any of these preembargo contracts, the Australian government could claim to be supporting the U.S. embargo by making no *new* sales, while all the time exporting to the Soviet Union larger volumes of grain than ever before in its history.[50] Prime Minister Malcolm Fraser was not eager to antagonize the United States, but found himself under intense pressure from the Australian Wheat Board (AWB) not only to deliver on all preembargo contracts, but to further expand grain sales to the Soviet Union. In May, therefore, the Australian government announced that it would authorize a limited number of *new* export contracts for sales of feedgrains—barley, oats, and grain sorghum—to the Soviet Union. These sales, in combination with 2.3 million tons of wheat sales to the Soviet Union already under contract for delivery through July, would bring Australia's total July–June 1979–80 grain shipments to the Soviet Union to an unprecedented level of approximately 4 million tons.

Fraser delayed for as long as possible any public decision on expanded sales for the 1980–81 year; U.S. officials continued to express hope that Australia would show restraint. "I've talked with the Australians and they're going to hold the Russian's feet to the fire," said Secretary Bergland in late June. The AWB was still holding relatively large quantities of unsold grain, however, so it argued that its unusually large 1979–80 sales to the Soviets ought to be established as the *new* "normal and traditional" level and therefore allowed to continue in the coming year. In July 1980 the Australian government finally yielded to this argument, and the AWB went ahead immediately to arrange new sales of an additional 2 million tons of wheat to the

Soviet Union, for delivery between August 1980 and May 1981.[51] U.S. officials accepted these new Soviet–Australian wheat contracts with a certain resignation. Although Australian grain shipments to the Soviet Union in the July–June 1980–81 year would total 2.9 million tons, once again well above the preembargo level, the White House decided not to challenge in public the dubious assertion that these sales were still within the "normal and traditional" range.[52]

As Argentina and Australia went ahead with larger-than-normal postembargo grain sales to the Soviet Union, pressure on Canada to do likewise became irresistible. Unlike Australia, Canada had not signed a new round of export contracts with the Soviet Union at the time the embargo was announced. It had been waiting for an expected rise in export prices in the new year. Simply to maintain a normal pace of grain sales to the Soviet Union, Canada was therefore obliged to undertake new sales within a month after having pledged not to take advantage of the embargo. In February 1980 the Canadian Wheat Board (CWB) announced plans to sell an additional 2 million tons of grain to the Soviet Union during the balance of the marketing year that would end in June. Although these sales were denounced by some in the United States as early evidence of a Canadian betrayal, they brought total Canadian grain exports to the Soviet Union during the July–June 1979–80 year to only 3.5 million tons, a sales volume somewhat above the average of the three previous years, but actually *below* the volume recorded following earlier Soviet harvest failures in both 1975–76 and 1972–73. In fact, the ratio of Canada's total wheat exports going to the Soviet Union fell in 1979–80, during the first year of the embargo, from 14 percent to 12 percent.[53]

This early Canadian restraint began to weaken after the defeat of Prime Minister Clark's Progressive Conservative government and its replacement by the Liberal government of Prime Minister Pierre Trudeau, who felt less personally committed to supporting the embargo. Moreover, by early summer, Canadian grain producers were becoming more vocal in their resentment, noting estimates that unrestrained sales to the Soviet Union could have boosted prices by as much as 75 cents a bushel.[54] Official support for the embargo had eroded by early July, when Hazen Argue, the minister in the Trudeau Cabinet responsible for the CWB, announced that Canada would have to seek a "change in the rules" governing its grain exports during the new crop year to begin on 1 August. Canada, said Argue, should be credited with normal and traditional yearly sales to the Soviet Union of "up to 5 million tons or more" of grain. To be sure, Canada had supplied the Soviet Union with 5.1 million tons of grain on one occasion in 1972–73, but U.S. officials felt it was hardly accurate to characterize this one-time-only record volume as "normal and traditional."[55]

Early in August, despite U.S. misgivings, Canada went forward with an authorization of new grain sales to the Soviet Union at an annual level of roughly 5 million tons, to be limited mostly by Canada's own constrained handling capacity, and by the uncertain final result of the summer crop. The government still claimed that it was standing by the earlier pledge to hold sales to normal and traditional levels, but for all practical purposes it had abandoned its original position of support for the embargo.

Canada did not formally announce its withdrawal from the embargo until late November, by which time Carter's election defeat appeared to render any future Canadian support for the embargo meaningless. Upon withdrawal it simultaneously announced that a new sale of 2.1 million tons of wheat and barley had just been arranged, pushing Canada's 1980–81 grain exports to the Soviet Union well *above* the 5 million ton level. The justification offered for abandoning the embargo in this fashion was a U.S. decision, made public the month before, to sign a long-term bilateral grain trade agreement with China. Canada (along with Australia) had long coveted the Chinese grain market, and resented this incursion of U.S. wheat sales seemingly occasioned by the embargo. With the United States unloading its embargoed grain in Canada's export markets, why should Canada any longer show restraint? Equally upsetting to Canadian grain producers had been the October resumption of U.S. long-term agreement sales to the Soviet Union. If U.S. producers could continue to sell 8 million tons of grain to the Soviet Union every year, why should Canadian producers restrict themselves to any less?

Over the course of the entire July–June 1980–81 year, Canadian grain exports to the Soviet Union would actually reach a record-breaking level of 6.8 million tons. Considering specifically the sixteen-month period of the embargo, Canadian grain exports to the Soviet Union totaled 6.5 million tons, and two-thirds of these exports were recorded during the second half of the 1980 calendar year, helping to sustain the Soviet Union in the aftermath of their second bad grain harvest.[56] The early restraint shown by the Canadian government was not sustained. By 1981 Canada had emerged second only to Argentina as a supplier of larger-than-usual quantities of grain to the Soviet Union, further undermining the punitive potential of the embargo.

Argentina, Australia, and Canada were by far the largest suppliers of non-U.S. grain to the Soviet Union during the period of the embargo, but other traders also got into the act. The response of the European Community was of particular interest in this regard. To a surprising degree, the European Community lived up at least to the letter of its formal pledge not to take commercial advantage of the embargo. Grain exports from the European Community to the Soviet Union increased only modestly during the July–June 1979–80 year, up from the previous year's level of 200,000 tons to about 800,000 tons.[57] In the 1980–81 year, even though most others had abandoned all restraint, European Community grain sales to the Soviet Union expanded only modestly, to a total of 1.1 million tons. This was despite the fact that the European Community had plenty of grain to sell. Total exportable supplies of wheat were actually increasing during the embargo period, and pressure from grain producers within the Community to boost exports was increasing as well. Early in 1980, French representatives had specifically urged additional authorizations for subsidized wheat exports, to further strengthen internal prices and to hold down surplus stocks.[58]

European restraint on grain sales to the Soviet Union did not, however, reflect any exceptional European deference to the U.S. embargo strategy. The European Community only recently had become a wheat surplus region, and had no history of providing significant quantities of grain to the Soviet Union. Equally important, the budgetary cost to the European Community of a dramatic increase in its subsidized grain sales to the Soviet Union would have been prohibitive. European grains, grown behind a protective barrier of variable import levies, are priced so high that they cannot be sold abroad without the application of expensive "restitution payments." When European Community officials discontinued offering grain export subsidies to the Soviet Union in January 1980 as their way of supporting the U.S. grain embargo, they were actually *saving* money.[59] In fact, just before the embargo was lifted they refused to authorize an additional 600,000 tons of wheat sales to the Soviet Union despite the fact that the French ambassador in Washington had already solicited and received approval for such a sale from the U.S. secretary of state.[60]

Whenever the European Community found itself in a position to sell food products that did *not* require costly subsidies, it showed much less restraint. Soybeans, for example, which could be purchased duty-free from abroad by European processors, could be reexported to the Soviet Union at competitive prices, without subsidy. Taking every advantage of this option, European companies imported (and processed) as much as 1 million tons of U.S. soybeans during the period of the embargo, for resale to the Soviet Union as soybean meal, a high-protein animal feed.[61] European millers meanwhile used a parallel scheme to expand wheat flour exports to the Soviet Union. The rules of the Community permitted European companies to import inexpensive foreign wheat, levy-free, so long as they reexported that wheat in the form of milled flour. Taking maximum advantage of this loophole, North German millers were able to sell a record volume of wheat flour to the Soviet Union (as much as 250,000 tons by midsummer 1980), much of it processed from U.S. wheat. Before the embargo, the Soviet Union had been only a minimal buyer of foreign wheat flour; by February 1981 Soviet purchases from European mills had reached 700,000 tons, about 15 percent of the world trade total.[62]

Obviously, the U.S. grain embargo was not supported in every respect by the European Community. For reasons of financial convenience to the Community, direct sales of European grains were not conspicuously expanded, but an expansion of food sales was nonetheless accomplished, in a less conspicuous but more profitable fashion, as wheat and soybeans were purchased, processed, and then reexported to the Soviet Union, at higher prices, capturing value-added along the way.

Additional damage was done to the embargo by a variety of smaller actors within the world's food-trading system. Unable to resist the commercial trade opportunity, a number of minor producers—including Hungary, Thailand, Spain, Sweden, and India—combined during the embargo to provide the Soviet Union with an additional 4.7 million tons of much-needed non-U.S. grain.[63] U.S. efforts to discourage these sales were fitful and unavailing. Thailand remained particularly defiant in the face of early U.S. diplomatic pressure to restrain its food and feed exports to the Soviet Union. "We are not a satellite of the U.S.," announced the Thai deputy minister of commerce in March 1980; in December his government entered into a ten-year bilateral trade agreement with the Soviet Union, to cover annual Soviet purchases of roughly 500,000 tons of tapioca (a high-value animal feed), plus 450,000 tons of corn and 230,000 tons of rice.[64] One month earlier, in November 1980, Spain had seized upon the occasion of an unusually large wheat harvest at home (up 33 percent from the level of the previous year) to announce that it too would begin direct wheat sales to the Soviet Union. Spain, which until then had been consistently a net *importer* of wheat, supplied the Soviet Union with 700,000 tons of wheat and barley in the new year beginning January 1981.[65] India's rice exports to the Soviet Union were also expanded, as noted in chapter 2, and the repayment of it earlier 2 million ton Soviet wheat loan was accelerated during the period of the embargo.

The cumulative effect of these trade shifts, during the sixteen months of the embargo, was a near-total replacement of grain sales embargoed by the United States: Soviet grain imports from all sources did not shrink but continued to expand (Table 9).

Amid this continued growth of Soviet grain imports, several events that some feared might weaken the embargo did *not* occur. First, large quantities of U.S. grain were not transshipped to the Soviet Union through satellite states in Eastern Europe. About 1.4 million tons of grain were shipped to the Soviet Union from Hungary, Bulgaria, and Romania in 1979–80, but this was only slightly more than the quantity of grains normally traded between these countries.[66] Suspicions that grain was being heavily transshipped had been understandably aroused when U.S. grain sales to Eastern Europe suddenly increased

Table 9. Total Soviet grain imports by country of origin

Country of origin	Preembargo (calendar year 1979)		Embargo (Jan. 1980–Apr. 1981)	
	Volume (million metric tons)	% of Total	Volume (million metric tons)	% of Total
United States	19.4	77.6	10.96	27.1
Non-U.S. total	5.6	22.4	29.51	72.9
Argentina	1.9	7.4	11.13	27.5
Australia	1.2	5.0	5.34	13.2
Canada	2.1	8.3	6.48	16.0
European community	0.2	0.8	1.88	4.6
Other	0.2	0.9	4.68	11.6
All-origin total	25.0	100.0	40.47	100.0

Source: U.S. Department of Agriculture, *Foreign Agricultural Circular*, FG-25-82, 12 August 1982, p. 5; FG-19-81, 12 May 1981, p. 5; January–June 1979 figures from personal communication with U.S. Department of Agriculture.

during 1979–80, up to 11.6 million tons, in contrast to only 5.6 million tons the previous year. Department of Agriculture officials found no evidence that this grain, most of which had been sold to Poland, was moving on to the Soviet Union. Poland's larger grain imports had been an independent response to its own much larger internal needs, due to a very poor harvest in 1979 and the labor unrest in 1980. Grain shipments *from the Soviet Union to Poland* were in fact on the rise while the embargo was in place.

A second kind of slippage that was anticipated but did *not* occur was the widespread sale of U.S. grain to the Soviet Union through the foreign subsidiaries of U.S.-based multinational grain-trading companies. Such firms, which handle the vast majority of U.S. grain exports, enjoy a well-deserved reputation for ingenuity and discretion when servicing the import needs of large and steady cash-paying customers such as the Soviet Union. The U.S. government could scarcely hope to control all of the highly secretive sale and resale operations that these firms conduct overseas. During the period of the embargo, however, most fears of corporate duplicity were quickly laid to rest. The private companies had been mollified by the marketing opportunities that had become available elsewhere and by the extraordinary protection and compensation provided to them under the terms of the "exporter's agreement" patched together in Washington immediately following the embargo announcement. To protect themselves from unwelcome federal investigation, they went out of their way to demonstrate good faith, even to the extent of honoring an informal request from the administration, made on 12 January 1980, that they refrain from using their foreign subsidiaries to sell *non-U.S.* grain to the Soviet Union. This so-called gentleman's agreement, which went well beyond the official scope of the embargo, was terminated at the end of the crop year in June, by which time official suspicions of company misbehavior had been eased. Investigations of "alleged" instances of diversion or transshipment of U.S. grain to the Soviet Union continued under the direction of the Commerce Department, but in midsummer 1980 it was announced by the Department of Agriculture that no violation of the terms of the embargo by any private trading firm had yet been demonstrated.[67]

Food power advocates should not conclude too much, however, from this "leak-proof" appearance of the embargo. U.S. grain did not "leak" through the 1980–81 embargo because it did not have to. Recall that the Soviet Union found ways to meet almost all of its import needs through the purchase of non-U.S. grain, while U.S. exporters likewise discovered ways to keep their sales volume up without resorting to duplicity. As larger quantities of non-U.S. grain began to move toward the Soviet Union, embargoed U.S. grain found compensating opportunities to move elsewhere. International grain shipments were substantially rerouted after the embargo announcement, but neither the Soviet Union—nor the United States—had been forced by the embargo into a dramatic downward adjustment in the total volume of its trade. On the contrary, U.S. grain exports as well as Soviet grain imports continued to grow during the embargo (Table 10).

This growth is the key to understanding the sixteen-month duration of the embargo. Within the international grain-trading system the embargo not only failed to deny short-run import opportunities to the Soviet Union; it also failed to deny short-run export opportunities to the United States. Soon after the embargo was declared, the United States merely "traded customers" with other exporters. The United States gave up a large share of its annual sales to the Soviet Union, but gained a compensating share of annual sales to numerous non-Soviet customers, such as Mexico and China, who wished to avoid paying more for the purchase of Argentine, Australian, or Canadian grain. The fact is that total U.S. grain exports never declined during the period of the embargo. As predicted by Bergland, the volume of those sales *increased* during the first marketing year affected by the embargo by no less than 22 percent, from 89.2 million tons in 1978–79 to 108.8 million tons in 1979–80. Even the U.S. *share* of world grain exports managed to increase during the period of the embargo; it was greater when the embargo finally ended than it had been in 1978–79, the last

Table 10.   U.S. grain exports and Soviet grain imports, 1979–1980

	U.S. grain exports		Soviet grain imports	
	Total volume*	% to Soviet Union	Total volume*	% from U.S.
1979 (Preembargo)	100.8	21.3	25.0	77.6
1980 (Embargo)	109.8	6.2	28.7	24.0
Rate of growth (%)	8.9		4.8	

Sources: U.S. Department of Agriculture, *Foreign Agriculture Circular,* FG-19-81, 12 May 1981, p. 5. Calendar year trade figures provided by Trade and Economic Information Division, International Agricultural Statistics, Foreign Agricultural Service, U.S. Department of Agriculture.

*In millions of metric tons.

Table 11.   U.S. share (%) of world grain exports

	1978–79	1979–80 (July–June Year)	1980–81
Wheat and wheat flour	44.9	43.3	44.8
Coarse grains	63.1	71.0	69.0
Total grains	55.0	58.2	57.5

Source: U.S. Department of Agriculture, *Foreign Agriculture Circular*, FG-26-82, 16 August 1982.

complete marketing year prior to the embargo (Table 11). Because U.S. grain export prices were also on the rise, from the middle of 1980 into 1981, this unbroken expansion of U.S. grain exports during the embargo period produced record dollar export earnings for U.S. grain traders and producers.

The Carter administration had done its best, from the start, to take full advantage of these new export openings in non-Soviet markets. As early as 16 January 1980, after two days of hasty negotiations, the United States announced an agreement whereby Mexico would purchase larger-than-expected quantities of U.S. agricultural commodities in 1980 (4.76 million tons in all), a portion of which (about 1 million tons of corn) would come directly from embargoed grain supplies previously destined for the Soviet Union. In September the total quantity of Mexican agricultural purchases covered by this agreement would be increased to 7.2 million tons, almost twice the level of Mexico's annual imports from the United States over the three previous years. Then in October, the United States signed a landmark four-year minimum grain sale agreement with the People's Republic of China.[68] As Carter would later claim, "Secretary Bob Bergland and other administration officials marshaled a world-wide effort to sell American corn and wheat, concentrating on such countries as Mexico and China. . . . We were to be very successful, breaking all-time world records in grain sales during 1980, in spite of the restraints on Soviet trade."[69] Of course, by working so hard to push grain into these non-Soviet markets, the United States gave its export competitors further cause to ignore the embargo and to redirect still more of their own sales to the Soviet Union.

In several respects, therefore, the 1980–81 grain embargo was less than a perfect test of the ability of the United States to deny grain sales to the Soviet Union. Such a test would have required that the United

States first discontinue all sales to the Soviet Union—including the 8 million tons guaranteed under the long-term agreement—and then restrain the impulse to dump its own embargoed grain into non-Soviet markets. By behaving otherwise, to protect its share of world markets and to relieve some domestic pressures to terminate the embargo, the government ensured in the end a minimal impact on the Soviet Union.

Impact on the Soviet Union

The embargo never had much of a chance to show what it could do within the Soviet Union, since it failed to halt the growth of Soviet grain imports. The Soviet Union was not even forced to pay a heavy price to import its way around the embargo. Arguably, the U.S. grain embargo was even helpful to the Soviet leadership, by providing a foreign scapegoat for flawed domestic food policies, while also providing a timely inducement to initiate some modest reform of those policies.

When considering the sort of damage that a grain embargo might do within the Soviet Union, not even the most optimistic food power advocate would expect damage to Soviet supplies of bread and bakery products. These are readily available from domestic food grain production. Brezhnev himself confidently promised the Soviet people, in a *Pravda* interview soon after the U.S. embargo announcement, that "plans of providing Soviet people with bread and bakery products will not be lessened by a single kilogram."[70] Soviet bread supplies during the embargo period were, indeed, unaffected by the trade disruptions that took place.

The meat and livestock sector of the Soviet economy provided a more inviting food power target, because of its significant import dependence. Even a relatively brief denial of imported feed supplies might do long-lasting damage to Soviet livestock inventories, and hence to meat production trends. In 1975, following a weather-related harvest failure, the Soviet Union had been forced to reduce the use of grains for feed by 17 percent (from 107 million tons to 89 million tons) in a single year. Livestock inventories could not be maintained under these circumstances; in a brief span of five months poultry and pork numbers were reduced by 36 percent and 26 percent, respectively. This "distress slaughter" resulted in larger meat supplies available for immediate consumption in the short run, but made a sustained increase in meat production vastly more difficult in the long run. After the distress slaughter, despite good weather and unrestricted access to grain imports, three years were required to rebuild livestock inventories to the previously established level. Total meat production in the meantime fell, from 15 million tons in 1975 to only 13.6 million tons in 1976.[71] When bad weather—and the U.S. embargo—struck in 1979–80, per capita meat production in the Soviet Union had only just begun to resume its upward trend. The punitive intent behind the embargo was to trigger a renewed round of cutbacks in Soviet livestock inventories, thereby retarding further the growth of Soviet meat production.

The meat and livestock sector of the Soviet economy was politically inviting as a food power target because of the clear priority Brezhnev had placed upon the upgrading of Soviet meat supplies. Beginning in 1965 and especially during the 1970s, Brezhnev had allowed himself to become personally associated with a pledge to increase per capita Soviet meat consumption. Facing a poor grain harvest at home on the eve of the embargo, Brezhnev made clear on several occasions in 1979 the importance he still attached to meat production. Late in September 1979, he personally instructed that livestock numbers should be maintained. Then at the November plenum of the Central Committee, he reiterated that "the primary obligation . . . is that of achieving a considerable increase in meat production throughout the country."[72] Soviet citizens had come to view meat availability as a "barometer" of their economic well-being; the United States expected that they would hold the Brezhnev leadership responsible for any new meat production setback. Never had such a significant Soviet economic target been so exposed to U.S. food power. U.S. press reports soon after the embargo decision dwelt upon the confidence of White House aides that Carter's grain embargo would set the Soviet diet back for "a decade."[73]

These grandiose expectations were to be sadly disappointed. In the end, the reductions in Soviet meat production caused by the grain embargo were much less than the 20 percent estimate originally provided by the CIA. These reductions were even less than the modest 1–3 percent estimate more prudently offered by the Department of Agriculture.

A quarterly analysis of Soviet grain imports from all sources reveals that the impact of the embargo on Soviet trade objectives was confined almost entirely to the first nine months of 1980 (Table 12). According to one private trade estimate, during the tightest period of the embargo, April–September 1980, total Soviet grain imports did fall about 6 million tons below the preembargo "programmed level."[74] This in-

Table 12. Soviet total grain imports, 1979–1981

Quarter	1979	1980 (million metric tons)	1981
I	2.3	7.0	9.1
II	6.2	6.9	10.2
III	9.0	5.9	10.8
IV	7.5	8.9	10.0
Total	25.0	28.7	40.1

Source: U.S. Department of Agriculture, *Foreign Agriculture Circular*, FG-19-81, 12 May 1981; FG-25-82, 12 August 1982; 1979 quarters I and II supplied by U.S. Department of Agriculture, Economic Research Service.

terlude of embargo-induced import reductions did not, however, translate into an equally large or equally long reduction in the feeding of grain to livestock. The availability of reserve stocks of grain, plus the eventual onset of the Soviet Union's own summer harvest, in July 1980, did much to ease the strain.

An estimated 13 million tons of grain were drawn out of Soviet stocks in 1979–80, stocks that had fortunately been replenished in the preceding year due to the record harvest of 1978–79.[75] Even assuming the imminent exhaustion of these reserve stocks of grain, import reductions suffered during the second half of the summer could also be covered in the short run, from newly harvested home-grown supplies. It was hoped that a heavy drawdown of these newly harvested grain supplies could be made up during the winter ahead, presuming better luck by then in the search for alternative foreign sources of supply. Total Soviet foreign purchases did expand in just this fashion by early 1981. It is therefore clear, in retrospect, that the only period during which the trade reductions caused by the embargo might have actually threatened Soviet livestock production was the six-month January–June 1980 period, immediately after the embargo announcement and immediately before the onset of the 1980 Soviet harvest.

In this more restricted time period, the modest grain import reductions caused by the embargo did translate into some reduced feed use. One way to estimate these embargo-caused feed use reductions is to compare the actual postembargo experience to preembargo Department of Agriculture projections for the entire year ending in June 1980 (Table 13).

From the comparison in Table 13 it may be noted that the estimated 5 million ton reduction in total feed use, slightly less than the predicted

Table 13. Soviet grain imports and feed use

	Imports	Feed use
	(million metric tons)	
July–June 1979–80 preembargo projection	37.5	128.0
July–June 1979–80 actual	31.0	123.0
Estimated January–June 1980 reductions attributable to embargo	6.5	5.0

Source: U.S. Department of Agriculture, *Foreign Agriculture Circular*, FG-23-79, 11 December 1979; FG-35-82, 12 November 1982; FG-12-80, 10 April 1980.

6.5 million ton reduction in imports, brings us closest to judging the possible damage to Soviet livestock production. During the six-month period in question, this feed use reduction represented a 7.8 percent cutback in Soviet feed levels attributable directly to the embargo. Such a cutback was less than half the magnitude of the feed use reduction undertaken following the weather-induced Soviet harvest failure of 1975. But does it nonetheless signify a measurable degree of damage done to Soviet livestock production?

In fact, this small 7.8 percent embargo-induced reduction in grain fed to Soviet livestock during the first six months of 1980 had little measurable impact on the maintenance of Soviet livestock inventories, or on Soviet meat production. Despite this embargo-induced reduction in the feed use of grains, Soviet livestock numbers managed to *expand* during the 1980 season overall. Some above-trend slaughtering was noted briefly early in the year, but by 1 November 1980, Soviet inventories of cattle, hogs, and poultry all stood *above* the preembargo level. These expanded Soviet livestock inventories were also maintained throughout 1981, despite four more months of the embargo and, even more remarkably, despite a third bad domestic grain harvest later in that year (Table 14).

The ability of the Soviet Union to maintain (and even to expand) its livestock herds over the sixteen months of the embargo despite actual reductions in the availability and use of grain for animal feed is a matter of some interest. Retention of livestock inventories reflects at least two separate policy decisions taken by the Soviet leadership in the wake of the embargo. The first of these was to accept some continued decline in average animal slaughterweights. Livestock were to be kept for as long as before, but fed and fattened somewhat less. Livestock slaughterweights had begun to decline in the Soviet Union before the

1980 embargo in the aftermath of the bad domestic harvest of 1979, and the Soviet leadership permitted this decline to continue during the ensuing period of the embargo itself (Table 15).

A second leadership decision that contributed to the successful retention of Soviet livestock inventories during the grain embargo—an adjustment in feeding rations—was mentioned in chapter 3. Grains and pulses until the embargo accounted for about one-third of total animal feed consumed in the Soviet Union.[76] Soviet planners had known for some time that this ratio was actually *too high*. The grain embargo gave these planners their occasion to press for a significant reform of feed ration policies. By making heavier use of home-grown nongrain feed sources (such as silage, feed roots, hay, and alfalfa) both during and after the embargo, they were able to improve the efficiency of their livestock sector while making room to reduce feedgrain imports. Some Soviet officials even went so far as to express their appreciation for the stimulus to this reform that the embargo had provided.[77]

If the grain embargo did not force the Soviet Union into a dramatic distress slaughter of livestock, did it at least cause some short-run decline in Soviet meat production? The reduced slaughterweight of Soviet livestock during the embargo seems to raise this possibility. Perhaps farmers were able to keep their animals alive in stubborn pursuit of long-term objectives but at some cost to adequate meat production in the short term.

At this point it becomes necessary to draw a distinction between whatever damage was done to Soviet meat production by the embargo and the damage that would have been done—due to poor Soviet harvests—without the embargo. The Soviet meat economy would have

Table 14.   Soviet cattle, hog, and poultry inventories on state and
collective farms

Year (1 Nov.)	Cattle	Hogs (million head)	Poultry
1978	88.6	57.7	573.1
1979	89.3	57.5	616.1
1980	90.0	57.7	655.5
1981	90.3	58.4	674.2
1982	91.0	58.6	713.0

Source: U.S. Department of Agriculture, *Foreign Agriculture Circular*, FG-38-83, 13 December 1983, p. 3.

Table 15.   Soviet average liveweights at slaughter
of cattle and hogs

Year	Cattle	Hogs
	(kilograms)	
1978	366	105
1979	363	104
1980	355	101
1981	350	101

Source: U.S. Department of Agriculture, *Foreign
Agriculture Circular*, FG-45-81, 11 December 1981,
p. 3.

faltered in 1980 and 1981 even without an embargo, because of an extraordinary sequence of below-average grain harvests—largely a consequence of bad weather. In 1979, the harvest had fallen to 179 million tons, 58 million tons below the preceding year's record harvest of 237 million tons. In 1980, the harvest was only 189 million tons. Then, in 1981, the worst year of all, the Soviet grain harvest fell to no more than an estimated 160 million tons. These three sequential harvest failures contributed *much more,* in combination, to lagging Soviet meat production during the period than any import or feed use reduction attributable to the U.S. grain embargo. Although the embargo perhaps denied a total of 5 million tons of grain to the Soviet livestock sector during the first six months of 1980, bad weather in 1979 had denied much more (Table 16). Nikolai K. Baibakov, chief of the Soviet State Planning Committee, had announced two months *before* the embargo that meat, chicken, and milk production were going to fall short of planning targets in 1980 because of "inadequate grain and fodder supplies" due entirely to the country's own poor domestic harvest.[78]

When this decline did take place in 1980, some U.S. observers erroneously attributed it to the grain embargo. In July 1980, for example, a Department of Agriculture report on the "impact" of the embargo correctly noted that Soviet meat production was about 1.2 percent lower during the first half of 1980 than it had been during the corresponding period in 1979.[79] Soon thereafter, State Department spokesmen explained, in misleading fashion, that Soviet meat production was dropping "as a result of our restrictions."[80] Of the small decline that had taken place, only a minor part could be attributed to the embargo. One study later confirmed that the drop in Soviet meat output noted in 1980 was far more the result of the Soviet Union's below-trend harvest than of denied imports. This study found that denied imports were responsible in 1980 for reductions in beef output of a miniscule 0.16 percent, in milk output of only 0.73 percent, in pork 0.19 percent, and poultry 0.64 percent; it concluded that "the embargo's impact on livestock product output in the Soviet Union was all but eclipsed by the crop failures in 1979 and 1980."[81]

By one line of reasoning, perhaps the damage done by poor weather could have made the U.S. food weapon *more potent* as a means of punishing the Soviet Union in 1980. With the livestock sector already under stress, and with meat production already lagging, perhaps *any* added measure of denial—however trivial it might be in absolute terms—would be magnified to constitute a legitimate U.S. food power advantage. The dynamic of Soviet domestic politics was to produce just the opposite effect, however. The Soviet leadership came to view the embargo as a propaganda windfall—not as an added source of consumer discontent, *but as a convenient opportunity to shift the focus of that discontent.*

Rather than downplaying the embargo, Soviet press reports cleverly highlighted its magnitude and punitive intent. In fact, it was only during the U.S. embargo that the Soviet people were told, for the first time, of their country's significant dependence on imported grains. And what they were told amounted to a momentarily convenient exaggeration of that dependence. In a January 1980 *Pravda* interview, Leonid Brezhnev stressed only that *bread supplies* would not be affected. By mentioning only bread, Brezhnev left a clear public impression that the U.S. embargo might very well add to the *meat* shortages already being experienced by Soviet consumers. Alec Nove, an expert on Soviet agriculture at the University of Glasgow, noted immediately that this unprecedented public admission of some dependence on

Table 16.   Soviet meat and milk production

Year	Total meat	Milk
	(million metric tons)	
1978	15.5	94.7
1979	15.3	93.3
1980	15.0	90.6

Source: U.S. Department of Agriculture, "USSR: Review of Agriculture in 1981 and Outlook for 1982," Suppl. 1 to WAS-27, May 1982, Table 4, p. 24.

Western grain, in combination with an omission of official assurances on meat supplies, was highly significant: "The public admission [to the Soviet people] is very interesting because it constitutes an alibi—'We are very sorry for you, but it is the fault of the wicked imperialists.'"[82]

A variety of techniques were employed in the following weeks to establish more firmly in the minds of Soviet consumers this convenient connection between widespread domestic food shortages (which were then occurring anyway) and the embargo. In February, the illustrated weekly *Ogonyok* published a defiant poem by a fifty-one-year-old Leningrader, addressed to "James Carter," which recalled the patriotic food sacrifices made while his city was under siege by German armies in World War II.[83] Later in February, the same theme of patriotic sacrifice was developed in a full-page "Open Letter to U.S. President Carter," published in *Literaturnaya Gazeta,* the weekly of the Union of Writers. The editor wrote:

> . . . vain attempts like this to create famine in another country, to force it to make concessions, are truly unspeakable and disgraceful. During the war, Hitler gave hunger an assignment the generals of the Wehrmacht could not carry out: to defeat blockaded Leningrad. Need I remind you, Mr. President, how this effort ended?[84]

With such evocative memories of wartime victory and sacrifice thus aroused, the Soviet leadership probably found itself (thanks to the embargo) in a better position to deal with any public dissatisfactions that might arise over the upcoming meat shortages. Shortages which were almost entirely the result of problems encountered at home, could now be explained through reference to a Hitler-like adversary abroad. One U.S. official who had dutifully helped to manage the embargo, later conceded that it had been built around a misunderstanding of its likely psychological impact within the Soviet Union:

> Rationing and economic hardships are a way of life in the USSR. . . . [O]vert external pressures provide a handy scapegoat for failures of the internal system and may even rally the population to accept new hardships. One should remember that during the Arab oil embargo we [in the U.S.] got angry at the Arabs, not at the U.S. government.[85]

Not that the Soviet leadership was ever close to losing its political grip due to the poor performance of its food programs: with or without a foreign scapegoat, Soviet leaders probably had little to fear from domestic economic frustrations. In the summer of 1980, reports began reaching the United States of strikes and work stoppages in Soviet motor vehicle plants, allegedly the result of consumer dissatisfaction with shortages of meat and dairy products; Secretary of Agriculture Bergland attempted at one point to present these reports as indirect confirmation that the embargo was having an impact.[86] More cautious and creditable assessments were being made by those on the scene, such as Thomas J. Watson, Jr., the U.S. ambassador in Moscow at the time. Watson criticized the "wishful thinkers" back home "who were ready to seize on such reports as evidence that the Soviet system could not long survive." "Nothing," said Watson, "could be further from the truth."[87] Even dissidents within the Soviet Union were pessimistic about the political impact of the embargo. Roy A. Medvedev, a dissident Marxist historian, explained to foreign visitors early in 1980 that the United States had misperceived the way in which the grain embargo would be received within the Soviet Union: "[I]f anybody suffers from the embargo, it will not be the leaders who ordered the invasion of Afghanistan. They will have meat in their special stores, embargo or no embargo. It will be the common man, who had nothing to do with the invasion and cannot exert any pressure on those who did."[88]

To the degree that Soviet leaders were affected by the embargo, U.S. foreign policy interests were probably not well served. Within the Soviet leadership, those who had been the strongest advocates of détente were no doubt discredited. It now became much more difficult to push for closer commercial and diplomatic ties with the United States. Even Brezhnev gave expression to his personal disappointment in this regard:

> As a result of the Carter Administration's actions, the impression is increasingly forming in the world of the United States as an absolutely unreliable partner in interstate ties, as a state whose leadership, prompted by some whim, caprice or emotional outbursts, or by considerations of narrowly understood immediate advantages, is capable at any moment of violating its international obligations.[89]

Soviet leaders were also able to use the embargo to initiate several modest but invigorating internal food policy reforms. In the words of one Soviet scholar speaking soon after the embargo was imposed, "Jimmy Carter has made a terrible mistake. By embargoing grain he has proved to the Soviet people that agriculture has strategic importance, and it must be developed the same way we develop our rockets." According to Zhores Medvedev, a dissident biochemist and specialist in Soviet agriculture living in London, "The grain embargo made things better [for the Soviets] rather than worse. It forced the Soviet leadership to mobilize everything to prove their independence. A reformist tendency developed."[90]

The new "food program" conceived by Brezhnev during the embargo was lavish, but not altogether wasteful, as it sought to redirect investment toward weak links in the food-production chain.[91] As argued previously, the rewards from these postembargo reforms so far are quite modest. Still, *any* advantage gained for Soviet agriculture from the embargo must be counted as a disadvantageous development for the United States, given the punitive intent of the embargo.

It remains possible, of course, that a rededication of administrative energy and resources to Soviet agriculture might draw energy and resources away from the Soviet military sector. If so, a derivative form of "food power" might have been exercised. Unfortunately, no such diminution of military efforts appears to have occurred.[92] If anything, the hostile U.S. reaction to the Afghan crisis probably reinforced Soviet determination to build its military strength. In a speech to the Central Committee in October 1980, while calling for greater efforts in agriculture, Brezhnev promised that nothing would be permitted to detract from the capability to defend the state against foreign threats. Until his death some two years later, Brezhnev continued to argue in public for attaching equal priority to arms and agriculture. In his last widely noted speech to high-ranking military and political officials in late October 1982, Brezhnev reasserted that a great deal of work was required to "eliminate in the future the need for grain purchases abroad." Yet he also took this occasion to argue that "the time now is such that the level of combat readiness of the army and navy should be even higher."[93] Soviet planners thus far have refused to accept any short-run "guns for butter" trade-off. They prefer instead to spend more for both arms and agriculture, perhaps sacrificing some long-run capital investments in other areas.[94] The Soviet leadership was not in the process of selecting "butter over guns" in the aftermath of the grain embargo; it was pressing ahead in its quest for both guns and butter, most likely at the expense of some future growth.

If the postembargo agricultural policy reforms adopted in the Soviet Union can do anything to restore productivity growth to agriculture, they might even *boost* the long-run growth of Soviet military expenditures. Expensive investments in agriculture can be helpful to total growth rates, as the Soviet farm sector remains seriously under-capitalized. Fixed assets per farm worker stand at only half the level of fixed assets per industrial worker (in the United States fixed assets per worker are 60 percent higher in the agricultural sector than in the industrial sector).[95] Investments that are beneficial for the long-run development of Soviet agriculture will help to expand the total economic base upon which Soviet defense spending must ultimately depend.

Another possible U.S. advantage from the embargo deserves to be considered. By setting in motion such a hasty diversification of Soviet grain imports away from the United States, toward a variety of smaller high-priced foreign suppliers, perhaps the embargo was at least costly to the Soviet Union in terms of foreign currency. Midway through 1980, the Defense Intelligence Agency estimated that the cost to the Soviet Union of purchasing foreign grain that year would be about $1 billion higher, due to the embargo policy. It was argued that the Soviet Union would also experience costly logistical bottlenecks during the embargo, because they were now obliged to handle an irregular mix of much smaller shipments of grain from a wide variety of suppliers, rather than a steady flow of bulk shipments from the United States.

In retrospect, such costs of buying non-U.S. grain during the embargo were probably not great enough to be considered a derivative form of punishment. By some accounts, in fact, the Soviet Union absorbed no additional hard currency expense at all. Department of Agriculture economists observe that before the embargo the Soviet Union was about to purchase large amounts of U.S. grain *at high 1979 prices,* roughly 20–25 percent above the lower world market price that prevailed by mid-1980. By releasing the Soviet Union from these more expensive 1979 U.S. grain contracts, the embargo may have actually provided Exportkhleb with as much as a $500 million hard currency windfall, enough to offset the subsequent expense of briefly offering price premiums for Argentine grain.[96] Even with these "premiums," the prices paid to Argentina in mid-1980 were in some instances actually lower than the prices contracted earlier for U.S. grains under embargo. Due to the embargo the Soviet Union also imported a slightly reduced total volume of grain, while using home-grown feed supplies more efficiently. For such reasons overall, according to the chief economist in the Department of Agriculture at the time, "[I]t's hard to argue that the embargo cost them any additional loss of foreign exchange."[97] Nor did the transportation bottlenecks experienced during the embargo present lasting problems. By 1981 the Soviet Union had installed five new floating docks at ports in the Baltic Sea and in the Black Sea, increasing their total port capacity for handling grain by roughly 50 percent.[98]

Did the grain embargo secure some advantage for the United States by way of "signaling" to the Soviet Union the high level of U.S. concern about the Afghanistan invasion, thereby helping to "deter" a subsequent Soviet intervention in Poland? Even though the embargo failed to "punish" the Soviet Union for Afghanistan, could it be credited with cautioning Soviet behavior in subsequent conflicts? There are several reasons to discount this sort of justification for the embargo. If President Carter's purpose had been to caution the Soviet Union against similar actions, it might have made greater sense in January 1980 for him to permit grain sales to continue, *conditioned on good behavior*. With new sales discontinued after Afghanistan, one incentive for good Soviet behavior in Poland was actually gone. From the Soviet viewpoint, why not commit the crime, now that the penalty had already been paid? Not even Reagan's 1981 resumption of grain sales was sufficient to restore the full deterrent value of those sales, as the new U.S. share of the Soviet market remained only a fraction of what it had been in 1979. Without the post-Afghanistan embargo (and the trade diversification it prompted) the United States might well have been in a position to exercise a "deterrent" form of food power, through a tacit threat to interrupt sales. By the time of the Polish crisis, however, the U.S. food weapon had already been discharged.

When considering the possibility that a grain embargo can serve as a useful "signal" of U.S. resolve, it is necessary to remember the context in which such signals are given and received. Does the United States in fact communicate "resolve" when it selects a *grain embargo* as its most visible response to a decisive show of Soviet military strength? And how much resolve is signaled when the United States then exempts a substantial volume of its own exports from that embargo, and falls into an unseemly squabble with its allies over their reluctance to provide support? Finally, what sort of signal was sent by the decision of the Reagan administration, under obvious domestic pressure, to terminate the embargo? Rather than a clear signal of resolve, of U.S. determination to take all measures necessary to counter Soviet military might, the tortured grain embargo episode was perhaps read by the

Soviet Union as further evidence of indecision and confusion in U.S. foreign policy. To the war-toughened leaders in Moscow, the decision to rely on a "food weapon" might well have been seen as further evidence that the United States had yet to emerge from its enfeebling "post-Vietnam syndrome" and was not yet prepared to take genuine military risks to protect its vital interests overseas. Rather than being taken as a signal of resolve, the grain embargo could well have been dismissed in Moscow as a "fake-tough" policy, dictated at every turn by domestic political expediency.

Summary

What, then, are the final lessons of the 1980–81 grain embargo? The first lesson drawn by the Soviet Union was to diversify its grain trade away from the United States. After the embargo was lifted, significant Soviet purchases of U.S. grain were resumed, especially in 1981–82, a year of unprecedented need. But by 1983, the year in which a new long-term agreement for grain purchases was finally concluded with the United States, Soviet import needs were momentarily moderating, and were well enough satisfied from other sources, so that the United States was forced to become the supplicant in the negotiations. U.S. agricultural policy officials, by then desperate to revive the growth of U.S. grain exports, found themselves courting the Soviet Union rather than the other way around.

The immediate lesson drawn in the United States, at least by those in the Reagan administration who favored lifting the embargo, was never again to use the food weapon against the Soviet Union without being sure in advance that other Western grain-exporting countries would follow suit. It is possible, however, that the actual circumstances under which such an inclusive embargo could be arranged might also generate new opportunities for absorbing sacrifice within the Soviet Union. In the instance of a more severe crisis in East–West relations, such as would be necessary to call forth a well-disciplined multilateral embargo, the Soviet leadership would find it that much easier to conjure up images of a foreign threat, and thus would be better positioned to demand sacrifice from its own citizens. By a perverse logic, the very conditions of intense East–West conflict that might be necessary to call forth an effective multilateral grain embargo from the Western food-trading system would simultaneously permit a more determined resistance to that embargo within the Soviet Union.

A second lesson drawn in the United States was never again to single out agricultural products when designing economic sanctions policies. Additional "embargo insurance" and "contract sanctity" provisions, written into law by farm state legislators in 1981 and 1983, foreclosed this option in any case. Having made the 1980–81 grain embargo something of a scapegoat for their export and income losses early in the 1980s, U.S. agriculturalists became united in their political determination to prevent its recurrence. During the 1981–82 martial law crisis in Poland and after the shooting down of the Korean airliner in 1983, renewed U.S. sanctions policies never included stoppage of grain exports.

The final lesson of the U.S. grain embargo must be a more cautious attitude about the minimal foreign policy advantage an exporter can hope to gain from a selective food trade interruption. The commercial or coercive power that derives from food exports is uncertain to begin with; it will be further reduced when exports are actually cut off. The United States appeared, in January 1980, to enjoy an unprecedented food power advantage over the Soviet Union. Nonetheless, the embargo was a considerable foreign policy failure. Not even the minor food power advantage enjoyed over India fifteen years earlier accrued to the United States on this occasion, when it actually terminated food sales to the Soviet Union.

Yet the similarity in these two cases may outweigh the differences. In both, the presumed existence of a U.S. "food weapon" added little to the options and advantages that would have been available through the manipulation of more traditional foreign policy assets. The food weapon had some arguable effect against India, a much weaker country. It proved to be of negligible value when directed against the Soviet Union, a nation of estimable strength, and a nation with greater incentives to resist coercion. How valuable is a weapon that can only be used, in the best of circumstances, against weak nations that are already vulnerable to so many other instruments of coercion? A food weapon that only works against the weak, when conditions are ideal, under circumstances in which many less controversial weapons would work as well, is no weapon at all. And a food weapon that fails under ideal conditions when used against the strong, causing frustration and a sense of defeat, may be worse than no weapon at all.

Conclusion

Our purpose has been to examine the connections presumed to exist between food trade and foreign policy. In India, the Soviet Union, and the United States, one is struck most of all by the *disconnections* between these two policy realms. We must question the popular notion that nations seek to manipulate their food trade in search of external advantages, and that food exporters gain the most advantage in the event of such manipulations. The analysis of these three cases over the past several decades leads to the conclusion that these nations seldom altered their food trade policies in search of external gains and when they did, the exporter (in these cases, the United States) did not gain the expected foreign policy advantage. The two-part food power presumption is therefore challenged on both counts.

Why did these three nations seldom seek food power? It was not for any lack of imagination on the part of foreign policy leaders, who frequently made rhetorical reference to their external food trade prospects and objectives. Indian foreign policy officials, ever since independence, had endorsed the presumed external gains to be had from foodgrain "self-sufficiency." Soviet foreign policy officials, who were the first in this century to speak of food as an international "weapon," had not only warned against grain imports; for decades they had used their own grain *exports* to earn foreign hard currency and to consolidate control over client states within their sphere of influence. U.S. foreign policy officials were also experienced practitioners as well as theorists of food power, having gained significant external political advantages from food exports during both World Wars and the period of the Marshall Plan. They subsequently discovered the trade gains to be made from commercial food export expansion, and began to speculate out loud about diplomatic "food power." This, needless to say, reconfirmed the diplomatic anxieties of food importing countries such as India and the Soviet Union.

But this rhetorical fascination with food power has recently had little impact on behavior. At no time in recent years have foreign policy officials—in India, the Soviet Union, or the United States—been strong enough to act at will on their inclinations or presumptions concerning food power. In India, grain trade policies are formulated first of all to satisfy the ever-changing requirements of that nation's internal food-grain distribution system. Considerations such as the conservation of foreign exchange, or the avoidance of a "dependent" trade posture, consistently take a backseat. In fact, as the practice of importing grain under negotiated "food aid" agreements has been superseded by the practice of making commercial purchases abroad, the presumed connection between Indian food trade and Indian foreign policy has grown weaker. A comparable trend is noted in the Soviet Union, where domestic food needs, once sacrificed to sustain exports, are now given precedence, resulting in a diplomatically awkward growth of expensive grain imports. These imports may be secure, however, since food power policies are also now being rejected by the United States. U.S. foreign policy leaders have met enormous frustration in their occasional efforts to manipulate grain exports for external economic or diplomatic gains. Shifting coalitions of powerful domestic interest groups, including consumers and labor leaders as well as producers and traders, have repeatedly taken the food weapon out of their hands.

Grain trade policies in these three nations thus have become significantly disconnected from foreign policy, for reasons that go beyond carelessness or inadvertence. In each instance the presumed "primacy" of foreign policy gave way to the more enduring and inward-looking primacy of domestic food and farm policy.

Moreover, on those exceptional occasions when "food power" confrontations did occur, the presumed power advantage available to the United States, as the food-exporting nation, failed to materialize. Even when examining two food power confrontations that provided extreme contextual advantages to the United States—such as Lyndon Johnson's short-tether policy on food aid to India, or Jimmy Carter's embargo on commercial grain sales to the Soviet Union—the coercive advantage presumably available to the exporter falls short of expectations. In the Indian case, a determined use of U.S. food power, in combination with several parallel instruments of influence, did for a time accelerate some economic policy changes already under way in India. But food power failed, in this case, to induce the desired change in Indian foreign policy. In fact, it brought undesired changes, which were arguably disadvantageous to the United States. In the Soviet case, the presumed food power advantage available to the United States was even more elusive. The 1980–81 grain embargo failed in the Soviet Union to produce any of its intended objective or subjective consequences.

Food power failures are attributable to the cumulative difficulty of simultaneously implementing a food denial strategy at each of the three vital points in the food power process—the domestic system of the exporting state, the international food-trading system, and the domestic system of the "target" country. Even when a food trade denial is somehow successful at points one and two, it can still fail to gain its intended effect at point three. Ironically, the only means to accomplish denial abroad may be to incur economic costs at home. The expectation of such costs, and the weak prospect of foreign policy benefits, usually combine to discourage an exporter's recourse to food power.

What are the larger lessons that might be drawn from such observations? For students of national food policy, the lesson is clear enough, and to a large extent supportive of views long held by agricultural policy specialists. This book offers new evidence to support the time-honored belief that national food trade policies most often evolve as an extension or an outward expression of *inward-looking* domestic food and farm policies. This tendency may even be growing stronger. It is now a dominant tendency not only in the United States, an advanced industrial democracy, but also in India, a nonindustrial democracy, and in the Soviet Union, a nondemocratic industrial state.

For students of the "world food system," the implications are equally clear, but somewhat more difficult to digest. The so-called world food system that emerges from this study is little more than the residual external consequence of many separately determined, inward-looking national food and farm policy actions, suggesting that it may not be a "system" at all. Each of the three governments examined here adopted grain trade policies with remarkably little prior regard for the external circumstances or consequences. Rather than consistently pursuing external objectives as is often expected, each approached the international grain market with inward-looking objectives uppermost in mind. They most often considered the world food system as an afterthought, using it either as an outlet for surplus production brought on by domestic farm subsidy programs, or as a supplementary source of supplies when domestic consumption objectives could not be met from home production. They seldom saw the international grain market as a system, to be shaped or managed in a self-conscious fashion through outward-looking food trade initiatives.

This discovery is on the one hand unsettling. Those who prefer self-conscious "management" as a means to improve the security and stability of global food markets might be troubled. Over the past dozen years, the share of the world's grain consumption satisfied through international trade has nearly doubled. Nations appear to be growing more dependent upon a "less dependable" international grain-trading system, one which takes its shape from an increasing number of un-coordinated national policy actions, seemingly self-centered or at best haphazard in character.

On the other hand, the management of today's enlarged international grain-trading system would not necessarily improve if habits were to change and if these separate nations were to opt for more outward-looking food trade policies. Instead of a dumping ground for domestic surplus, or a shopping place for marginal consumption needs, the world food-trading system might be transformed into something even less attractive—a battleground for international diplomatic and commercial competition. The competitive pursuit of food power, which has proved troublesome enough as an occasional reality, might take hold as a permanent reality, displacing altogether any ideal of sound global food management. The outward-looking policy instincts of national governments, once engaged, can be no less menacing to food security and market stability. Better, perhaps, to live with a world food system that is not the product of any one nation's outward-looking policy actions or ambitions. Better to trust in the relative absence of self-conscious management at the system level.

For students of foreign policy, this analysis is a useful reminder that the "primacy" of a nation's foreign policy concerns, at least in peacetime, should not be taken for granted. Foreign policy leaders often try to enlist the full array of their nation's resources in a pursuit of commercial or diplomatic advantage abroad, but they are frequently frustrated in this effort by their nation's larger preoccupation with perceived policy opportunities and prior political commitments at home. This generalization may not apply with equal force in every nation, or in every issue area. Food policy, however, seems to revolve around domestic priorities not only in advanced industrial democracies such as the United States. The impulse to assign highest priority to inward-looking food policy objectives was also noted in India and in the Soviet Union. However frustrating this tendency may be at times to practitioners of foreign policy, others should see it as cause for reassurance. The greatest gains waiting to be made from political action in the food policy arena are those to be made through improved production and consumption initiatives taken at home.

This brings us to a lesson that students of international relations might draw from this study. In the postwar period the economic interdependence of nations has indeed been enlarged. Each nation's economic prosperity, as well as its military security, is now determined by numerous cross-border interactions. Yet the fashionable conclusion, that these vital international economic relations must now be managed by outward-looking *foreign* policy officials, may be unwarranted. Why should this expanded network of international economic relations be added to the agenda of "foreign policy"? To entrust global economic management to practitioners of international diplomacy might reduce opportunities for some mutually advantageous economic relations to evolve. We saw here the growth of advantageous international grain trade relations, among diplomatic rivals, in part because the diplomatic community (at both ends) had been denied control over those relations. Since conflictual behavior is so often contagious across issue areas, this disconnection between food trade and foreign policy might be regarded as a healthy development, a prudent "compartmentalization" of international policy concerns, self-protective for all concerned. It is one useful means by which national governments, properly mindful of their prior food policy responsibilities at home, can minimize the damage done by their instinct for destructive competition abroad.

Notes

Introduction

1. "Talking Paper" used by Alexander Haig to prepare for 6 January 1981 meeting with the president-elect, as obtained by *Washington Post*. Published in *Boston Globe*, 13 July 1982, p. 7.
2. Alexander M. Haig, Jr., *Caveat: Realism, Reagan, and Foreign Policy* (New York: Macmillan, 1984), p. 111.
3. U.S. Department of State, Bureau of Public Affairs, *U.S. Foreign Policy and Agricultural Trade*, Current Policy no. 535 (Washington, 10 January 1984), p. 4.
4. "Food: Potent U.S. Weapon: Interview with Earl L. Butz, Secretary of Agriculture," *U.S. News and World Report*, 16 February 1976, p. 27.
5. U.S. Central Intelligence Agency, Office of Political Research, *Potential Implications of Trends in World Population, Food Production, and Climate*, OPR 401 (Washington, August 1974), p. 39.
6. Geoffrey Barraclough, "Wealth and Power: The Politics of Food and Oil," *The New York Review of Books* 22:13 (7 August 1975): 23.
7. *Washington Post*, 19 September 1974, p. 1.
8. *Time*, 21 January 1980, p. 12.
9. U.S. Department of State, *U.S. Foreign Policy and Agricultural Trade*, p. 1.

1 The Food Power Presumption

1. Karl W. Deutsch, *The Analysis of International Relations*, 2d ed. (Englewood Cliffs, N.J.: Prentice-Hall, 1978), p. 129. See also Kenneth N. Waltz, *Theory of International Politics* (Reading, Mass.: Addison-Wesley, 1979), pp. 65–71.
2. Thomas R. Grennes, Paul R. Johnson, and Marie Thursby, *The Economics of World Grain Trade* (New York: Praeger, 1978), p. 14.

3. Lazar Volin, *A Century of Russian Agriculture* (Cambridge: Harvard University Press, 1970).

4. U.S. Department of Agriculture, Foreign Agriculture Service, *Foreign Agriculture Circular,* FG-28-81 (Washington, 14 July 1981), p. 3.

5. For a discussion see Robert O. Keohane and Joseph S. Nye, Jr., *Power and Interdependence* (Boston: Little Brown, 1977), pp. 27–28.

6. D. Gale Johnson, *World Agriculture in Disarray* (London: Macmillan, 1973), p. 20. For similar arguments, see Harald B. Malmgren, *International Economic Peacekeeping in Phase II,* rev. ed. (New York: Quadrangle, 1972), p. 119.

7. See Theodore W. Schultz, ed., *Distortions of Agricultural Incentives* (Bloomington: Indiana University Press, 1978).

8. J. P. O'Hagan, "National Self-Sufficiency in Food," *Food Policy* 1:5 (November 1976): 355–66.

9. Peter J. Katzenstein, ed., *Between Power and Plenty: Foreign Economic Policies of Advanced Industrial States* (Madison: University of Wisconsin Press, 1978), p. 588.

10. I. M. Destler, *Making Foreign Economic Policy* (Washington: Brookings, 1980) pp. 20–21.

11. Frances Moore Lappe and Joseph Collins, *Food First* (New York: Ballantine, 1977), p. 248.

12. G. Edward Schuh, "Agriculture and Foreign Policy: The Economic Framework," speech presented to Agriculture and Foreign Policy Conference, Spring Hill Center, Minneapolis, 29 April 1982.

13. "Food: Potent U.S. Weapon: Interview with Earl L. Butz, Secretary of Agriculture," *U.S. News and World Report,* 16 February 1976, p. 27. See also U.S. Library of Congress, Congressional Research Service, *Food Power: The Potential Use of U.S. Grain Exports as a Tool in International Affairs* (Washington, January 1977), p. 10.

14. For a representative sampling of such diplomatic and security gains attributed to food power—specifically U.S. food power—see Richard Gilmore, *A Poor Harvest* (New York: Longman, 1982), chap. 8; Dan Morgan, *Merchants of Grain* (New York: Viking, 1979), chaps. 11–12; Mitchel B. Wallerstein, *Food for War—Food for Peace* (Cambridge: MIT Press, 1980), chap. 6.

15. "Food Power: The Ultimate Weapon in World Politics?" *Business Week,* 15 December 1975, pp. 54–60.

16. Lester Brown asserted in 1975 that this collective market power could be put to a particularly humane use, if Canada and the United States could agree to ration their exports in times of tight supplies to foreign customers that were making a contribution to solving global food and population problems. Without such a coordinated exporter's strategy, in Brown's view, the potential food power of the "North American Breadbasket"

would continue to be frittered away. Lester R. Brown, "The Politics and Responsibility of the North American Breadbasket," Worldwatch Paper 2 (Washington: Worldwatch Institute, 1975), p. 6.

17. Samuel P. Huntington, "Trade, Technology, and Leverage," *Foreign Policy* no. 32 (Fall 1978): 70.

18. U.S. Library of Congress, *Food Power: The Potential Use of U.S. Grain Exports as a Tool in International Affairs*, p. 16.

19. Henry Kissinger, *White House Years* (Boston: Little Brown, 1979), p. 1270. Kissinger's assessment of Soviet vulnerability to U.S. food power on this occasion is in serious error. Mass starvation in the Soviet Union was never a prospect. Grains imported by the Soviet Union from *all sources* in 1972–73 accounted for only 12 percent of total internal use, and most of these imported grains were used as animal feed.

20. U.S. Congress, House, Committee on Foreign Affairs, *Data and Analysis Concerning the Possibility of a U.S. Food Embargo as a Response to the Present Arab Oil Boycott*, 93d Cong., 1st sess., 21 November 1973, p. 1.

21. Emma Rothschild, "Food Politics," *Foreign Affairs* 54:2 (January 1976): 285–307.

22. Cheryl Christensen, "Food and National Security," in Klaus Knorr and Frank N. Trager, eds., *Economic Issues and National Security* (Lawrence: Regents Press of Kansas, 1977), p. 292.

23. Joseph M. Willett and Sharon B. Webster, " 'Food Power'—Food in International Politics," paper presented to the Conference on Political Aspects of the World Food Problem, Kansas State University, 5 March 1977, p. 14.

24. Dan Morgan, "The Politics of Grain," *Atlantic Monthly*, July 1981, p. 31.

25. Lauren Soth, "The Grain Export Boom: Should It Be Tamed?" *Foreign Affairs* 59:4 (Spring 1981): 909.

26. For a review of long-term trends in real export prices of wheat and corn see *Journal of Agricultural Economics* 65:1 (February 1983): 158–59.

27. "Export Act Should Include Embargo Protections," *Cargill Bulletin*, May 1983, p. 2.

2   India: Domestic Sources of Grain Trade Policy

1. Fred H. Sanderson and Shyamal Roy, *Food Trends and Prospects in India* (Washington: Brookings, 1979), p. 1.

2. Shlomo Reutlinger, "The Level and Stability of India's Foodgrain Consumption," in *India: Occasional Papers*, World Bank Staff Working Paper no. 279 (Washington, May 1978), pp. 95–97.

3. John Wall, "Foodgrain Management: Pricing, Procurement, Distribution, Import and Storage Policy," in *India: Occasional Papers*, p. 89.

4. Government of India, *Sixth Five Year Plan, 1980–85,* Planning Commission (New Delhi, January 1981), p. 113.

5. World Bank, *World Development Report 1980* (New York: Oxford University Press, 1980), p. 110.

6. Government of India, *Sixth Five Year Plan,* p. 16.

7. Raj Krishna, "The Economic Development of India," *Scientific American* 243:3 (September 1980): 169.

8. Ibid., p. 166.

9. Government of India, *Sixth Five Year Plan,* p. 16; Krishna, "The Economic Development of India," p. 166.

10. Sanderson and Roy, *Food Trends and Prospects in India,* p. 106. See also Krishna, "The Economic Development of India," p. 173.

11. R. N. Chopra, *The Evolution of Food Policy in India* (New Delhi: Macmillan India Ltd., 1981), p. 218.

12. Marcus Franda, "The Dynamics of Indian Food Policy," in Barbara Huddleston and Jon McLin, eds., *Political Investments in Food Production* (Bloomington: Indiana University Press, 1979), p. 107.

13. When government grain stocks later fell, the FFWP was denied any further allocations of wheat or rice from India's central government supply. Lacking in political organization, India's rural poor had no means to resist this sort of decision. Some complaints came from the state of West Bengal, where the rural poor had become a more significant political force. But from the view of Congress party leaders in New Delhi, such complaints registered by an isolated opposition party in West Bengal could receive low priority.

14. Uma Lele, *Food Grain Marketing in India* (Ithaca, N.Y.: Cornell University Press, 1971), p. 44.

15. Chopra, *The Evolution of Food Policy in India,* p. 204.

16. Ibid., p. 176.

17. The high profits earned by a few Indian traders derive less from market control than from large sales volume. Transport bottlenecks in the countryside also contribute to the very high profit margins taken by Indian traders during the immediate postharvest season. Government interventions in the market, which often restrict the free movement of grain from surplus to deficit regions, can unwittingly increase these profit margins. Lele, *Food Grain Marketing in India,* pp. 215–17.

18. U.S. Department of Agriculture, *India: Quarterly Grain and Feed,* Attache Report IN-1032 (New Delhi, 13 May 1981), p. 3.

19. Chopra, *The Evolution of Food Policy in India,* p. 189.

20. Ibid., p. 191. See also Wall, "Foodgrain Management," p. 53.

21. The Indian Food Department uses its overseas Supply Missions to make foodgrain purchases, and then arranges shipment to India, where FCI takes control. Purchases are made on a competitive bid basis from private

grain companies, or through negotiations with government marketing boards in surplus countries, usually on a deferred payment cash basis, with only a small grant element. Imports of other foods, such as pulses, are handled through a less centralized procedure, with India's own private traders permitted to purchase from abroad under Open General License. India's grain *export* procedures allow more room for separate state initiatives. India's rare wheat exports have been arranged and managed from the Centre, by a variety of ministries in coordination with each other (Commerce, Agriculture, Finance, and External Affairs). But exports of rice, and more recently of maize and barley, are merely authorized by the Centre, with maximum quantities and minimum export prices specified. The Centre then allocates export quotas to a variety of state export organizations, as well as to FCI, on a first-come-first-served basis. India's long-standing exports of *basmati* rice are made under Open General License; exports of non-*basmati* rice more recently have been made on a commercial basis, and at times in the form of commodity loans to friendly countries, or more significantly in the form of rice-for-oil barter agreements with the Soviet Union. See U.S. Department of Agriculture, *India Quarterly Grain and Feed*, Attache Report IN-1032.

22. United Nations Food and Agriculture Organization, *The Rice Policy of India*, CCP-RI 80/3 (Rome, December 1980).
23. U.S. Department of Agriculture, *India Quarterly Grain and Feed*, Attache Report IN-1053 (New Delhi, 11 August 1981).
24. Chopra, *The Evolution of Food Policy in India*, p. 245; U.S. Department of Agriculture, *India: Quarterly Grain and Feed*, Attache Report IN-1053, p. 3.
25. United Nations Food and Agriculture Organization, *The Rice Policy of India*, pp. 3–6.
26. Ibid. See also U.S. Department of Agriculture, *India Quarterly Grain and Feed*, Attache Reports IN-0086 and IN-1053 (New Delhi, 13 November 1980, and 11 August 1981).
27. U.S. Department of Agriculture, *India Quarterly Grain and Feed*, Attache Report IN-1053, p. 4.
28. Government of India, *Sixth Five Year Plan*, p. xx.
29. *New York Times*, 6 July 1981, p. 1.
30. *Journal of Commerce*, 23 March 1982, p. 5A, and 22 March 1983, p. 9A.
31. The Planning Commission originally arrived at its 3 million ton export target figure by subtracting "projected internal consumption" from "projected domestic production," a further indication that internal needs remained paramount.
32. *The Economist*, 31 May 1980, p. 48.
33. *The Statesman*, 10 September 1981, p. 7.
34. *New York Times*, 14 December 1980, p. 1; 13 September 1981, p. 4.

35. Minister of Agriculture Rao Birindra Singh, Opening General Statement to Sixth Ministerial Session of World Food Council, Arusha, Tanzania, June 1980, p. 2.
36. Prime Minister Indira Gandhi, speech presented to Food and Agriculture Organization of the United Nations, Rome, 9 November 1981, pp. 7–8.
37. U.S. Department of Agriculture, *India: Quarterly Grain and Feed*, Attache Report IN-1032, p. 9.
38. Chopra, *The Evolution of Food Policy in India*, pp. 54–59.
39. Ibid., p. 292; p. 85.
40. John W. Mellor, *The New Economics of Growth* (Ithaca, N.Y.: Cornell University Press, 1976), p. 56.
41. *Times of India*, 15 August 1956, p. 1.
42. Chopra, *The Evolution of Food Policy in India*, p. 51.
43. Ibid., p. 101.
44. Mitchel B. Wallerstein, *Food For War—Food For Peace* (Cambridge: MIT Press, 1980), p. 186.
45. Chester Bowles, *Promises to Keep* (New York: Harper and Row, 1971), p. 491.
46. *Times of India*, 10 July 1956, p. 1.
47. Bowles, *Promises to Keep*, p. 439.
48. Chopra, *The Evolution of Food Policy in India*, p. 119.
49. Cited in ibid., p. 118.
50. Ibid., p. 119.
51. C. Subramaniam, *The New Strategy in Indian Agriculture*, (New Delhi: Vikas, 1979), p. 10.
52. Mellor, *The New Economics of Growth*, p. 56.
53. Henry Kissinger, *White House Years* (Boston: Little Brown, 1979), pp. 868–69.
54. *Times of India*, 30 December 1971, p. 11.
55. Ibid., 24 November 1971, p. 4; 30 December 1971, p. 11.
56. Chopra, *The Evolution of Food Policy in India*, p. 137.
57. *Economist Intelligence Unit*, Quarterly Economic Review, India (Fourth Quarter 1972), p. 4.
58. Ibid.
59. Chopra, *The Evolution of Food Policy in India*, p. 292.
60. *Times of India*, 28 May 1973, p. 1; 10 June 1973, p. 1; 26 July 1973, p. 1; 6 September 1973, p. 1.
61. Ibid., 9 October 1973, p. 5.
62. *Economist Intelligence Unit*, Quarterly Economic Review, India, p. 11.
63. Ibid., p. 13.
64. U.S. Department of Agriculture, *India: Quarterly Grain and Feed*, Attache Report IN-1032, p. 4.
65. Ibid.
66. *The Statesman*, 24 July 1981, p. 9.

67. These farmers pointed out that the government would be paying a higher price per ton for its wheat imports from the United States than it was presently offering to producers at home. If the government was willing to pay such a high price to U.S. farmers for additional wheat, why not first raise the procurement price at home? From the viewpoint of Indian officials, higher procurement prices within India had not been considered an attractive short-run policy alternative. Once set at the beginning of a harvest season, procurement prices cannot be changed. Moreover, any increase in the procurement price would imply a budgetary commitment perhaps difficult to reverse. Imports, it was hoped, could always be terminated; procurement prices, once raised, have never been lowered. *Financial Express*, 18 July 1981, p. 1.

68. Prime Minister Gandhi was singled out for having acquiesced in the decisions taken by Chief Ministers in several northern states to delay official procurement efforts for a critical two-week period early in the market season, apparently to give politically powerful private traders a chance to acquire significant quantities of wheat without any competition from FCI. See *The Statesman*, 22 July 1981, p. 7.

69. India's exchange position was so weak that the IMF would agree later in the year to extend to India an unprecedented $5.5 billion balance of payments loan. *The Statesman*, 9 September 1981, p. 1; 24 July 1981, p. 8.

70. For similar reasons, between 1972 and 1976 India had purchased roughly two-thirds of its imported wheat from the United States, despite its difficult diplomatic relations with Washington at the time.

71. U.S. Department of Agriculture, *Foreign Agriculture* (Washington, November 1982), p. 20.

72. *U.S. Wheat Associates Newsletter*, 24 September 1982, p. 1.

73. *U.S. Wheat Associates Newsletter*, 14 September 1984, p. 4.

74. *The Economist*, 3 March 1984, p. 67.

3 The Soviet Union: Retreat from Food Power

1. Lazar Volin, *A Century of Russian Agriculture* (Cambridge: Harvard University Press, 1970), p. 174.

2. Ibid., p. 58.

3. Ibid., p. 63.

4. In 1921 an "unofficial" joint appeal for emergency food assistance was sent from Maxim Gorky and from the Patriarch of the Russian Orthodox Church to the American Relief Association headed by Herbert Hoover. Over the next two years the American Relief Association undertook food relief operations inside the Soviet Union which, at their peak, fed 10 million daily.

5. Volin, *A Century of Russian Agriculture*, p. 176.

6. Ibid., p. 211.

7. Ibid., p. 176.

8. Marshall I. Goldman, "The Changing Role of Raw Material Exports and Soviet Foreign Trade," U.S. Congress, Joint Economic Committee, *Soviet Economy in a Time of Change*, vol. 1 (Washington, 10 October 1979), p. 181.

9. Volin, *A Century of Russian Agriculture*, pp. 281, 175, 292.

10. Dmitri V. Pavlov, *Leningrad, 1941: The Blockade* (Chicago: University of Chicago Press, 1965), p. 127.

11. Victor Perlo, "How Agriculture is Becoming an Advanced Section of Socialist Society," in Harry G. Shaffer, ed., *Soviet Agriculture* (New York: Praeger, 1977), p. 132.

12. U.S. Department of Agriculture, Economic Research Service, *The World Food Situation and Prospects to 1985*, Foreign Agricultural Economic Report no. 98 (Washington, December 1974), p. 14.

13. Khrushchev was deeply resentful of this grain export requirement, however, due to the hardships which it created in the Soviet Union, particularly in his native Ukraine where a drought had further reduced supplies. As Khrushchev later wrote, "Stalin made major concessions for the Poles, creating great difficulties. . . . Bread was sent to Poland from the Ukraine while Ukrainians were bloated from starvation and in some cases were eating each other." *Khrushchev Remembers: The Last Testament* (Boston: Little Brown, 1974), p. 159.

14. Roy Medvedev, *Khrushchev* (Garden City, N.Y.: Anchor Press/Doubleday, 1983), p. 76.

15. David M. Schoonover, "Soviet Agricultural Policies," in Joint Economic Committee, *Soviet Economy in a Time of Change*, vol. 2, p. 94.

16. Volin, *A Century of Russian Agriculture*, p. 200.

17. Novosti Press Agency, "The Socialist Transformation of Agriculture," in Shaffer, ed., *Soviet Agriculture*, p. 159. See also Douglas B. Diamond and W. Lee Davis, "Comparative Growth in Output and Productivity in U.S. and U.S.S.R. Agriculture," in Joint Economic Committee, *Soviet Economy in a Time of Change*, vol. 2, p. 20.

18. Medvedev, *Khrushchev*, pp. 76–77.

19. M. Gardner Clark, "Soviet Agricultural Policy," in Shaffer, ed., *Soviet Agriculture*, p. 17. See also Schoonover, "Soviet Agricultural Policies," p. 92, and Volin, *A Century of Russian Agriculture*, pp. 485–93.

20. Medvedev, *Khrushchev*, p. 116.

21. Volin, *A Century of Russian Agriculture*, p. 343.

22. Judith G. Goldich, "U.S.S.R. Grain and Oilseed Trade in the Seventies," in Joint Economic Committee, *Soviet Economy in a Time of Change*, vol. 2, p. 146.

23. Michael D. Zahn, "Soviet Livestock Feed in Perspective," in ibid., p. 174.

24. Khrushchev later recalled his deep irritation with Poland, in particular, on

this occasion: "[E]ven then [in 1963] Gomulka came to us asking for increased shipments. I spoke to him very directly . . . 'You know per capita meat consumption in the Soviet Union is lower than in your country. . . . Yet here you are asking us to give you extra shipments.'" *Khrushchev Remembers: The Last Testament*, p. 214.

25. Volin, *A Century of Russian Agriculture*, p. 343.

26. Romania, having enjoyed a good harvest, was in some position to help. Medvedev, *Khrushchev*, p. 173.

27. He was immediately ridiculed in the Chinese press for having at last produced an agricultural miracle, by planting wheat in Siberia and harvesting a bountiful crop in Kansas.

28. James Trager, *The Great Grain Robbery* (New York: Ballantine, 1975), pp. 15–16.

29. Clark, "Soviet Agricultural Policy," p. 43.

30. Schoonover, "Soviet Agricultural Policies," p. 93. See also David W. Carey and Joseph F. Havelka, "Soviet Agriculture: Progress and Problems," in Joint Economic Committee, *Soviet Economy in a Time of Change*, vol. 2, p. 58, and Diamond and Davis, "Comparative Growth in Output and Productivity in U.S. and U.S.S.R. Agriculture," p. 21.

31. U.S. Department of Agriculture, Economic Research Service, *U.S.S.R.: Review of Agriculture in 1981 and Outlook for 1982*, suppl. 1, WAS-27 (Washington, May 1982), pp. 16–17.

32. On collective farms, which are largely dependent on their own earnings, labor is used according to the dictates of the collective farm chairman. Above a low minimum wage, labor receives whatever remains after other obligations have been met. State farms, by contrast, are funded and operated directly by the state, and the labor force is paid—like industrial labor—on a fixed wage independent of net farm earnings.

33. Clark, "Soviet Agricultural Policy," p. 10.

34. Ann Lane, "U.S.S.R.: Private Agriculture on Center Stage," in U.S. Congress, Joint Economic Committee, *Soviet Economy in the 1980's: Problems and Prospects*, vol. 2 (Washington, 31 December 1982), p. 38.

35. The Brezhnev leadership removed all limits on household livestock holdings early in 1981, but only if private production was contracted to count toward the state farm's sales plan.

36. Ivan Khudenko, an innovative former senior agricultural official of the Kazakh Republic, conducted several successful experiments with the link system over nearly a decade. But early in 1973, shortly after his experimental farms had demonstrated a level of labor productivity twenty times higher than on neighboring farms, Khudenko was arrested on a trumped-up charge of having tried to steal 1,000 rubles from the state. He died in prison in 1974. Clark, "Soviet Agricultural Policy," p. 42. See also Hedrick Smith, *The Russians* (New York: Ballantine, 1976), p. 283.

37. Douglas B. Diamond, Lee W. Bettis, and Robert E. Ramsson, "Agri-

cultural Production," unpublished manuscript prepared for Conference on The Soviet Economy Toward the Year 2000 (Airlie House, Va., 23–25 October 1979), p. 3.

38. U.S. Department of Agriculture, Foreign Agriculture Service, *Foreign Agriculture Circular,* FG-14-83 (Washington, 11 May 1983).

39. "Statement of Henry Rowen, Chairman, National Intelligence Council," to Subcommittee on International Trade, Finance, and Security Economics, 1 December 1982. U.S. Congress, Joint Economic Committee, *Allocation of Resources in the Soviet Union and China—1982* (Washington, 1983), p. 184.

40. Zahn, "Soviet Livestock Feed in Perspective," p. 174.

41. U.S. Department of Agriculture, Economic Research Service, *Prospects for Agricultural Trade with the U.S.S.R.,* ERS—Foreign 356 (Washington, April 1974), pp. 4–6.

42. By one account, factories closed for three days both in Novocherkassk and in Rostov-on-Don following the rioting, as unofficial martial law prevailed. See Medvedev, *Khrushchev,* p. 171.

43. Soviet meat price subsidies (which increased by 15 percent in 1978 alone) now provide demanding consumers with an effective 40 percent price markdown in state retail outlets. Over 1976–80, Soviet subsidies for meat and milk cost the state nearly 100 billion rubles, roughly four times the total agricultural investment in 1975, and nearly one and one half times more than agriculture's total contribution to Soviet GNP in 1977. D. Gale Johnson, "Prospects for Soviet Agriculture in the 1980's," in Joint Economic Committee, *Soviet Economy in the 1980's,* vol. 2, pp. 8–9.

44. M. Elizabeth Denton, "Soviet Consumer Policy: Trends and Prospects," in Joint Economic Committee, *Soviet Economy in a Time of Change,* vol. 1, p. 760.

45. U.S. Department of Agriculture, Economic Research Service, *U.S.S.R.: Review of Agriculture in 1981 and Outlook for 1982,* p. 28.

46. Ibid., *Prospects for Agricultural Trade with the U.S.S.R.,* p. 10.

47. Daniel L. Bond and Herbert S. Levine, "The 11th Five-Year Plan, 1981–85," unpublished manuscript prepared for Conference on the Twenty-Sixth Congress of the Communist Party of the Soviet Union, The Rand Corporation—Columbia University (Washington, 23–25 April 1981), p. 3.

48. Denton, "Soviet Consumer Policy," p. 761.

49. Lawrence J. Brainard, "Foreign Economic Constraints on Soviet Economic Policy in the 1980's," in Joint Economic Committee, *Soviet Economy in a Time of Change,* vol. 1, p. 104.

50. Valentine Zabijaka, "The Soviet Grain Trade 1961–70: A Decade of Change," *The ACES Bulletin* 16:1 (Spring 1974): 6; Dan Morgan, *Merchants of Grain* (New York: Viking Press, 1979), p. 142.

51. U.S. Congress, Senate, Committee on Government Operations, *Russian Grain Transactions*, Report no. 93-1033, 93d Cong., 2d sess., 29 July 1974, p. 10.

52. Zabijaka, "The Soviet Grain Trade 1961–70," p. 6.

53. As Kissinger recalled:

> During the summit Nixon had commented several times to Brezhnev and Kosygin about the beneficial impact of grain sales on our public opinion, but the Soviet leaders had feigned little interest. Kosygin told Rogers that as a special favor the Soviets might buy $150 million. I advised Nixon that this sum was too insignificant to merit inclusion in the summit communique.

See Henry Kissinger, *White House Years* (Boston: Little Brown, 1979), p. 1269.

54. When U.S. officials proudly announced the long-delayed agreement on credit terms, early in July, they were not aware that the Soviet Union had already purchased, for cash, during the previous week, 8.5 million tons of U.S. wheat and corn, or almost as much as the credit agreement had originally been designed to finance over the next three years. See U.S. Senate, *Russian Grain Transactions*, p. 9.

55. Paul G. Ericson and Ronald S. Miller, "Soviet Foreign Economic Behavior: A Balance of Payments Perspective," in Joint Economic Committee, *Soviet Economy in a Time of Change*, vol. 2, pp. 241–42.

56. Indeed, it was only due to a physical upper limit on import volume (only a bit more than 2 million tons of grain per month could then be unloaded at Soviet port facilities and moved inland by barge and rail) that Soviet grain imports in 1975 were not even larger.

57. David W. Carey and Joseph F. Halveka, "Soviet Agriculture: Progress and Problems," in Joint Economic Committee, *Soviet Economy in a Time of Change*, vol. 2, p. 66.

58. Goldman, "The Changing Role of Raw Material Exports and Soviet Foreign Trade," pp. 191–92.

59. The Soviet debt service ratio (on total foreign exchange earnings) never became dangerously large, but it did increase as a result of this stepped-up borrowing from 0.09 in 1974 to 0.15 by 1976.

60. Ericson and Miller, "Soviet Foreign Economic Behavior," p. 241; Denton, "Soviet Consumer Policy," p. 726.

61. For such purposes during the 1960s, 58.0 percent of Soviet wheat and wheat flour exports had gone to Eastern Europe, 13.1 percent to Cuba, 2.6 percent to North Korea, and 3.0 percent to North Vietnam. In addition to these exports of its own grain, the Soviet Union had also transshipped significant quantities of grain to its allies "on Soviet account." Zabijaka, "Soviet Grain Trade 1961–70," p. 8.

62. In a personal letter to Prime Minister Indira Gandhi explaining his reason

for the loan, Brezhnev mentioned "the aspiration to develop friendly Soviet-Indian relations." The Indian government, which had discreetly asked for the loan, immediately conveyed its "warm appreciation." *Times of India,* 29 September 1973, p. 1.

63. U.S. Department of Agriculture, Foreign Agriculture Service, *Foreign Agriculture Circular,* Grains, FG-40-81 (Washington, 13 November 1981).
64. Morgan, *Merchants of Grain,* pp. 274–76.
65. Ericson and Miller, "Soviet Foreign Economic Behavior," p. 230; Philip Hanson, "Economic Constraints on Soviet Policies in the 1980's," *International Affairs* 57:1 (Winter 1980–81): 36.
66. Even when oil prices began to decline, after 1980, Soviet production capacity was sufficient to keep export earnings high, through an increase in export volume—to as much as 1.5 million barrels a day in 1982.
67. Sales of gold in 1979 dropped 44 percent below the 410 tons that had been sold in 1978. During 1980 and 1981, sales dropped to an estimated average level 50 percent lower than the average during 1977–79, even though annual production remained high. Total Soviet gold stocks, estimated at 1,900 tons in 1981, were worth over $25 billion at the prices then prevailing. Statement of Henry Rowen, p. 19. See also Angel O. Byrne, James E. Cole, Thomas Bickerton, and Anton F. Malish, "U.S.–U.S.S.R. Grain Trade," in Joint Economic Committee, *Soviet Economy in the 1980's,* vol. 2, p. 71.
68. Ericson and Miller, "Soviet Foreign Economic Behavior," p. 214.
69. U.S. Department of Agriculture, *Foreign Agriculture Circular,* FG-30-81, 13 August 1981, p. 7.
70. U.S. Department of Agriculture, *Update, Impact of Agricultural Trade Restrictions on Soviet Union,* Foreign Agricultural Economic Report no. 160 (Washington, July 1980).
71. The Soviet Union had earlier heard Jimmy Carter's promise to American farmers that he would never embargo grain exports, but they had also seen, in 1975, that anti-Soviet U.S. labor organizations (specifically the International Longshoremen's Association) could effectively disrupt grain exports on their own initiative, with or without the president's approval.
72. U.S. Department of Agriculture, *Update, Impact of Agricultural Trade Restrictions on Soviet Union.*
73. *Wall Street Journal,* 23 April 1981, p. 46.
74. "Argentine Grain Production, Exports Rise," *Cargill Crop Bulletin,* February 1982, pp. 8–9. U.S. Department of Agriculture, *Foreign Agriculture Circular,* FG-13-83, 12 May 1983, pp. 10–11.
75. U.S. Department of Agriculture, *Foreign Agriculture Circular,* FG-13-83, 12 May 1983, pp. 10–11.
76. *Journal of Commerce,* 22 October 1982, p. 9A.
77. *U.S. Wheat Associates Newsletter,* 20 May 1983, p. 1.

78. See *Boston Globe,* 17 October 1982, p. 13.
79. Quoted in *Business Week,* 7 June 1982, p. 36, and *New York Times,* 28 October 1982, p. A7.
80. Soviet officials could calculate, moreover, that per capita meat consumption would increase only modestly (to 64 kilograms of meat *and* fat, still well below the earlier endorsed "consumption norm" of 82 kilograms), even in the unlikely event that the grain production goals of the Eleventh Plan were met. Johnson, "Prospects for Soviet Agriculture in the 1980's," p. 21.
81. In a parallel step, "consumption norms" were modified modestly downward as well, in October 1981, from 82 kilograms per capita to 78 kilograms. See U.S. Department of Agriculture, *U.S.S.R.: Review of Agriculture in 1981 and Outlook for 1982,* p. 28.
82. Schoonover, "Prospects for U.S.–U.S.S.R. Agricultural Trade," pp. 10–11.
83. *London Times,* 17 November 1981, p. 1.
84. It remains this high because retail prices are held artificially low, and because there are few alternative outlets for disposable income. Schoonover, "Prospects for U.S.–U.S.S.R. Agricultural Trade," p. 4.
85. David M. Schoonover, "Overview," in Joint Economic Committee, *Soviet Economy in the 1980's,* vol. 2, p. 3.
86. Russell A. Ambroziak and David W. Carey, "Climate and Grain Production in the Soviet Union," in Joint Economic Committee, *Soviet Economy in the 1980's,* vol. 2, p. 118.
87. Schoonover, "Overview," p. 5.
88. Anton F. Malish, "The Food Program: A New Policy or More Rhetoric?" in Joint Economic Committee, *Soviet Economy in the 1980's,* vol. 2, p. 51.
89. Quoted in "Statement of Lt. Gen. James A. Williams, Director, Defense Intelligence Agency," to Subcommittee on International Trade, Finance, and Security Economics, 29 June 1982. U.S. Congress, Joint Economic Committee, *Allocation of Resources in the Soviet Union and China—1982* (Washington, 1983), p. 62.
90. *Economist,* 7 May 1983, p. 32.
91. *Journal of Commerce,* 28 March 1984, p. 9A.
92. U.S. Department of Agriculture, *Foreign Agriculture Circular,* SG-12-84, 12 October 1984, p. 1. See also *New York Times,* 24 October 1984, p. 3.
93. U.S. Central Intelligence Agency, *U.S.S.R.: Long Term Outlook for Grain Imports* (Washington, January 1979), p. 18.
94. Specialists such as N. P. Alexsandrov had pointed out by 1978 that the share of grain used in Soviet feed rations, for cattle and sheep in particular, was increasing unnecessarily, and that "other types of feed" were "more appropriate to the needs of these animals." By various estimates, the expanded use of nongrain feed sources such as succulents and roughages,

at no extra cost to the Soviet Union, could result in an annual savings of as much as 20–30 million tons of grain. Allan P. Mustard, "Impact of the U.S. Grain Embargo on World Grain Trading Patterns and Soviet Livestock Output," diss., University of Illinois, Urbana-Champaign, 1982, p. 73. See also U.S. Department of Agriculture, *U.S.S.R.: Review of Agriculture in 1981 and Outlook for 1982,* p. 4.

95. U.S. Central Intelligence Agency, *U.S.S.R.: Long Term Outlook for Grain Imports* (Washington, January 1979), p. 18.

96. U.S. Department of Agriculture, *Foreign Agriculture Circular,* SG-12-84, 12 October 1984, p. 3. In the view of one specialist in the Department of Agriculture at the time: "[The embargo] seems to have jolted Soviet thinking, and a flurry of articles appeared bemoaning the 'overconsumption' of grain and urging the correction of the protein deficiency in Soviet livestock rations. In fact, the Soviets seem to have achieved some greater efficiencies in 1980, and this new development is institutionalized in the new Plan." Anton F. Malish, Jr., "Internal Policy, Decision Making, and Food Import Demand in the Soviet Union," unpublished manuscript prepared for third meeting of the Trade Research Consortium (Washington, 23–26 June 1981), p. 10.

4   The United States: Food Power Forgone

1. Dan Morgan, *Merchants of Grain* (New York: Viking Press, 1979), p. 36.

2. Murry R. Benedict, *Farm Policies of the U.S.: 1790–1950* (New York: Octagon, 1953), p. 85.

3. Ibid., pp. 120–43.

4. With wheat production in France, Belgium, and Italy suddenly reduced by 60 percent after 1914, and with imports from Russia and the Balkan States no longer available, governments in Western Europe turned to North America for a larger share of their grain requirements. The United States and Canada responded, providing more than two-thirds of Western Europe's total wartime grain import needs, up from a level of only 30 percent before the war. In response to the wartime emergency, total U.S. wheat exports after 1913 more than doubled, increasing from 4 million tons to 9 million tons.

5. The Food Administration Grain Corporation fixed U.S. wheat prices at terminal markets and issued export licenses only with the approval of the Treasury Department, which coordinated allied buying in the United States. Trudy H. Peterson, *Agricultural Exports, Farm Income, and the Eisenhower Administration* (Lincoln: University of Nebraska Press, 1979), p. 2.

6. Grain producers did approve of, in the so-called McNary–Haugen Bill (1924), a plan to have the government support domestic farm prices at a

"fair exchange value," through the sale of surplus farm products abroad at prices below the supported domestic price. President Calvin Coolidge vetoed this plan in 1927 and again in 1928.

7. Benedict, *Farm Policies of the United States*, p. 184.
8. U.S. Congress, Senate, *World Trade Barriers in Relation to American Agriculture*, Document no. 70, 73d Cong., 1st sess., 5 June 1933, p. 17.
9. Benedict, *Farm Policies of the United States*, pp. 299–307.
10. Meat consumption per capita rose 9 percent during the war; consumption of dairy products rose 22 percent. Don Paarlberg, *American Farm Policy* (New York: John Wiley and Sons, 1964), p. 27.
11. Willard W. Cochrane and Mary E. Ryan, *American Farm Policy, 1948–1973* (Minneapolis: University of Minnesota Press, 1976), p. 266.
12. Paarlberg, *American Farm Policy*, p. 156.
13. Peterson, *Agricultural Exports*, p. 4.
14. Benedict, *Farm Policies of the United States*, p. 482.
15. Cochrane and Ryan, *American Farm Policy*, p. 360.
16. Quoted in Peterson, *Agricultural Exports*, p. xii.
17. Jon McLin, "Surrogate International Organization and the Case of World Food Security, 1949–1969," *International Organization* 33:1 (Winter 1979): 52.
18. Peterson, *Agricultural Exports*, p. 79.
19. McLin, "Surrogate International Organization and the Case of World Food Security, 1949–1969," p. 52.
20. The Council on Foreign Economic Policy in 1956 was solidly opposed to an extension of the program, endorsing in the end a modified extension proposal only because of the certainty that farm state legislators would accept nothing less. Peterson, *Agricultural Exports*, pp. 55–57, 76.
21. U.S. Department of Agriculture, Economic Research Service, *Foreign Agricultural Trade of the U.S. (FATUS)* (Washington, 1977), p. 21.
22. Mitchel B. Wallerstein, *Food for War—Food for Peace* (Cambridge: MIT Press, 1980), pp. 32–33.
23. P.L. 480 sales of U.S. wheat to the Nehru government in India, the Nasser government in Egypt, and the Sukarno government in Indonesia performed a function that regular assistance programs, subject as they were to closer congressional scrutiny, could not.
24. At one point in the negotiations India hinted improbably that it could always meet its agricultural import needs from Communist China. U.S. officials (upon learning that the Indian minister of agriculture was actually in Peking) quickly met India's terms. In similar fashion, Egypt had at one point bargained for U.S. wheat sales on the best terms possible, by threatening to turn to the Soviet Union. Peterson, *Agricultural Exports*, pp. 31, 64.
25. For just such reasons, the initiation of this loan program, in 1957, had also

drawn complaints from the State Department, which predicted that it would "further complicate the already difficult administration of P.L. 480." Peterson, *Agricultural Exports*, p. 66.

26. Morgan, *Merchants of Grain*, p. 104.

27. Peterson, *Agricultural Exports*, p. 82.

28. Cochrane and Ryan, *American Farm Policy*, p. 79.

29. Report to the President Submitted by the Commission on International Trade and Investment Policy, *United States International Economic Policy in an Interdependent World* (Washington, July 1971), p. 900 (hereafter cited as the Williams Commission Report).

30. Don Paarlberg, *Farm and Food Policy: Issues of the 1980's* (Lincoln: University of Nebraska Press, 1980), p. 35.

31. Well into the 1960s, even mainstream agricultural economists continued to view external markets not as a promising commercial outlet for U.S. grain but as a source of *instability*, from which U.S. producers required the "protection" that high commodity loan rates appeared to provide. Dale Hathaway, who years later became responsible for promoting U.S. grain exports, as an undersecretary of agriculture in the Carter administration (by which time attitudes had changed) offered the following textbook view of U.S. grain exports in 1963:

> [T]he impact of this source of [foreign market induced] instability has been substantially reduced by the operation of the federal price support programs for most of the major export crops. . . . Shifts in export demand have been substantially reduced and are unlikely to be a major destabilizing force on U.S. farm prices and income as long as present programs are continued.

See Dale E. Hathaway, *Government and Agriculture* (New York: Macmillan, 1963), pp. 135–36.

32. Farm Export Education Project, *U.S. Farm Export Strategies for the Eighties* (Washington: Agriculture Council of America, 1981), p. 150.

33. *New York Times*, 7 February 1961, p. 16; 29 January 1961, sect. III, p. 1; and 26 January 1961, p. 1.

34. Ibid., 17 March 1961, p. 14; 11 October 1961, p. 19; 4 December 1961, p. 24; and 25 March 1962, p. 52.

35. Morgan, *Merchants of Grain*, pp. 104–5.

36. Richard Gilmore, *A Poor Harvest* (New York: Longman, 1982), pp. 187–88; McLin, "Surrogate International Organization and the Case of World Food Security, 1949–1969," p. 51; and Cochrane and Ryan, *American Farm Policy*, p. 275.

37. Trudy H. Peterson, "Sales, Surpluses, and the Soviets: A Study in Political Economy," *Policy Studies Journal* 6:4 (Summer 1978): 531–32.

38. This presidential endorsement was intended to satisfy legal concerns raised by the terms of the Export Control Act, which directed the president to

prohibit exports that might contribute to the "military or economic potential" of nations threatening U.S. security. Although the anticipated sales were to be made for cash, they also risked violating the Johnson Act of 1934 (which prohibited loans or commercial credits to nations in default on debts to the United States), due to the existing U.S. wheat export subsidy program. *New York Times,* 10 October 1963, p. 1.

39. The International Longshoremen's Association signaled its determination to police this restriction by refusing at one point to load any grain at all on ships bound for the Soviet Union.

40. James Trager, *The Great Grain Robbery* (New York: Ballantine, 1975), pp. 14–16.

41. *New York Times,* 17 March 1965, p. 73.

42. McLin, "Surrogate International Organization and the Case of World Food Security, 1949–1969," p. 51.

43. Wallerstein, *Food for War—Food for Peace,* p. 44.

44. The mixed success he enjoyed on this occasion is examined in detail in chapter 5.

45. Gilmore, *A Poor Harvest,* pp. 154–55.

46. Wallerstein, *Food for War—Food for Peace,* p. 46.

47. As Secretary of Agriculture Earl Butz noted in the aftermath of one trip to the Middle East, in 1974, "[I] went down to Cairo with a little wheat in my pocket" and "they had the red carpet out for me there. . . . I went to Syria. I got a royal welcome. . . . I was speaking the language of food, and they understand." Gilmore, *A Poor Harvest,* p. 155.

48. John W. Sewell, *The United States and World Development, Agenda 1980* (New York: Praeger, 1980), p. 234; *Journal of Commerce,* 30 October 1981, p. 9A.

49. Robert Paarlberg, "Food, Oil, and Coercive Resource Diplomacy," *International Security* 3:2 (Fall 1978): 9.

50. This P.L. 480 share did rise to 18 percent of the total in 1976, but it then fell once more, back down to only 9 percent of all wheat exports by 1978. Gilmore, *A Poor Harvest,* pp. 90–91.

51. Butz anticipated some objection from Henry Kissinger's State Department, but was reported to have concluded, "If Henry needs it, let the money come out of his budget." I. M. Destler, *Making Foreign Economic Policy* (Washington: Brookings, 1980), p. 68.

52. Williams Commission Report, pp. 7, 9, 58, 142.

53. The grains policies of the CAP, which imposed particularly stiff variable levies on U.S. foodgrain and feedgrain exports to the European Community, had become fully effective in 1966, and by 1970 U.S. exports to the Community of products subject to this variable levy had fallen by $360 million (about 50 percent) from the 1966 level.

54. Williams Commission Report, pp. 144–56. If Canada were to lose its

privileged Commonwealth Preference in the British food market, Canadian exporters would doubtless seek other markets, in an even more intense competition with U.S. exporters. See U.S. Congress, Senate, Committee on Agriculture and Forestry, *Agricultural Trade and the Proposed Round of Multilateral Negotiations,* 93d Cong., 1st sess., 30 April 1973, p. 57 (hereafter cited as the Flanigan Report).

55. Private lobbyists for U.S. grain export companies were still being told, by State Department officials, that "European unity is more important to the U.S. than your grain exports." Morgan, *Merchants of Grain,* p. 133.

56. McLin, "Surrogate International Organization and the Case of World Food Security, 1949–69," p. 53.

57. Williams Commission Report, pp. 821–24, 855; Flanigan Report, p. 41.

58. This official preoccupation was most clearly revealed in a confidential report prepared early in 1972, by a team from the Department of Agriculture at the request of Peter Flanigan, then assistant to the president for International Economic Affairs. The Flanigan Report stressed that the most important U.S. food trade opportunities were waiting to be exploited in the "grain-feed-livestock sector," where U.S. corn producers in particular held an unbeatable competitive edge. It was noted that meat consumption elsewhere in the industrial world had enormous growth potential. In the European Community specifically, it was noted that 1969 beef consumption per capita was only half the U.S. level. If the United States could price its grain and livestock exports in a competitive fashion, and if effective pressure could then be brought to bear *on the European Community and Japan* to adopt new internal price policies and to open their markets to trade, the benefits to U.S. export earnings (as well as farm income) could be considerable. If trade liberalization were achieved, the report concluded, the U.S. trade balance might improve by as much as $8 billion. Alternatively, without any change in the trade policies of traditional customers such as the European Community and Japan, total U.S. agricultural exports would increase only slightly, and U.S. feedgrain exports specifically, might even *decline* from their 1970–71 levels in the decade ahead. Flanigan Report, p. 90.

59. Daniel T. Morrow, *The Economics of International Stockpiling of Wheat,* Research Report no. 18 (Washington: International Food Policy Research Institute, September 1980), p. 17. See also World Food Institute, "World Food Trade and U.S. Agriculture" (Iowa State University, August 1981), fig. 6, p. 13.

60. U.S. Department of Agriculture, *The World Food Situation and Prospects to 1985,* Foreign Agricultural Economic Report no. 98 (Washington, December 1974), pp. 1–3.

61. Annual GNP growth rates among the developed countries, in real terms, rose from 3.6 percent in 1971 to 5.5 percent in 1972, up to 6.3 percent by

1973. Growth rates among the developing countries rose even more rapidly, to 6.2 percent in 1972 and 7.4 percent in 1973.

62. Destler, *Making Foreign Economic Policy,* pp. 40–44.

63. Morgan, *Merchants of Grain,* p. 142. Moreover, when Nixon asked Congress for an extension of the Export Control Act, due to expire in that year, he sought no change in the prohibition on sales that might contribute to the "economic potential" of a communist country. It was not the Nixon administration that was more anxious to promote exports to the Soviet Union, at this early point, but rather Nixon's partisan critics in the Senate. *New York Times,* 19 June 1969, p. 9.

64. Henry Kissinger, *Years of Upheaval* (Boston: Little Brown, 1982), p. 247.

65. The Longshoremen's resistance was at last overcome in October 1971. A series of pleadings by numerous White House officials, plus the promise of sundry favors, at last enticed the maritime unions to relent. By the end of 1971, the number of shipboard jobs for U.S. seamen had dropped to a twenty-year low, and so the prospect of new exports to any market was welcomed by the unions. As one union official put it at the time, when considering the alternative, "50 percent of nothing is nothing."

66. A wave of dollar selling in spring and summer would eventually force Nixon to take even more drastic steps, including the imposition in August of a 10 percent surcharge on all dutiable imports, and the suspension of convertability of the dollar into gold.

67. *Washington Post,* 7 December 1971, p. A10.

68. See especially Seymour M. Hersh, *The Price of Power* (New York: Summit, 1983), pp. 334–49.

69. U.S. Congress, Senate, Committee on Government Operations, *Russian Grain Transactions,* Report no. 93-1033, 93d Cong., 2d sess., 29 July 1974, p. 27. See also Henry Kissinger, *White House Years* (Boston: Little Brown, 1979), pp. 1134, 1269.

70. Kissinger himself later recalled that the Soviet Union, on that occasion, gave us a lesson in the handicaps a market economy has in negotiating with a state trading enterprise. Each of our grain companies, trying to steal a march on its competitors, sold the largest amount possible and kept its sale utterly secret, even from the U.S. government. Not for several weeks did we realize that the Soviets had, by a series of separate transactions, bought up nearly one billion dollars worth of grain in one year.

Kissinger, *White House Years,* p. 1270.

71. Extensive congressional investigations led to the conclusion that the Department of Agriculture was acting in ignorance and in confusion, rather than in a willful design to favor the Soviet Union or to enrich private traders. See U.S. Senate, *Russian Grain Transactions,* p. 60.

72. Kissinger, *White House Years,* p. 1269.

73. Ibid., p. 1270.
74. Destler, *Making Foreign Economic Policy*, p. 110.
75. For a detailed examination of the U.S. policy-making process during the period of the 1975 sales suspension, see Roger B. Porter, *Presidential Decision Making: The Economic Policy Board* (New York: Cambridge University Press, 1980).
76. Destler, *Making Foreign Economic Policy*, p. 31.
77. Ibid., pp. 50–59.
78. Senior food and commodity specialists in the State Department learned of the export suspension decision just five minutes before it was announced to the public. Ibid., pp. 60–61.
79. *National Farmers Union Washington Newsletter*, 5 October 1979, p. 1.
80. *Agreement between the Government of the United States of America and Government of the Union of Soviet Socialist Republics on the Supply of Grain*, Moscow, 20 October 1975. Reprinted in U.S. House of Representatives, Committee on Appropriations, *Hearings before Subcommittees, Part One* (Washington, 1975), pp. 351–52.
81. Morton I. Sosland, "U.S.–U.S.S.R. Agreement on Grains," (Cambridge: Harvard University Russian Research Center, 5 November 1979), p. 5.
82. Samuel P. Huntington, "Trade, Technology, and Leverage," *Foreign Policy* no. 32 (Fall 1978): 75.
83. Trager, *The Great Grain Robbery*, p. 197.
84. Farm Export Education Project, *U.S. Farm Export Strategies for the Eighties*, p. 178.
85. *New York Times*, 4 October 1979, p. 1; *Great Plains Wheat Newsletter*, 5 October 1979, pp. 2–3.
86. U.S. Congress, Senate, *Agriculture and Food Act of 1981*, Conference Report no. 97-290, 97th Cong., 1st sess., 10 December 1981, pp. 66–67.
87. Alexander M. Haig, Jr., *Caveat: Realism, Reagan, and Foreign Policy* (New York: Macmillan, 1984), p. 251.
88. Ibid., p. 111.
89. Ibid., p. 82.
90. In each instance the president's restraint was being forced by his concern for producer interests at home. A resolution calling for a new agreement had by April 1983 accumulated forty-six cosponsors in the Senate. When a new agreement was then finally negotiated, in July 1983, U.S. officials disassociated the pact from any larger drift in foreign policy. It was hailed instead as "a happy hour for American Agriculture." Secretary of Agriculture John Block, rather than the secretary of state or the U.S. trade representative, had led the negotiations.
91. *U.S. Wheat Associates Newsletter*, 14 January 1983, and 29 April 1983.
92. Unclassified telegram, Department of State 124393, from secretary of

state to all diplomatic and consular posts, "Promotion of U.S. Agricultural Exports," 13 May 1981.

93. *U.S. Wheat Associates Newsletter*, 12 November 1982, p. 2.

94. U.S. Department of Agriculture, *Foreign Agriculture* (Washington, July 1981), pp. 5–6.

95. *Cargill Bulletin*, May 1983, p. 20; and March 1983, p. 12.

96. *Journal of Commerce*, 12 July 1983, p. 9A.

97. These same budgetary constraints that stood in the path of competitive export pricing were also placing an upper limit on the expansion of export credits and export credit guarantees. Department of Agriculture requests for expanded export credit guarantees in 1983 encountered firm resistance from Office of Management and Budget Director David Stockman, who argued that "increased federal credit alone is not the answer to U.S. export expansion." *Cargill Bulletin*, July 1983, p. 1.

5   Testing Food Power: U.S. Food Aid to India, 1965–1967

1. When U.S. food aid shipments were at their peak, in 1966, the steady arrival of two ships daily, loaded with U.S. grain, provided the minimum daily food requirements of 50 million Indian citizens. R. N. Chopra, *The Evolution of Food Policy in India* (New Delhi: Macmillan India Ltd., 1981), pp. 113, 116, 292.

2. Calculated from tables 5, 6, 7 in ibid., pp. 291–92.

3. C. Subramaniam, *The New Strategy in Indian Agriculture* (New Delhi: Vikas, 1979), p. 9; Chester Bowles, *Promises to Keep* (New York: Harper and Row, 1971), p. 525.

4. Francine R. Frankel, *India's Political Economy, 1947–1977* (Princeton, N.J.: Princeton University Press, 1978), p. 284.

5. Carolyn Castore, "The United States and India: The Use of Food to Apply Economic Pressure—1965–67," in Sidney Weintraub, ed., *Economic Coercion and U.S. Foreign Policy* (Boulder, Colo.: Westview Press, 1982), pp. 130–38.

6. Under the U.S.–Indian food aid agreements then in effect, most U.S. wheat shipments arrived under Title I of P.L. 480. The Indian government would normally pay at least half the shipping costs, receive the wheat as a "gift," and sell it through the subsidized PDS. The local currency accumulated from these sales would then be distributed as follows: 10–15 percent to pay for local U.S. administrative expenses; 80–85 percent to finance mutually agreed development projects in India.

7. P. J. Eldridge, *The Politics of Foreign Aid in India* (London: Weidenfeld and Nicholson, 1969), p. 115.

8. In that year (when P.L. 480 surplus wheat shipments to India rose to equal

about 20 percent of total annual U.S. production), food aid to India was judged to have reduced total U.S. surplus storage payments by $200 million. These shipments also contributed, in the year that followed, to a $869 million reduction in CCC expenditures. Castore, "The United States and India," p. 141.

9. *Times of India,* 15 July 1966, p. 1.
10. Memorandum from Orville L. Freeman to the president, 2 July 1965, cited in Mitchel B. Wallerstein, *Food for War—Food for Peace* (Cambridge: MIT Press, 1980), p. 186.
11. Cited in ibid., p. 182.
12. Lyndon B. Johnson, *The Vantage Point* (New York: Holt, Rinehart and Winston, 1971), p. 231.
13. Chester Bowles, *Promises to Keep* (New York: Harper and Row, 1971), p. 500.
14. He noted specifically that "the U.S. had not insisted on measurable progress as a *quid pro quo* for food and technical assistance. Rather, we had provided India with increasing food assistance and had insisted on very little progress in return." Orville L. Freeman, *World Without Hunger* (New York: Praeger, 1968), p. 152.
15. James W. Bjorkman, "Public Law 480 and the Policies of Self-Help and Short-Tether: Indo-American Relations, 1965–68," in Appendices (Case Studies, Economic Policy), *Commission on the Organization of the Government for the Conduct of Foreign Policy* (Washington, June 1975), p. 204.
16. Wallerstein, *Food for War—Food for Peace,* p. 279 n. 16.
17. Subramaniam, who had by then pushing for major Indian policy reforms for more than a year, recalls that the explicit conditions now to be placed upon shipments of U.S. food aid, in combination with the month-by-month manner in which that aid was to be authorized, was not immediately helpful to his cause within the Cabinet:

> President Johnson sent word through his Secretary of Agriculture Freeman, that there should be some sort of an understanding that we would get on with increasing production in a meaningful way and that we should provide them with details of the steps we were taking. This requirement—to tell them what we were doing—was another unfortunate step taken by President Johnson. It perhaps implied also that they would be monitoring whether or not we were proceeding correctly. It enabled the communist group in particular to launch a further attack on the steps we were taking.

Subramaniam, *The New Strategy in Indian Agriculture,* p. 53.
18. *Times of India,* 2 December 1965, p. 1. See also Subramaniam, *The New Strategy in Indian Agriculture,* p. 37.
19. *Times of India,* 7 December 1965, p. 1.

20. Frankel, *India's Political Economy*, p. 286; Freeman, *World Without Hunger*, p. 158.
21. Johnson, *The Vantage Point*, p. 226.
22. *Times of India*, 13 December 1965, p. 7; 10 December 1965, p. 1; 8 December 1965, p. 1.
23. Castore, "The United States and India," p. 135.
24. Bowles, *Promises to Keep*, p. 558.
25. Sidney Weintraub, ed., *Economic Coercion and U.S. Foreign Policy* (Boulder, Colo.: Westview Press, 1982), pp. 52–53.
26. Frankel, *India's Political Economy*, pp. 288–92; Subramaniam, *The New Strategy in Indian Agriculture*, p. 25.
27. Johnson, *The Vantage Point*, p. 225.
28. Cited in ibid., p. 225.
29. Wallerstein, *Food for War—Food for Peace*, p. 189.
30. Bjorkman, "Public Law 480," p. 197–200.
31. Ibid., p. 200–201.
32. Bowles reported Johnson's words:

    I am persuaded that we may stand, at this moment, on the threshold of a great tragedy. The facts are simple; their implications are grave. India faces an unprecedented drought. Unless the world responds, India faces famine. . . . It is not our nature to drive a hard mathematical bargain where hunger is involved. . . . I, therefore, ask your endorsement of this emergency action. India is a good and deserving friend. Let it never be said that "bread should be so dear, and flesh and blood so cheap" that we turned in indifference from her bitter need.

    Bowles, *Promises to Keep*, pp. 524–25.
33. Ibid., p. 525.
34. Johnson, *The Vantage Point*, p. 228.
35. *Times of India*, 27 November 1966, p. 1; 28 November 1966, p. 1.
36. Bowles, *Promises to Keep*, p. 528; Johnson, *The Vantage Point*, p. 228.
37. Castore, "The United States and India," p. 141–42.
38. Johnson, *The Vantage Point*, p. 229. Republican Congressman Robert Dole of Kansas, a member of this study mission, stated that he had found the dimensions of India's food crisis to be "alarming." Bowles, *Promises to Keep*, p. 529.
39. Johnson, *The Vantage Point*, p. 229.
40. *Times of India*, 5 April 1967, p. 1.
41. Bowles, *Promises to Keep*, p. 532.
42. Walt W. Rostow, *Diffusion of Power* (New York: Macmillan, 1972), p. 423.
43. Chopra, *The Evolution of Food Policy in India*, p. 292; Wallerstein, *Food for War—Food for Peace*, p. 68.

44. Quoted in Castore, "The United States and India," pp. 137–38.
45. *Times of India*, 7 April 1966, p. 8.
46. Ibid., 23 December 1966, p. 1; 18 December 1966, p. 1; Johnson, *Vantage Point*, p. 230.
47. Only at the end of the year did Johnson finally become personally active, coaxing some additional food aid out of both Canada and Australia, through direct telephone conversations with the respective heads of state. *Times of India*, 24 December 1966, p. 1; 18 December 1966, p. 1.
48. Ibid., 7 April 1967, p. 1; Johnson, *The Vantage Point*, p. 236.
49. Wallerstein, *Food for War—Food for Peace*, p. 151; *Times of India*, 22 April 1966, p. 1.
50. India's basic Industrial Policy Resolution of 1948, as revised in 1956, had specified that the nation's fertilizer industry was to become "progressively state-owned." Freeman, *World Without Hunger*, p. 149.
51. *Times of India*, 19 April 1966, p. 1.
52. Ibid., 7 April 1966, p. 10; Bjorkman, "Public Law 480," p. 205; Frankel, *India's Political Economy*, pp. 297–98.
53. Frankel, *India's Political Economy*, pp. 296–98; *Times of India*, 8 June 1966, p. 7.
54. *Times of India*, 20 July 1966, p. 1.
55. In April 1966 Prime Minister Gandhi denied having yielded to any U.S. pressure, and defended her new fertilizer policy in particular as honorable and in the best interests of India. Before the rupee devaluation announcement, Planning Minister Mehta vehemently denied having even discussed the matter while in Washington. *Times of India*, 20 April 1966, p. 7, p. 9; 29 April 1966, p. 1.
56. Ibid., 10 June 1966, p. 1; 17 June 1966, p. 1.
57. *New York Times*, 23 January 1967, p. 1; 30 November 1966, p. 1.
58. Frankel, *India's Political Economy*, p. 284.
59. Ibid., p. 297; Lawrence A. Veit, *India's Second Revolution* (New York: McGraw-Hill, 1976), p. 293; Eldridge, *The Politics of Foreign Aid in India*, p. 113.
60. India also refused some of the conditions which had been placed upon management of its fertilizer industry. The Indian government refused full import liberalization, insisting for example that foreign investors use India's own indigenous sources of naphtha, rather than importing ammonia from Iraq and Kuwait, as was being suggested. *Times of India*, 22 April 1966, p. 1.
61. Frankel, *India's Political Economy*, p. 323; Veit, *India's Second Revolution*, p. 293.
62. Subramaniam, *The New Strategy in Indian Agriculture*, pp. 52–53.
63. Castore, "The United States and India," pp. 135–36.
64. Subramaniam, *The New Strategy in Indian Agriculture*, p. 6.
65. Frankel, *India's Political Economy*, pp. 259–68.

66. Ibid., pp. 274–75.
67. Subramaniam, *The New Strategy in Indian Agriculture*, p. 45; Frankel, *India's Political Economy*, p. 277.
68. Cited in Veit, *India's Second Revolution*, p. 193.
69. Bowles, *Promises to Keep*, pp. 558–59.
70. *Times of India*, 28 June 1966, p. 1.
71. *New York Times*, 23 January 1967, p. 1.
72. When challenged by Ambassador Bowles, who had argued that India's views of U.S. bombing policy in Vietnam were actually quite mild (no more critical than those of United Nations Secretary General U Thant, or of the Pope) one White House official captured the president's views with a reply that "the Pope and U Thant don't need our wheat." Bowles, *Promises to Keep*, p. 526.
73. James W. Bjorkman describes Indian criticism on Vietnam as "[A] necessary trade off between sovereignty (in foreign policy) and dependency (in agriculture) . . . a type of symbolic horse-trading for domestic consumption. . . . The relationship should have been intuitively obvious to a consummate politician, but President Johnson did not always appreciate the domestic imperatives of other countries." Bjorkman, "Public Law 480," p. 205.
74. Prior to that trip, her public views on U.S. policy in Vietnam had been mild enough. Indeed, on a brief stop in Moscow earlier in the year she had responded in a surprisingly uncritical fashion to a reporter's leading question about how the Vietnam War might be ended, not even mentioning her well-known preference for a U.S. bombing halt. When she returned to Moscow in July, a part of her purpose was to propose a negotiated solution to the Vietnam conflict which would *not* require a prior withdrawal of all U.S. military forces, a position far more acceptable to the United States at the time than it was to the Soviet Union. *Times of India*, 15 July 1966, p. 1.
75. Bowles, *Promises to Keep*, p. 515; *Times of India*, 22 July 1966, p. 8.
76. *New York Times*, 26 January 1967, p. 16.
77. Ibid., 23 January 1967, p. 1.
78. Bjorkman, "Public Law 480," p. 207.
79. *Times of India*, 30 November 1966, p. 1; Frankel, *India's Political Economy*, p. 308.
80. *New York Times*, 11 June 1967, sect. IV, p. 3; Wallerstein, *Food for War—Food for Peace*, p. 191.

6   Testing Food Power: Embargo on U.S. Grain to the Soviet Union, 1980–1981

1. U.S. Department of Agriculture, *Update: Impact of Agricultural Trade Restrictions on the Soviet Union*, Foreign Agricultural Economic Report

no. 160 (Washington, July 1980), p. 3; ibid., Foreign Agriculture Service, *Foreign Agriculture Circular,* FG-26-79 (Washington, 28 December 1979), p. 3.

2. Ibid., *The U.S. Sales Suspension and Soviet Agriculture: An October Assessment,* suppl. 1, WAS-23 (Washington, October 1980), p. 4.

3. Ibid., *Foreign Agriculture Circular,* FG-26-79, p. 1. This Department of Agriculture estimate of import intentions was later increased during the embargo to 37.5 million tons.

4. Ibid., *The U.S. Sales Suspension and Soviet Agriculture,* p. 3.

5. The Soviet Union does import high-quality bread grains from the United States, but it does so to free up its own lower-quality wheat for feed use at home.

6. U.S. Department of Agriculture, *Update: Impact of Agricultural Trade Restrictions,* p. 4.

7. Bergland sought to deflect complaints from the farm community after the embargo decision by arguing quite properly that U.S. agriculture could well afford to lose some of its direct sales of grain to the Soviet Union, so long as exports to other customers continued to expand. He expressed his hope that the embargo would "help us shake off this [mistaken] notion that the Kremlin and our export fortunes are synonymous." "Statement of Hon. Bob Bergland, Secretary, U.S. Department of Agriculture," to Senate Committee on Agriculture, Nutrition, and Forestry, 22 January 1980. U.S. Senate, Committee on Agriculture, Nutrition, and Forestry, *Embargo on Grain Sales to the Soviet Union* (Washington, 1980), pp. 54–65.

8. *New York Times,* 5 January 1980, p. 6.

9. Jimmy Carter, *Keeping Faith* (New York: Bantam, 1982), p. 474.

10. John C. Roney, "Grain Embargo as Diplomatic Lever: Fulcrum or Folly?" *SAIS Review* no. 4 (Summer 1982), p. 192.

11. Zbigniew Brzezinski, *Power and Principle* (New York: Farrar, Straus, Giroux, 1983), p. 430.

12. Carter, *Keeping Faith,* p. 474.

13. Ibid., p. 473.

14. Brzezinski, *Power and Principle,* p. 431.

15. Although he later claimed to have requested such estimates, none of the top Department of Agriculture officials involved in the decision recalls such a request.

16. Roney, "Grain Embargo as Diplomatic Lever," p. 192.

17. Ibid., p. 193. Brzezinski argues that the president did not make up his mind until 4 January, but couples this argument with a dubious assertion that the Department of Agriculture estimate presented by Bergland actually encouraged the president's action. See Brzezinski, *Power and Principle,* p. 431.

18. Roney, "Grain Embargo as Diplomatic Lever," p. 193.

19. It is of interest that the president felt obliged to begin his 4 January grain embargo speech to the American people with a reference not to the invasion of Afghanistan, but to the "outrage and impatience" he felt over the continuing hostage crisis in Iran. *New York Times*, 5 January 1980, p. 6.

20. U.S. Library of Congress, Congressional Research Service, *Agriculture: U.S. Embargo of Agricultural Exports to U.S.S.R.*, Issue Brief IB80025 (Washington, August 1981), p. 2.

21. Under the terms of that act, an export suspension justified for reasons of "foreign policy" alone could have been overturned by a vote of both houses of Congress within thirty days of its implementation. But by citing reasons of "national security" as well as "foreign policy," Carter avoided this danger. U.S. Library of Congress, *Agriculture: U.S. Embargo*, p. 2.

22. It was not until after the 1980–81 embargo that U.S. producers inserted a parallel provision into the 1981 farm bill to provide even stronger protection in the event of selective export suspensions undertaken for reasons of national security or foreign policy.

23. U.S. Library of Congress, *Agriculture: U.S. Embargo*, p. 2.

24. Carter, *Keeping Faith*, p. 476.

25. *Cargill Crop Bulletin*, March 1980, p. 10.

26. The CCC proposed at first to hold the wheat off the domestic market altogether, as a part of an "emergency food security reserve," and it promised either to take physical delivery of the corn or to resell corn for domestic or export use at prices no lower than the preembargo level.

27. Farmers were suspicious of this retendering process, however, believing that prices for feedgrains in particular should have been allowed to move even higher, according to seasonal patterns, to well above the preembargo level. When soybean producers accused the CCC at one point of selling soybean contracts for less than preembargo prices, the CCC responded by purchasing additional soybeans on the open market.

28. U.S. Library of Congress, *Agriculture: U.S. Embargo*, pp. 5–6.

29. Roney, "Grain Embargo as Diplomatic Lever," p. 204.

30. *Milling and Baking News*, 23 June 1980, p. 12.

31. Ibid., 8 July 1980, p. 8.

32. Ibid., 8 July 1980, p. 8; 19 August 1980, p. 8.

33. Ibid., 5 August 1980, p. 9.

34. In a confused and unrecorded voice vote on 26 September, a narrow Senate majority did vote to cut off all funding for the enforcement of the embargo, but this was never more than a preelection gesture, certain to be dropped in conference because the House had earlier voted so heavily against similar proposals.

35. *New York Times*, 27 September 1980, p. D2.

36. Reagan used these foreign policy arguments to turn back for a time the growing wave of complaints from farmers, and the public pleas from his

own secretary of agriculture, John Block, as well as direct appeals, early in February, from the heads of fifteen major farm and commodity organizations, reinforced by a visit to the White House from eleven farm state senators.

37. *New York Times*, 29 April 1981, p. A24.
38. An entry in Carter's diary on 4 January noted only that Canada and Australia were being "asked" to cooperate. Argentina is once again disregarded as not having any grain on hand to make additional sales to the Soviets. Roney, "Grain Embargo as Diplomatic Lever," p. 197; Carter, *Keeping Faith*, p. 476.
39. Roney, "Grain Embargo as Diplomatic Lever," p. 195.
40. John C. Roney's reconstruction of the embargo decision shows "no evidence that either Carter, any top White House official, or any Cabinet member ever spoke with officials of other grain-exporting countries before the embargo." Ibid., 195.
41. *New York Times*, 12 January 1980, p. D1.
42. Carter, *Keeping Faith*, p. 477.
43. *New York Times*, 11 January 1980, p. D13.
44. Roney, "Grain Embargo as Diplomatic Lever," p. 198.
45. U.S. Department of Agriculture, *Foreign Agriculture Circular*, FG-4-81, 28 January 1981; *U.S. Wheat Associates Newsletter*, 11 April 1980, p. 2.
46. U.S. Department of Agriculture, *Foreign Agriculture Circular*, FG-4-81.
47. *U.S. Wheat Associates Newsletter*, 8 February 1980, p. 2; U.S. Department of Agriculture, *Foreign Agriculture Circular*, FG-15-80, 9 May 1980, p. 3.
48. *U.S. Wheat Associates Newsletter*, 11 July 1980, p. 3.
49. U.S. Department of Agriculture, *Foreign Agriculture Circular*, FG-25-82, 12 August 1982, p. 5.
50. U.S. Library of Congress, *Agriculture: U.S. Embargo*, p. 13.
51. As a public justification for this new sale, AWB Chairman Leslie Price explained that Australia was forced into expanded sales to the Soviet Union because of certain "abberations" in world grain trade patterns that had been caused by the embargo—most notably a large increase in U.S. wheat sales to China, a growing market that Australia coveted. In private, AWB officials had come to view the embargo as a rare opportunity to gain access to the Soviet market on a long-term basis.
52. *Milling and Baking News*, 8 July 1980, p. 14.
53. Allan P. Mustard, "Impact of the U.S. Grain Embargo on World Grain Trading Patterns and Soviet Livestock Output," diss., University of Illinois, Urbana-Champaign, 1982, p. 41.
54. In early June, the Saskatchewan Wheat Pool announced that it would independently withdraw its support for the embargo on 31 July, when the current crop year came to an end. The president of the Pool, Ted Turner,

argued that Canadian restraint was no longer called for because the United States was selling so much grain to Eastern Europe, a region he characterized as a likely transshipment point to the Soviet Union.

55. *National Farmer's Union Washington Newsletter,* 13 June 1980, p. 3; *Milling and Baking News,* 8 July 1980, p. 14.

56. U.S. Department of Agriculture, *Foreign Agriculture Circular,* FG-25-82, 12 August 1982; FG-19-81, 12 May 1981.

57. Most of these larger 1979–80 shipments were delivered under licenses issued before the embargo announcement, and so did not represent any willful European effort to undercut the embargo. *Wall Street Journal,* 27 October 1980, p. 32.

58. *U.S. Wheat Associates Newsletter,* 18 April 1980, p. 2.

59. *Le Monde,* 8 January, 1980, p. 5.

60. Because of its unique budgetary exposure, the European Community was even obliged at times during the embargo to place additional restraints on its food sales to the Soviet Union. Soviet purchasing agents, eager during the embargo to find affordable supplies of animal feed, had discovered in 1980 that the European export subsidies no longer available to them for most grain products were still available for some kinds of European grain "mixtures." European Community officials were upset to discover in late October that the Soviet Union had used this loophole to purchase an unprecedented 500,000 tons of mixed animal feed from two West German firms, at a cost to the Community budget of $23 million in export subsidies. Export subsidies on mixed grains were thereafter suspended, and overseas grain sales were more tightly monitored. *U.S. Wheat Associates Newsletter,* 10 April 1981, p. 1; 30 October 1980, p. 1.

61. U.S. Library of Congress, *Agriculture: U.S. Embargo,* p. 15.

62. Unclassified telegram, Department of State 27224, from U.S. Embassy Paris to U.S. Department of Agriculture, "EC Flour Sales to USSR," 28 August 1980. See also *Milling and Baking News,* 3 February 1981, p. 1.

63. U.S. Department of Agriculture, *Foreign Agriculture Circular,* FG-25-82, 12 August 1982, p. 5; FG-19-81, 12 May 1981, p. 5.

64. *Economist,* 15 March 1980, p. 36; U.S. Department of Agriculture, *Foreign Agriculture,* April 1982, p. 21.

65. U.S. Department of Agriculture, *Foreign Agriculture Circular,* FG-2-81, 15 January 1981; *New York Times,* 29 November 1980, p. D30.

66. Hungary's wheat exports during the first calendar year of the embargo increased to a significant 1.1 million tons (more than twice the average level of the three previous years) but these larger exports were facilitated, at least in part, by a record domestic harvest. Hungary was a regular exporter of its own agricultural products in Eastern Europe, and not a transshipment point for Western-origin grains. Romania, which did increase both its imports and exports of grain in 1979–80, to levels ap-

proaching 2 million tons, was the more likely focal point for those few transshipments through Eastern Europe that did occur. U.S. Library of Congress, *Agriculture: U.S. Embargo,* p. 15.

67. *Milling and Baking News,* 24 June 1980, p. 9; U.S. Department of Agriculture, *Update: Impact of Agricultural Trade Restrictions,* p. 2.

68. U.S. Library of Congress, *Agriculture: U.S. Embargo,* pp. 25–28.

69. Carter, *Keeping Faith,* p. 478.

70. *Wall Street Journal,* 24 January 1980, p. 1.

71. U.S. Department of Agriculture, *Agricultural Situation in the U.S.S.R.,* suppl. 1, WAS-18 (Washington, April 1979), p. 10.

72. Ibid., *The U.S. Sales Suspension,* pp. 3–4.

73. *Newsweek,* 28 January 1980, p. 17.

74. Robbin Johnson, "Recent Foreign Policy Developments: What They Can Tell Us about Future U.S. Grain Policy," speech presented to Agriculture and Foreign Policy Conference, Spring Hill Center, Minneapolis, 29 April 1982.

75. U.S. Department of Agriculture, *Foreign Agriculture Circular,* FG-38-83, 13 December 1983, p. 5.

76. Ibid., FG-2-82, 12 January 1982, p. 3.

77. Arnold Litvinov, an agribusiness expert at the Institute of U.S. and Canadian Studies in Moscow, explained to a visiting U.S. reporter that "The grain embargo was a pleasure for our country. Because we had come to rely on imported feed and coarse grain from the U.S., we weren't forced to do anything about increasing the production of high protein forage and coarse grain in our own country." Soviet emigré scientist Zhores Medvedev had earlier reached a parallel judgment: "In general, I find that the U.S. embargo, which was designed to expose the vulnerability of the Soviet Union, has in reality made a rather positive impact on the Soviet economy, helping to mobilize its resources and potentialities." *New York Times,* 10 February 1981, p. 23.

78. *New York Times,* 29 November 1979, p. 9.

79. U.S. Department of Agriculture, *The U.S. Sales Suspension,* p. 6.

80. "Statement of Richard N. Cooper, Under Secretary for Economic Affairs, U.S. Department of State," to Senate Committee on Banking, Housing, and Urban Affairs, 20 August 1980. U.S. Senate, Committee on Banking, Housing, and Urban Affairs, *Suspension of United States Exports of High Technology and Grain to the Soviet Union* (Washington, 1980), p. 123.

81. Mustard, *Impact of the U.S. Grain Embargo,* p. 115.

82. Quoted in *Wall Street Journal,* 24 January 1980, p. 1.

83. This poem read in part, "Congress is full of noise and spite, / But I'll be direct and straight: / Would I my Kabul brothers betray / For a loaf of Texas white?" Quoted in *New York Times,* 7 February 1980, p. A8.

84. Ibid.

85. Dale Hathaway, "Foreign Policy and Agricultural Trade," speech presented to Agriculture and Foreign Policy Conference, Spring Hill Center, Minneapolis, 29 April 1982.
86. "Statement of Hon. Bob Bergland, Secretary, U.S. Department of Agriculture," to Senate Committee on Banking, Housing, and Urban Affairs, 20 August 1980. U.S. Senate, Committee on Banking, Housing, and Urban Affairs, *Suspension of United States Exports of High Technology and Grain to the Soviet Union* (Washington, 1980), p. 105.
87. Thomas J. Watson, Jr., "Dealing with Moscow," *New York Times OPED*, 19 January 1981.
88. Quoted in *New York Times*, 7 February 1980, p. A8.
89. Ibid., 13 January 1980, p. 16.
90. *Newsweek*, 21 January 1980, p. 25; *New York Times*, 8 February 1981, p. 1.
91. Financial incentives offered to Soviet agriculture were increased both during and after the experience of the embargo. Early in 1981 the official purchase price for key agricultural commodities was increased, and bonus payments for above-plan sales were converted into an integral part of the state procurement price. These higher procurement prices implied an increase in subsidy costs. It was projected that in 1983 alone 16 billion rubles would be added to subsidies on food production, roughly 11 billion rubles in long-term credits to farms would be canceled and exempted from repayment, and 3 billion rubles would be invested in improvements to rural living conditions. All the while, major capital outlays were continued. Capital investment in the agricultural sector increased by 3 percent in 1981 to reach 37 billion rubles, equal to 27 percent of total capital investment in the economy. "Statement of Lt. Gen. James A. Williams, Director, Defense Intelligence Agency," to Subcommittee on International Trade, Finance, and Security Economics, 29 June 1982. U.S. Congress, Joint Economic Committee, *Allocation of Resources in the Soviet Union and China—1982* (Washington, 1983), p. 62.
92. Revised CIA estimates of Soviet military spending, released late in 1983, revealed that a previously unnoticed slowdown in new arms procurements might have taken place in 1976, coincident with slower overall economic growth, but that no slowdown occurred since 1979, Afghanistan, and the embargo. *New York Times*, 19 November 1983, p. 6.
93. Quoted in ibid., 28 October 1982, p. A7.
94. According to one Defense Intelligence Agency assessment, offered in June 1982,

> The high priority Soviet leaders place on military power has resulted in continued increases in expansion of military production facilities even as economic growth has slowed. There has been no significant reduction, to date, in the rate of expansion of such facilities. In addi-

tion, the number of weapons systems in development and testing has remained virtually constant for the past decade. Both of these trends point to on-going increases in military production and procurement. The Soviets are planning to allocate substantial additional resources to the military, with full recognition of the harm to the economy.

"Statement of Lt. Gen. James A. Williams, Director, Defense Intelligence Agency," to Subcommittee on International Trade, Finance, and Security Economics, 29 June 1982. U.S. Congress, Joint Economic Committee, *Allocation of Resources in the Soviet Union and China—1982* (Washington, 1983), p. 82.

95. U.S. Department of Agriculture, Economic Research Service, *U.S.S.R.: Review of Agriculture in 1981 and Outlook for 1982*, suppl. 1, WAS-27 (Washington, May 1982), p. 17.

96. Johnson, "Recent Foreign Policy Developments."

97. Subsequent analysis by the Congressional Research Service found the source of the original Defense Intelligence Agency $1 billion additional cost figure to be "not clear." See also Roney, "Grain Embargo as Diplomatic Lever," p. 201. See also Hanns-D. Jacobsen, "Economic Asymmetries and Economic Sanctions: The Partial Grain Embargo of the US against the USSR, 1980/81," unpublished manuscript prepared for the eleventh World Congress of the International Political Science Association (Rio de Janeiro, 9–14 August 1982), p. 10.

98. U.S. Department of Agriculture, *U.S.S.R.: Review of Agriculture in 1981 and Outlook for 1982*, p. 12. See also Johnson, "Recent Foreign Policy Developments."

Bibliography

Agreement between the Government of the United States of America and Government of the Union of Soviet Socialist Republics on the Supply of Grain. Moscow, 20 October 1975. Reprinted in U.S. House of Representatives. Committee on Appropriations. *Hearings before Subcommittees, Part One,* pp. 351–52. Washington: Government Printing Office, 1975.

Barraclough, Geoffrey. "Wealth and Power: The Politics of Food and Oil." *The New York Review of Books* 22:13 (7 August 1975):23ff.

Benedict, Murry R. *Farm Policies of the United States: 1790–1950.* New York: Octagon, 1953.

Bergland, Bob. "Statement of Hon. Bob Bergland, Secretary, U.S. Department of Agriculture," pp. 54–65. In U.S. Senate, Committee on Agriculture, Nutrition, and Forestry. *Embargo on Grain Sales to the Soviet Union.* Hearing, 22 Jan. 1980. Washington: Government Printing Office, 1980.

Bergland, Bob. "Statement of Hon. Bob Bergland, Secretary, U.S. Department of Agriculture," pp. 105–10. In U.S. Senate. Committee on Banking, Housing, and Urban Affairs. *Suspension of United States Exports of High Technology and Grain to the Soviet Union.* Hearing, 20 August 1980. Washington: Government Printing Office, 1980.

Bjorkman, James W. "Public Law 480 and the Policies of Self-Help and Short-Tether: Indo-American Relations, 1965–68." In Appendices (Case Studies, Economic Policy), *Commission on the Organization of the Government for the Conduct of Foreign Policy,* pp. 192–209. Washington, D.C.: Government Printing Office, June 1975.

Bond, Daniel L., and Levine, Herbert S. "The 11th Five-Year Plan, 1981–85." Unpublished manuscript prepared for Conference on the Twenty-Sixth Congress of the Communist Party of the Soviet Union, The Rand Corporation—Columbia University. Washington, D.C., 23–25 April 1981.

Bowles, Chester. *Promises to Keep.* New York: Harper and Row, 1971.

Brown, Lester R. "The Politics and Responsibility of the North American

Breadbasket." Worldwatch Paper 2. Washington, D.C.: Worldwatch Institute, 1975.

Brzezinski, Zbigniew. *Power and Principle.* New York: Farrar, Straus, Giroux, 1983.

Carter, Jimmy. *Keeping Faith.* New York: Bantam, 1982.

Castore, Carolyn. "The United States and India: The Use of Food to Apply Economic Pressure—1965–67." In *Economic Coercion and U.S. Foreign Policy,* ed. by Sidney Weintraub, pp. 130–42. Boulder, Colo.: Westview Press, 1982.

Chopra, R. N. *The Evolution of Food Policy in India.* New Delhi: Macmillan India Ltd., 1981.

Christensen, Cheryl. "Food and National Security." In *Economic Issues and National Security,* ed. by Klaus Knorr and Frank N. Trager, pp. 285–95. Lawrence: Regents Press of Kansas, 1977.

Clark, M. Gardner. "Soviet Agricultural Policy." In *Soviet Agriculture,* ed. by Henry G. Shaffer, pp. 1–55. New York: Praeger, 1977.

Cochrane, Willard W., and Ryan, Mary E. *American Farm Policy, 1948–1973.* Minneapolis: University of Minnesota Press, 1976.

Cooper, Richard N. "Statement of Richard N. Cooper, Under Secretary for Economic Affairs, U.S. Department of State," pp. 122–24. In U.S. Senate. Committee on Banking, Housing, and Urban Affairs. *Suspension of United States Exports of High Technology and Grain to the Soviet Union.* Hearing, 20 August 1980. Washington: Government Printing Office, 1980.

Destler, I. M. *Making Foreign Economic Policy.* Washington, D.C.: Brookings, 1980.

Deutsch, Karl W. *The Analysis of International Relations.* 2d ed. Englewood Cliffs, N.J.: Prentice-Hall, 1978.

Diamond, Douglas B., Bettis, Lee W., and Ramsson, Robert E. "Agricultural Production." Unpublished manuscript prepared for Conference on the Soviet Economy Toward the Year 2000. Airlie House, Virginia, October 1979.

Eldridge, P. J. *The Politics of Foreign Aid in India.* London: Weidenfeld and Nicholson, 1969.

Farm Export Education Project. *U.S. Farm Strategies for the Eighties.* Washington, D.C.: Agriculture Council of America, 1981.

Franda, Marcus. "The Dynamics of Indian Food Policy." In *Political Investments in Food Production,* ed. by Barbara Huddleston and Jon McLin, pp. 105–28. Bloomington: Indiana University Press, 1979.

Frankel, Francine R. *India's Political Economy, 1947–1977.* Princeton, N.J.: Princeton University Press, 1978.

Freeman, Orville L. *World Without Hunger.* New York: Praeger, 1968.

Gandhi, Indira. Speech presented to Food and Agriculture Organization of the United Nations. Rome, 9 November 1981.

Gilmore, Richard. *A Poor Harvest.* New York: Longman, 1982.

Government of India. Planning Commission. *Sixth Five Year Plan, 1980–85.* New Delhi: January 1981.

Grennes, Thomas R., Johnson, Paul R., and Thursby, Marie. *The Economics of World Grain Trade.* New York: Praeger, 1978.

Haig, Alexander M. *Caveat: Realism, Reagan, and Foreign Policy.* New York: Macmillan, 1984.

Hanson, Philip. "Economic Constraints on Soviet Policies in the 1980's." *International Affairs* 57:1 (Winter 1980–81):21–42.

Hathaway, Dale. "Foreign Policy and Agricultural Trade." Speech presented to Agriculture and Foreign Policy Conference. Spring Hill Center, Minneapolis, 29 April 1982.

———. *Government and Agriculture.* New York: Macmillan, 1963.

Hersh, Seymour M. *The Price of Power.* New York: Summit, 1983.

Huntington, Samuel P. "Trade, Technology, and Leverage." *Foreign Policy* no. 32 (Fall 1978):63–80.

Jacobsen, Hanns-D. "Economic Asymmetries and Economic Sanctions: The Partial Grain Embargo of the US Against the USSR, 1980/81." Unpublished manuscript prepared for the eleventh World Congress of the International Political Science Association. Rio de Janeiro, 9–14 August 1982.

Johnson, D. Gale. *World Agriculture in Disarray.* London: Macmillan, 1973.

Johnson, Lyndon B. *The Vantage Point.* New York: Holt, Rinehart and Winston, 1971.

Johnson, Robbin. "Recent Foreign Policy Developments: What They Can Tell Us about Future U.S. Grain Policy." Speech presented to Agriculture and Foreign Policy Conference. Spring Hill Center, Minneapolis, 29 April 1982.

Katzenstein, Peter J., ed. *Between Power and Plenty: Foreign Economic Policies of Advanced Industrial States.* Madison: University of Wisconsin Press, 1978.

Keohane, Robert O., and Nye, Joseph S., Jr. *Power and Interdependence.* Boston: Little Brown, 1977.

Khrushchev, Nikita S. *Khrushchev Remembers: The Last Testament.* Boston: Little Brown, 1974.

Kissinger, Henry. *White House Years.* Boston: Little Brown, 1979.

———. *Years of Upheaval.* Boston: Little Brown, 1982.

Krishna, Raj. "The Economic Development of India." *Scientific American* 243:3 (September 1980):18–19, 166–69ff.

Lappe, Frances Moore, and Collins, Joseph. *Food First.* New York: Ballantine, 1977.

Lele, Uma. *Food Grain Marketing in India.* Ithaca, N.Y.: Cornell University Press, 1971.

Malish, Anton F., Jr. "Internal Policy, Decision Making, and Food Import

Demand in the Soviet Union." Unpublished manuscript prepared for third meeting of the Trade Research Consortium. Washington, D.C., June 1981.

Malmgren, Harald B. *International Economic Peacekeeping in Phase II.* Rev. ed. New York: Quadrangle, 1972.

McLin, Jon. "Surrogate International Organization and the Case of World Food Security, 1949–1969." *International Organization* 33:1 (Winter 1979):35–55.

Medvedev, Roy. *Khrushchev.* Garden City, N.Y.: Anchor Press/Doubleday, 1983.

Mellor, John W. *The New Economics of Growth.* Ithaca, N.Y.: Cornell University Press, 1976.

Morgan, Dan. *Merchants of Grain.* New York: Viking Press, 1979.

_____. "The Politics of Grain." *Atlantic Monthly* (July 1980):29–34.

Morrow, Daniel T. *The Economics of International Stockpiling of Wheat.* Research Report no. 18. Washington, D.C.: International Food Policy Research Institute, September 1980.

Mustard, Allan P. "Impact of the U.S. Grain Embargo on World Grain Trading Patterns and Soviet Livestock Output." Diss., University of Illinois, Urbana-Champaign, 1982.

Novosti Press Agency. "The Socialist Transformation of Agriculture." In *Soviet Agriculture,* ed. by Harry G. Shaffer, pp. 151–66. New York: Praeger, 1977.

O'Hagan, J. P. "National Self-Sufficiency in Food." *Food Policy* 1:5 (November 1976): 355–66.

Paarlberg, Don. *American Farm Policy.* New York: John Wiley and Sons, 1964.

_____. *Farm and Food Policy: Issues of the 1980's.* Lincoln: University of Nebraska Press, 1980.

Paarlberg, Robert. "Food, Oil, and Coercive Resource Diplomacy." *International Security* 3:2 (Fall 1978):3–19.

Pavlov, Dmitri V. *Leningrad, 1941: The Blockade.* Chicago: University of Chicago Press, 1965.

Perlo, Victor. "How Agriculture is Becoming an Advanced Section of Socialist Society." In *Soviet Agriculture,* ed. by Harry G. Shaffer, pp. 106–50. New York: Praeger, 1977.

Peterson, Trudy H. *Agricultural Exports, Farm Income, and the Eisenhower Administration.* Lincoln: University of Nebraska Press, 1979.

_____. "Sales, Surpluses, and the Soviets: A Study in Political Economy." *Policy Studies Journal* 6:4 (Summer 1978):531–33.

Porter, Roger B. *Presidential Decision Making: The Economic Policy Board.* New York: Cambridge University Press, 1980.

Report to the President Submitted by the Commission on International Trade and Investment Policy (the Williams Commission). *United States International Economic Policy in an Interdependent World.* Washington, D.C.: Government Printing Office, July 1971.

Reutlinger, Shlomo. "The Level and Stability of India's Foodgrain Consumption." In *India: Occasional Papers,* World Bank Staff Working Paper 279. Washington, D.C., May 1978.

Roney, John C. "Grain Embargo as Diplomatic Lever: Fulcrum or Folly?" *SAIS Review* no. 4 (Summer 1982):189–205.

Rostow, Walt W. *Diffusion of Power.* New York: Macmillan, 1972.

Rothschild, Emma. "Food Politics." *Foreign Affairs* 54:2 (January 1976):285–307.

Rowen, Henry. "Statement of Henry Rowen, Chairman, National Intelligence Council," pp. 178–233. In U.S. Congress, Joint Economic Committee. *Allocation of Resources in the Soviet Union and China—1982.* Hearing, 1 December 1982. Washington: Government Printing Office, 1983.

Sanderson, Fred H., and Roy, Shyamal. *Food Trends and Prospects in India.* Washington: Brookings, 1979.

Schuh, G. Edward. "Agriculture and Foreign Policy: The Economic Framework." Speech presented to Agriculture and Foreign Policy Conference. Spring Hill Center, Minneapolis, 29 April 1982.

Schultz, Theodore W., ed. *Distortions of Agricultural Incentives.* Bloomington: Indiana University Press, 1978.

Sewell, John W. *The United States and World Development, Agenda 1980.* New York: Praeger, 1980.

Singh, Rao Birindra. Opening General Statement to Sixth Ministerial Session of World Food Council. Arusha, Tanzania, June 1980.

Smith, Hedrick. *The Russians.* New York: Ballantine, 1976.

Sosland, Morton I. "U.S.–USSR Agreement on Grains." Cambridge: Harvard University Russian Research Center, 5 November 1979.

Soth, Lauren. "The Grain Export Boom: Should It Be Tamed?" *Foreign Affairs* 59:4 (Spring 1981):895–912.

Subramaniam, C. *The New Strategy in Indian Agriculture.* New Delhi: Vikas, 1979.

Trager, James. *The Great Grain Robbery.* New York: Ballantine, 1975.

United Nations. Food and Agriculture Organization. *The Rice Policy of India.* CCP-RI 80/3. Rome, December 1980.

United States Central Intelligence Agency. Office of Policy Research. *Potential Implications of Trends in World Population, Food Production, and Climate.* OPR 401. Washington, D.C.: Government Printing Office, August 1974.

———. *U.S.S.R.: Long Term Outlook for Grain Imports.* Washington, D.C.: Government Printing Office, January 1979.

United States Congress. House. Committee on Foreign Affairs. *Data and Anal-*

ysis Concerning the Possibility of a U.S. Food Embargo as a Response to the Present Arab Oil Boycott. 93d Cong., 1st sess. Washington, D.C.: Government Printing Office, 21 November 1973.

————. Joint Economic Committee. *Soviet Economy in a Time of Change.* 2 vols. Washington, D.C.: Government Printing Office, 10 October 1979.

————. Joint Economic Committee. *Soviet Economy in the 1980's: Problems and Prospects.* 2 vols. Washington, D.C.: Government Printing Office, 31 December 1982.

————. Senate. Committee on Agriculture and Forestry. *Agricultural Trade and the Proposed Round of Multilateral Negotiations (The Flanigan Report).* 93d Cong., 1st sess. Washington, D.C.: Government Printing Office, 30 April 1973.

————. Senate. *Agriculture and Food Act of 1981.* Conference Report no. 97-290. 97th Cong., 1st sess. Washington, D.C.: Government Printing Office, 10 December 1981.

————. Senate. Committee on Government Operations. *Russian Grain Transactions.* Report no. 93-1033, 93d Cong., 2d sess. Washington, D.C.: Government Printing Office, 29 July 1974.

————. Senate. *World Trade Barriers in Relation to American Agriculture.* Document no. 70. 73d Cong., 1st sess. Washington, D.C.: Government Printing Office, 5 June 1933.

United States Department of Agriculture. *Agricultural Situation in the U.S.S.R.* Suppl. 1, WAS-18. Washington, D.C.: Government Printing Office, April 1979.

————. *Foreign Agriculture.* Washington, D.C.: Government Printing Office, 1975–84.

————. *India: Quarterly Grain and Feed.* Attache Reports IN-0086 to IN-1053. New Delhi: 1980–81.

————. *Update: Impact of Agricultural Trade Restrictions on the Soviet Union.* Foreign Agricultural Economic Report no. 160. Washington, D.C.: Government Printing Office, July 1980.

————. *The U.S. Sales Suspension and Soviet Agriculture: An October Assessment.* Suppl. 1, WAS-23. Washington, D.C.: Government Printing Office, October 1980.

————. *The World Food Situation and Prospects to 1985.* Foreign Agricultural Economic Report no. 98. Washington, D.C.: Government Printing Office, December 1974.

————. Economic Research Service. *Foreign Agricultural Trade of the U.S. (FATUS).* Washington, D.C.: Government Printing Office, 1977.

————. *Prospects for Agricultural Trade with the U.S.S.R.* ERS—Foreign 356. Washington, D.C.: Government Printing Office, April 1974.

————. *U.S.S.R.: Review of Agriculture in 1981 and Outlook for 1982.* Suppl. 1, WAS-27. Washington, D.C.: Government Printing Office, May 1982.

_____. Foreign Agriculture Service. *Foreign Agriculture Circular*. Washington, D.C.: U.S. Department of Agriculture, 1975–84.

United States Department of State. Bureau of Public Affairs. *U.S. Foreign Policy and Agricultural Trade*. Current Policy no. 535. Washington, D.C.: Department of State, 10 January 1984.

United States Library of Congress. Congressional Research Service. *Agriculture: U.S. Embargo of Agricultural Exports to U.S.S.R.* Issue Brief IB80025. Washington, D.C.: Government Printing Office, August 1981.

_____. *Food Power: The Potential Use of U.S. Grain Exports as a Tool in International Affairs*. Washington, D.C.: Government Printing Office, January 1977.

Veit, Lawrence A. *India's Second Revolution*. New York: McGraw-Hill, 1976.

Volin, Lazar. *A Century of Russian Agriculture*. Cambridge: Harvard University Press, 1970.

Wall, John. "Foodgrain Management: Pricing, Procurement, Distribution, Import and Storage Policy." In *India: Occasional Papers,* World Bank Staff Working Paper 279. Washington, D.C., May 1978.

Wallerstein, Mitchel B. *Food for War—Food for Peace*. Cambridge: MIT Press, 1980.

Waltz, Kenneth N. *Theory of International Politics*. Reading, Mass.: Addison-Wesley, 1979.

Watson, Thomas J., Jr. "Dealing With Moscow." *New York Times OPED* (19 January 1981).

Willett, Joseph M., and Webster, Sharon B. " 'Food Power'—Food in International Politics." Paper presented to the Conference on Political Aspects of the World Food Problem. Kansas State University, March 1977.

Williams, James A. (Lt. Gen.). "Statement of Lt. Gen. James A. Williams, Director, Defense Intelligence Agency," pp. 54–159. In U.S. Congress. Joint Economic Committee. *Allocation of Resources in the Soviet Union and China—1982*. Hearing, 29 June 1982. Washington: Government Printing Office, 1983.

World Bank. *World Development Report 1980*. New York: Oxford University Press, 1980.

World Food Institute. "World Food Trade and U.S. Agriculture." Iowa State University, August 1981.

Zabijaka, Valentine. "The Soviet Grain Trade 1961–70: A Decade of Change." *The ACES Bulletin* 16:1 (Spring 1974):4–16.

Index

Library of Congress Cataloging in Publication Data

Paarlberg, Robert L.
  Food trade and foreign policy.

  Written under the auspices of the Center for International Affairs, Harvard
University.
  Bibliography: p.
  Includes index.
  1. Grain trade—Political aspects—United States. 2. Grain trade—Political
aspects—Soviet Union. 3. Grain trade—Political aspects—India. 4. United
States—Foreign relations. 5. Soviet Union—Foreign relations. 6. India—
Foreign relations. I. Harvard University. Center for International
Affairs. II. Title.
HD9035.P33   1985   382′.4131   84–29335
ISBN 0–8014–1772–4 (alk. paper)
ISBN 0–8014–9345–5 (pbk.: alk. paper)

0215